Catholic Social Conscience:
Reflection and Action on
Catholic Social Teaching

'International in outlook, European in origin these essays put British debates in their wider context presenting us with unique and fresh insights as to how we might renew the Christian social conscience.'

Professor the Lord Alton of Liverpool

'This book offers cutting-edge reflections on social issues that stir the Christian conscience across Europe. The breadth and topicality of its chapters makes *Catholic Social Conscience: Reflection and Action* inspiring and essential reading.'

Luke Coppen, Editor of The Catholic Herald

'This is an exceptional collection of essays, which showcases Roman Catholic theological reflection and social engagement at its very best. The editors have brought together a rich and vibrant range of contributors, and their work will provide fertile and fruitful material for discussion, study and further debate. This volume admirably highlights just how exciting and engaging theology can be when it turns outward to address public life, social thought and ethical issues of common concern. This is a fresh and original book that will reward all who read and engage with its ideas and insights.'

Rev Canon Professor Martyn Percy,
Principal of Cuddesdon College, Oxford.

Catholic Social Conscience: Reflection and Action on Catholic Social Teaching

Edited by

Keith Chappell & Francis Davis

GRACEWING

First published in England in 2011
by
Gracewing
2 Southern Avenue
Leominster
Herefordshire HR6 0QF
United Kingdom
www.gracewing.co.uk

The right of Keith Chappell and Francis Davis to be identified as the authors of this work has been asserted in accordance with the Copyright, Designs and Patents Act 1988.

ISBN 978 085244 773 4

Typeset by Gracewing

Contents

Foreword

During his visit to Britain in September 2010, Pope Benedict XVI highlighted the need for increased social engagement between the Church and questions of social concern and responsibility. The conference in Oxford from which this book has grown, in many ways formed a prelude to this call, bringing together over two hundred and fifty participants from around the world to consider the question how best to understand, strengthen and renew Catholic social teaching, conscience and action. The conference organisers, led by the present editors, were successful in gathering those who spanned boundaries which often remain uncrossed. Thus eminent theologians debated with world renowned political scientists and sociologists; policy makers shared insights with business leaders. NGO workers, parish activists, philanthropists and those from the political Centre, Right and Left, all participated in the conference as did representatives from the Jewish, Islamic and Sikh communities. Opus Dei was represented as was the Justice and Peace Movement; the *Semaines Sociales De France* were there as was *Aid to the Church In Need*. Lay men and women, Bishops, Religious Superiors, young and emerging Catholic leaders, CAFOD, Focolare, the charismatic movement, ecumenical representatives and the Vice-Chancellor of the University of Oxford all took part to create a community of enquiry and discussion. I was delighted to play an active part in the event, and continue to be excited by the ongoing debate relating to Catholic social engagement which has been stimulated both by the conference and the Holy Father's own comments.

In the time since the Pope's visit, the Church in the UK has continued to discuss how best to enhance its own social engagement.

As is clear from the contributions in this book, the challenges which face us are significant but so are the strengths which we already possess. We have a significant and growing group of academics in this country who are producing work of international standing as well as of direct relevance to our more local issues. We have dedicated and highly skilled practitioners working at national, diocesan and local levels to make the message of social justice real in the lives of millions. We must also remember that we cannot sit in isolation. We need to listen and learn from the wider Church. Again, this is a distinctive aspect of this book.

As a universal Church we have a great heritage of putting social teaching into action around the world. Here, we are forced to face challenges of accepting the transfer of skills, knowledge and spiritual insights from other parts of the world who have faced, and are facing, the same challenges that we are. Perhaps the first step is to look to our European neighbours with whom we share much in terms of heritage and a common future. The suffering experienced by the persecutions of societies under Soviet rule remind us of the social and economic hardships still faced by so many, including in the global South where the Church continues to grow.

So, we are faced by many challenges but also many opportunities. We are called to work together as a universal Church to make our rich heritage of social teaching a lived reality. We need to do so basing our actions on deep reflection and creative new approaches. I believe this book represents an important part of our efforts to make this happen in the UK and Europe, and provides a model for conversation and discussions beyond these shores. This is not to say that we will all agree with every word we find in its pages, but all the contributions are worthy of serious consideration. Just as the original conference formed an important part of the prelude to the visit of Pope Benedict XVI to Britain, I also believe that this book has the potential to form an important part of the legacy of that visit.

✠ DECLAN LANG
Bishop of Clifton

Introduction

Catholic social thought and teaching has been one of the mainstays of the Church's engagement with the world. The action of religious and lay groups, the political interventions of the hierarchy and the heroic efforts of individuals, sometimes leading to martyrdom, have often proved to be key expressions of her mission and a vital source of credibility in the public sphere. This book sets out to stimulate a conversation, and to contribute to an ongoing debate around the origins and potential of this vital part of Catholic life. A conversation regarding the spiritual and intellectual origins of Catholic thought and its historical development. And a debate regarding in which institutions, forms of charity and solidarity, a modern Catholic commitment to social justice, freedom, the common good may be discovered and encouraged to grow.

The essays contained in this volume arise from a conference which sought to bring together academics and practitioners from all over the world, Catholic and non-Catholic, with the aim of informing this debate. The experiences and wisdom of all faith communities, and those from no particular faith, were sought. Catholics joined with Jews and Muslims, Anglicans and Methodists to gain broader insight of the issues that transcend particular communities. Members of Opus Dei, Focolare, the charismatic movement, justice and peace groups and Caritas agencies small and large joined with Catholic intellectuals, policy makers, businesspeople, trade unionists and Bishops to explore the meaning and future of the Catholic social conscience, Catholic social thought and Catholic social action. From Eastern Europe to South Africa, Sweden to South-East Asia, Rome to Oxford, Malta and Dublin to Jerusalem they brought their insights and contributions from theology and other disciplines and vocations. As such this is a book for academics and activists, leaders at the Diocesan and parish levels and those seeking to tease out the theological and social constraints—and opportunities—which the Catholic social tradition today seeks to understand and address. For those interested in the evangelisation of Europe widely understood, and of Britain within Europe, it will be of especial interest.

That said, while the essays here cover key experiences in the European Union it is not a publication constrained by a specifically political view as to what constitutes 'Europe'. The Catholic Church has long held the view that the idea of Europe includes both the islands that comprise Britain and Ireland along with the mainland nations of the European Union, but also those regions stretching further east to include the Urals. In turn this 'Europe' is always seen, by the Church, as resting in the context of a wider global family, and beyond that within the universal communion of saints. Europe, for the Church, is a pastoral reality and so here we focus on concrete challenges for the Church and other Christian communities rather than those which relate to the leadership or management of institutions in the secular sphere.

While the tradition of Catholic social thought is an ancient one, it is the contention of our contributors that we have experienced recent trauma (such as the Soviet persecutions), fresh challenges (of decline, renewal, or morphing ideas of state welfare), and new directions (for the European community, for what it means to be human, in identifying Catholic strengths and weaknesses). These all need fresh inspiration, both from old resources (theologies of justice) and those less noticed in the present (personalism, prophecy, social research and politics). Such an effort is not without risk. 'May you live in interesting times', is a thinly-veiled Eastern curse which the Church can probably identify with at most times in its history but never more so than in the twenty-first century.

We do indeed live in interesting times. Times in which the Church faces internal and external challenges as it struggles to continue its mission in a world that is almost unrecognisable to the world in which her leaders were born. Political, economic, social, technological and religious shifts have, in some senses, been tectonic in scale in the era following the second world war. Globalization has diminished the role of the nation-state in political and economic spheres. The collapse of European and Soviet communism, the rise of China and India and—thus far—the dominance of the United States in these spheres has meant that American values have often been dominant, but are now open to profound challenge. As political and economic spheres have become global, there has, for many, been a drift towards the social and religious becoming increasingly individualistic. On the one hand the exponential rise of entrepreneurial Pentecostalism has offered challenges to hierarchical Catholicism, while on the other, personal choice in terms of morality and faith has become the norm with which Western society especially is most comfortable. As Stephen Morgan observes in his essay, even the most objectionable activities have come to be described as 'unacceptable' rather than simply 'wrong'. This is neither the vocabulary nor the view of the Church and so presents a fresh dynamic in addressing these challenges and the social evils of poverty.

The dramatic penetration of technology, and perhaps more specifically electronic communications, provides us with a conundrum. It is both globalized and highly individual. A blogger or tweeter in a remote corner of the world can influence matters well beyond their physical sphere, through simply using their mobile phone. Social networks can be used to generate 'flash-mobs' in which hundreds of strangers gather to dance or sing—or give to charity—in a public space. Similarly, they are used to mobilise crowds for rebellion, repression or riot. It depends on your point of view as to whether this is a 'good' or 'bad' thing. For example, in the summer of 2011 the British Prime Minister,

David Cameron, found himself both praising and condemning the use of social networking to unite common interests and bring people together. His praise was for its use in the 'Arab Spring' uprisings in Tunisia, Egypt, Syria and Libya (more complex though those contexts are). However, faced with disturbances in London, fuelled by the same networks, he discussed the possibility of state censorship of these channels. A position commended by the Chinese government. Interesting times indeed.

Amidst such complexity there can be little doubt that in developing a social conscience, thought and strategies for action, the Church is presented with continuing and ever fresh challenges as the world (and the Church's own flock) simply refuses to sit still. But there is hope: the thought of 'social action flash-mobs' is an intriguing and powerful one that could not only achieve much but could speak to younger people in a better way than the hand-wringing, 'what are we to do about the youth', that we tend to engage in. Similarly, both globalisation and individualism invite us to re-express our notion of the human person and of community. In doing this we are drawn to a deeper understanding of ourselves, the Church, society, freedom and God's kingdom. The scope for evangelisation is thus increased and, of course, so is the scope and imperative for renewal within the Church. Again, whether this is a good or bad thing depends upon your point of view .

This leads us to the fact that not all challenges are 'external'; if anything can be considered to be truly external or 'beyond' the universal Church. Throughout the twentieth Century debates of all sorts within the Church were conditioned by the secular notions of 'left and right' and 'conservative and liberal'. Debates on liturgical reform, the interpretation of Scripture, catechesis, governance and education were all bogged down by the tendency to take sides along lines that mirrored those of politics. Opponents condemned each other as 'out of touch with the faithful' or 'unfaithful to Tradition' in much the same way secular debates used—and use—terms such as 'reactionary' or 'unpatriotic'. Today communications technology has been drawn into the battle with combative and often vitriolic blogs and websites being used to disparage not only the arguments but even the reputation of opponents. As one observer commented in conversation recently, this is truly a scene to 'make the devil dance with joy'. The time for such in-fighting and self-destructive behaviour *within the Church* has never been right but surely it is now the right time to stop, especially when its luxuriance is benchmarked against the suffering of those oppressed or in poverty. We need no new Avignon.

Perhaps more than any other aspect of Church life, with the possible exception of liturgical reform and marital relationships, the praxis of social teaching and the development of new social thought has been fraught with the fighting defined by left and right. There has been much talk and little dialogue, huge arguments but little resolution.

Troubled by the on-going question of fidelity to Tradition, the development of social thought has also fallen victim to partisan politics. The spectre of atheistic communism hung heavily over the twentieth century and for some, such as Pope John Paul II and the then Joseph Ratzinger, its defeat became an important characteristic of the mission of the Church. Similarly, the often oppressive responses exacted by the West on client states, and especially those in the developing world, have resulted in popular backlashes that have understandably demonised western values often conflating them with Christian ones. Very recently the ability of the Church's leadership to even speak amidst such argument has been compromised following episcopal cover-ups of the clerical child abuse crisis encountered in so many countries.

So, a polarised debate has been exacerbated and Catholic social praxis has been drawn in, or squeezed out, with excellent initiatives being dismissed by all sides as being associated with left-wing or right-wing ideologies. The closure of debate has been detrimental intellectually, but above all in a practical sense in which help has been denied to many on the basis of incompatible ideology. And as we have begun to emerge from the strait jackets of such characterisation there is a danger that old habits are represented in new terms with a renewed stigmatisation of authentic spiritualities, theologies, apostolates and contributions as 'insufficiently orthodox' or 'excessively traditionalist'. The Church's understanding of humanity is compassionate, vast and demanding but need not be diluted by reaching for ideological totems of closure at the expense of the demanding journey into virtue.

Engagement is the key here. Just as Christ engaged with Pharisees and civic authorities in the street we must seek to engage with all who have opposing views; becoming immersed in a comfortable orthodoxy rich in conversation. St Francis, after all, learnt more from those he met in hovels than he often did from those ensconced in palatial abbeys while St Dominic and St Catherine of Siena's preaching challenged the most humble and the most mighty both within the Church and beyond. Gone are the days when a simple *anathema* would suffice to make an opinion we did not like go away. We must engage in sensible and mature debate internally and move beyond polemic and vitriol so as to be able to walk comfortably again in the highways and byways. It is hoped then that this volume, in seeking to provoke conversation and debate, represents part of that effort as we seek to bring together diverse perspectives into a mature and secure forum. As with the Church in Corinth, our internal squabbles do nothing to render glory to God. This, of course, brings other challenges.

As we have touched upon, perhaps the greatest challenge facing the Church in attempts to contribute to debates in society is one of credibility. Few disagree on this fact, but few agree on why. It is easy to fool ourselves that it is down to simple secularisation, or the rise of atheism, or 'the abortion crisis' or only a ' false' view of 'reason'. These are undoubtedly factors, but to settle on these is to attempt to look for the excuse 'out there'. Perhaps more significant is the decline in credibility in all institutions over recent years in the face of abuses of power, financial mismanagement and the erosion of democratic processes. The economic crisis, post 2008, and the political responses that have ensured the financial security of those who brought it about, allied with consequent public spending reductions, has meant that in the west, confidence in governments and financial institutions has been under intense pressure. Similar declines can also be seen in confidence relating to journalists, judges, police, doctors and teachers. Each sector has had its own crisis which has left it reformed to some extent, and with reduced respect despite, rather than because of, this reform.

Perhaps the most significant crisis to hit the Church over the last few decades which has impacted on its credibility has been the scandal of the sexual abuse of children by clergy and religious and most especially attempts to hide this by those who were in senior positions of trust. It has not been unique in facing this. Other faith communities, teachers and the medical profession have all faced similar revelations. Yet, the issue is associated in the common psyche with the Catholic Church. This is, no doubt, because higher standards are rightly expected but the real scandal that stands out is the mishandling of the issue by the hierarchy. Perpetrators were protected and placed in positions where they could commit these crimes again, whilst victims were hushed. The language used by the Church was also equivocal with abusers described as 'sinners' or 'sick men' rather than acknowledging that they were criminals who had committed heinous acts. The place for these men is prison and we must be clear about this. The result of the protection and the equivocation is that moral authority has been lost, in fact seized upon, and will take some regaining if our claims to credibility in the field of social ethics are to have any standing.

To recapture our credibility is going to take more than apology. The time for apologies was long ago and they did not come; they will sound very hollow now. True contrition is needed, expressed in word and deed. There are few areas where we can begin to show this contrition, and so regain credibility, more clearly than in the engagement with social issues and in listening to the poorest; in engaging with balanced and mature debate in academia, the public square and parish council as well as working tirelessly in practical selfless 'apostolic' action. This is perhaps our greatest opportunity springing from the challenges that face us in the world today. And it is one that we ought rightly to have sought in the face of an economic crisis rather than in reparation for our community's sins. This is part of the complexity of what will constitute Catholic social conscience, thought and action in the years to come.

Indeed, the demands of today are likely to mean that we have reached a point where we are called to move beyond 'social teaching' into an approach that we might call 'social virtue'. This is not to dismiss the great value of the Catholic social teaching tradition which must be upheld and encouraged to grow. However, just as personal morality is better expressed through the development of virtue rather than simply following rules, so too are social ethics and action.

Firstly, we need to take seriously and engage constructively with social thought wherever it springs from. If it is destructive or erroneous in and of itself it will likely have to be reconsidered or refreshed. We must not reject thought simply because it has come from the wrong place or arrives at challenging concrete conclusions that test us and the quality and efficacy of our response. Francis Davis's essays here show this fulsomely. Nor should we disregard it because it has not 'come down' as official teaching. Much of our tradition of social thought has come from laity, from small communities and religious working in the field. In the work, for example, of those such as Bartolomé de las Casas and the Salamanca School whose contribution predates so many better known European voices. Truth comes from God, even if we don't particularly like the way he communicates it to us.

This then is the challenge—to renew, to discuss and debate the Catholic social conscience, tradition and action in our times. And this book is but a beginning.

Acknowledgements

In preparing a book one incurs many debts of gratitude and a section entitled 'acknowledgements' can only do partial justice by way of thanks: Without Charlotte Jenkins the conference from which this publication emerges, and which we jointly directed, would never have happened and we would like to pay tribute to her hard work, dedication and enthusiasm over many hours. Indeed the Jenkins family were key with Charlotte's father, David Jenkins,—both in his capacity as Birmingham Archdiocesan representative for Aid to the Church In Need and as administrator of Archbishop Bernard Longley's Justice and Peace Commission—made a huge contribution as did the Rt Hon John Battle. As we mention in the book a unique feature of the event was that we were able to gather, in friendship and conversation, those from parts of the Church who never normally meet, those from diverse religious communities that would rarely explore Catholic social thought or action, and those from countries throughout Europe and further afield who may rarely find England a gathering place.

Particular thanks go to the Jesuit team at the University of Oxford Catholic Chaplaincy, especially Fr Roger Dawson SJ, who despite the event coinciding with the death of his mother was enormously supportive both before, during and afterwards. Fr John O'Connor OP was a gentle and warm host of significant parts of the conference at Blackfriars, Oxford. We were pleased that Fr Timothy Radcliffe OP, Fr David Goodill OP, Fr Richard Finn OP and Fr David Sanders OP chose to attend and that Fr Bob Eccles OP, Fr Simon Gaine OP and Fr Timothy Gardner OP made special trips to be present. The Prior Provincial, Fr John Farrell OP OP stayed throughout and preached at the closing Mass.

The late Fr Austin Milner OP was the strongest of our encouragers, while the most important Dominican in Oxford, Sr Winnie McGarry OP of the Bushey Congregation, deserves both our thanks and love. Fr Brendan Callaghan SJ (Master of Campion Hall, Oxford) and Fr Felix Stephens OSB (Master of St Benet's Hall, Oxford) were also generous hosts to delegates and helped in other ways and our thanks go to them.

More broadly the IXE initiative (http://www.initiative-ixe.eu/About-us/IXE-Who-we-are) leant many a helping hand notably by its members attending and by its President, M Jerome Vignon, giving the key opening address. For an English conference to have collaborated with the eminent *Semaines Sociales De France* is a first and was greatly helped by the internationalism of the conference's President, Rt Rev William Kenney CP, (Bishop for Europe) himself a former president of Caritas Europa, and long standing contributor to the work of COMECE. For one of us, of course, colleagues at Caritas Europa and European Caritas agencies have remained true sources of inspiration and Fr Ernie Gillen (President), Marius Wanders (former Secretary General), George Joseph (Caritas Sweden), Adriana Opromolla, Peter Verghaege, Sr Angelita Sokic (formerly Caritas Croatia), Katerina Sekula (Caritas Polska), Robert Urbe (Caritas Luxemburg) deserve particular mention with—although no list can be adequate—Chris Bain of CAFOD and Paul Chitnis (until recently Director of SCIAF). We were delighted that two alumni of the Caritas family, Stefan Wallner (Secretary General of the Austrian Green party) and Franz Karl Preuller (now a Director at the ground breaking Erste Foundation) were able to speak and be with us. Professor Phillip Booth of the IEA gave a keynote address and Dr Andrew Hegarty of the Thomas More Institute very kindly reorganised his schedule to chair the panel on education. Special mention must also go to the Benedictines at Douai, Christopher Jamison OSB, Sr Mary Clare Mason DJ and the De Le Mennais Brothers whose global *'Reseau Mennaisien'* sets a new model for linking education, fundraising, social action and a care for the poorest; as well as the Focolarini who both promoted the conference (Liz Taite) and welcomed one of us so warmly to the wedding of Ellen Van Stichel whose contribution is among the most passionate calls to justice found here. The birth of Ellen and Hans' son, Johannes, was a blessing and a joy as the book reached proof stage. For the other of us the continuing support of colleagues at the Maryvale Institute, Birmingham is greatly appreciated. In particular the wisdom and generosity of Fr Robert Letellier deserves special thanks. Thanks must also go to the Department for Pastoral Formation, Diocese of Portsmouth, directed by Nicky Stevens, who provided invaluable practical assistance to the conference.

Ultimately this eclectic work, and the accompanying special edition of the *International Journal of Public Theology* (Brill: Leiden) would not have been possible but for very concrete encouragement in this, and in many other endeavours, of Sr Anne Thomson DJ and the provincial council of the Daughters of Jesus, William Hampson DL and the trustees of the Epiphany Trust, Neville Kyrke-Smith and *Aid to the Church In Need*, Michael Phelan and the trustees of *The Tablet Trust*, Lord Alton of Liverpool, Luke Coppen, Kevin Flaherty of *The Catholic Times*, the late Robert Keen, Rev Stephen Morgan, Fr Kevin Robb OP, Captain Terry Drummond CA, Oliver Holt OSB, Michael and Catherine Davis, Mgr Vincent Harvey, Fr Peter Codd, Richard Zipfel, Fr Terry Tastard, Mgr John O'Shea, Fr John Docherty OAR, Jamie Bogle, Phil Gray, Professor Peter Coleman, Catherine Pepinster and Elena Curti. The Archdiocese of Westminster's Head of Pastoral Affairs, Edmund Adamus, has been a constant source of encouragement in debating some of the content and ideas and in other ways. The Archdiocese of Southwark Commission for Justice Peace and the Integrity of Creation helped with the launch and our thanks especially to Terry Brown, and also to Bishop Patrick Lynch SSCC, who spoke at the conference as part of his outstanding work on migration and refugees for the Catholic Bishops' Conference of England and Wales. We are greatly appreciative of moral and financial support of the MB Reckitt Trust and an anonymous donor. We would wish to thank our wives and wider families for their support and solidarity.

Without Gracewing and the infinite patience of Tom Longford (Managing Director) and Rev Prof Paul Haffner (Theological and Editorial Director) there would be no book at all. Our thanks to them.

And while this book emerges from a conference in Oxford, England, attended by those from tens of countries across Europe and further afield its editors have their roots, in the end, in a particular Church, namely the Diocese of Portsmouth. At the time of going to press the Diocese's long-standing Bishop, Rt Rev Crispian Hollis, is receiving treatment for cancer just at the point when he was due to retire and hand on to a new incumbent, yet to be announced. This book then is dedicated to Bishop Hollis, his successor and the clergy and families of Portsmouth Diocese, far and near, and its twin Diocese of Bamenda in the Cameroon for all they have been and will be to the local Church, the universal Church and to us.

Contributors

Erik Borgman is professor of systematic theology at the University of Tilburg, the Netherlands. He is the biographer of the Flemish theologian Edward Schillebeeckx. He was also the President of the International Society for Religion, Literature and Culture. He is a member of the Editorial Board and the Presidential Board of *Concilium*: International Journal for Theology.

Keith Chappell is lecturer in Catholic philosophy and social thought at the Maryvale Institute, Birmingham and a member of Blackfriars Hall, University of Oxford.

Francis Davis is a graduate of Ashridge and Warwick Business Schools. Aside from his work on Catholic and other religious communities, he is editor of the forthcoming *Decentralisation And the Big Society* (Routledge) and was previously Visiting Fellow in Social Policy at the London School of Economics.

Ellen Van Stichel is a research assistant for the Anthropos project at the Theological Ethics Research Unit of the Faculty of Theology (KU Leuven, Belgium). This interdisciplinary project aims to reinterpret the Christian anthropology from both a systematic-theological and theological-ethical perspective. She holds a Doctorate from the University of Leuven where she was supervised by Professor Johan Verstraeten.

Jolanta Babiuch works for the Oxfordshire Racial Equality Council and is a Lecturer at Oxford Brookes University, UK. She previously taught at the Institute of Sociology of Warsaw University in Poland, and the University of London. She has published numerous academic and press articles, as well as several books in the field of sociology, business ethics and religious studies.

Miroslav Marynovych is the Vice-Rector of the Ukrainian Catholic University in Lviv, founder of Amnesty International Ukraine, and a founding member of the Ukrainian Helsinki Group. He lived through ten years of hard labour and exile under the Soviet system having been sentenced in 1977.

Lukács László SchP is Professor Emeritus in the faculty of dogmatics, Sapientia University, Hungary of which university he was the founding Director. He is a former member of the Pontifical Council of Social Communications.

Jonathan Luxmoore is a journalist based in Warsaw and Oxford and a regular contributor to *The Tablet* and *The Universe*. He writes on social issues in Europe and has specialist knowledge on these issues in Poland and the UK.

Michael Sutton is Professor Emeritus of Modern History and International Relations, Aston University, UK.

Stephen Morgan is a Deacon of the Diocese of Portsmouth where he is Secretary to the Trustees of the Diocese of Portsmouth. He is a past-Chairman of the Conference of Financial Secretaries of England and Wales. He is also reading for a DPhil on the relationship between continuity and change at St Benet's Hall, University of Oxford.

Geoff Morgan is the Anglican chaplain at the Imperial College Healthcare NHS Trust in London and preparing a doctorate at King's College, University of London.

Gerald Grace is Professor and director of the Centre for Research and Development in Catholic Education (CRDCE), University of London, Institute of Education, UK He has researched and written widely about Catholic education in the UK and abroad.

Terry Prendergast is Chief Executive of Catholic Marriage Care, a UK charity which provides support for marriage and relationships through education, research and the provision of counselling services.

Part 1:
Principles and Contexts

To Go Over to the Side of the Barbarians: Re-inventing subsidiarity

ERIK BORGMAN

Introduction

At the beginning of the second decade of the century we witness the rise of anti-Islamic populism all over Europe. In the Netherlands we have Geert Wilders, of course, the man CNN once dubbed 'a right-wing, anti-Islamic politician who hopes to become the next Dutch prime minister'. The Scandinavian Countries have their fair share of anti-Islamism in the political arena, now strikingly brought to public attention by Anders Breivik. Following on from the publication of a militantly anti-immigration book by the then member of the Executive Board of the Deutsche Bundesbank and Social-Democratic politician Thilo Sarrazin,[1] in September 2010 anti-Islamic politician René Stadtkewitz drew a rather large crowd of followers in Germany for his anti-Islam party Die Freiheit. The amazing thing is not that, for instance, Wilders proposed to change the Dutch constitution and let it state that we have in the Netherlands a Judeo-Christian and humanist culture—and therefore not an Islamic culture. The amazing thing is that the debates on Islam have dominated the Dutch political scene for quite some time and that the other political parties in the Netherlands have not been able to come up with a convincing answer to Wilders' position. Wilders did not become the prime minister after the elections in June 2010, but where the German Christlich Demokratischen Union (CDU) expelled Stadtkewitz after he invited Geert Wilders to speak in Berlin and the Sozialdemokratische Partei Deutschlands did the same with Sarrazin after the publication of his book, the conservative Liberals and the Christian Democrats formed a government and closed a deal with Wilders to support it in order to give it a majority in parliament. Quite a few analysts have tried to understand and explain how the Netherlands, which for a long time were internationally famous for their tolerance and openness, could turn Islamophobic almost overnight.[2] I have no intention of joining them here. My question here is how to respond properly to the growth of this populism. I will suggest in this chapter that the tradition of Catholic Social Thought could help us, and claim that in a sense—and I will clarify in what sense—the answer is the principle of subsidiarity.[3]

The Issue of Populism

In order to make this claim plausible, it is necessary to see the anti-Islamism of contemporary populism as in a sense peripheral to its electoral attraction. This might seem a surprising proposal, because it is so obviously central in the message its propagandists emphasise. People come to this kind of populism because they feel—with the term used by the populist politician Pim Fortuijn who was murdered in 2002—'orphaned'.[4] Or to be more modest, that is what seems apparent in the behaviour of the followers of Geert Wilders. Because, strangely enough, when they are confronted with the fact that a lot of what Wilders proposes is impractical, or even impossible, people who voted for Wilders' Freedom Party tend to answer that they do not expect Wilders to act literally on what he said. Manifesto proposals such as responding to harassment by young Muslim men by proposing outlawing the wearing of headscarves by Muslim women, or even sending second and third generation migrants who are Dutch by birth and nationality back to 'where they came from', thus contravening international law are not expected to be implemented by voters. They are attracted to his position, they say, because they feel he names the problems they are confronted with every day, whereas other politicians are 'just talking', enjoying their power and 'filling their own pockets'.[5] This highly overstated, not seldom aggressively uttered message expresses, in my view, a real experience of a large segment of the people in contemporary societies in North-Western Europe. It is the experience of not being really part of things, not being seen or heard, not being paid attention to, not being taken seriously in their experiences and struggles, in their grief and their anxieties.[6]

The expression 'not taken seriously in their grief and their anxieties' echoes the opening phrase of the Pastoral Constitution on the Church in the modern world *Gaudium et Spes* (7 December 1965) of the Second Vatican Council:

> The joys and the hopes, the grief and the anxieties of the men of this age, especially those who are poor or in any way afflicted, these are the joys and hopes, the grief and anxieties of the followers of Christ. [...] United in Christ, they are led by the Holy Spirit in their journey to the Kingdom of their Father and they have welcomed the news of salvation which is meant for every man. That is why this community realizes that it is truly linked with mankind and its history by the deepest of bonds.[7]

Populism also challenges us to engage in a new way with the Gospel parable of the Prodigal Son (Luke 15:11–32).[8] In the parable we, the people in North-Western Europe, are in the position of both the sons. We can easily identify with the son who asked his father the share of his estate that should come to him. We have taken our ideological inheritance, living off it for a while, maybe not so much squandering it on a life of dissipation, as it is said in the parable about the youngest son, and certainly not swallowing it up with prostitutes, as his older brother suggests, but clearly not making it productive, not renewing it. A lot of ideals of the Welfare States in the sixties and seventies were directly or indirectly inspired by a Christian view on the good life and the responsibility of all for all.[9] But we did fail to let our experiences renew that tradition and that tradition inform our experiences again; thus the inspiration was 'freely spend', as the expression in the parable is. Now we are confronted with a crisis—what the parable calls 'a severe famine', not just the current economic crisis, but the cultural one that is surfacing within it[10]—and a lot of people experience themselves as 'in dire need'. Just like the youngest son in the parable, a lot of people manage to find ways to survive, but at the same time they were longing for something else or something more, longing to eat their fill of the pods on which the swine feed.

Populism is feeding on this feeling of being left out, of not even been given a share of what the swine are given. Populism suggests that it is like the father, being on the lookout for his son, seeing him when he is still a long way off, embracing him and welcoming him not just with compassion, but with festivity and restoring him as a member of the household. On closer look, however, populism embodies the logic of the elder brother, who feels that he has served his father for years not once disobeying any of his orders, but now complaining that he did not get even as much as a young goat to feast on with his friends. It is the feeling of not being valued for what you do, simply being taken for granted and claiming the right to be if not properly valued, then at least properly rewarded.[11]

The father in the parable in a way does the same thing to both his sons. He goes out to them, makes clear how he considers them to be part of the community and the household. Both sons made a profound mistake. The younger one went away and sought freedom by leaving behind the community in which he is at home and taken care of, and to which he is responsible. The older one stays, but apparently sees his responsibilities as part of a bargain, as doing something to receive something else in return. The father invites them both to see how they in fact depend on the household they are obliged to contribute to and which he embodies. They simply belong to it because they are what they are, because they depend on it and at the same time contribute to it. Society and community ultimately are not based on contract, but on the simple fact that humans are dependent beings, dependent on what they receive from one another and therefore obliged to give to others what they need. Ultimately, human beings receive by giving. By giving others what they long for we receive from others where we long for: community, a place that is ours and where we can truly live. At least, that is what the parable suggests to be the divine logic, the original logic of which we moved away—fundamentally through sin, concretely by institutionalising a logic according to which we can and have to deserve, produce and conquer our living. Although this logic is presented as embodying the ultimate liberation, it installs a mechanism of attributing to human beings an irredeemable guilt.[12]

Catholic Social Thought after Vatican II

It is central to Catholic social thought that human beings find the good life for which they are created by trying to realise it, in their own way and in their own contexts, as a common good in which they, together with others, participate. To do this they do not need to be forced from the outside, by law or threat of violence, but they simply have to follow their true nature.

However, in order to see Catholic Social Thought in this way—and, for instance, not as a static body of doctrine, or a teaching to be condoned because it is presented with the highest ecclesial authority—and in order to show what it can mean in our contemporary debates, it is necessary to develop a post-Vatican II reading of it.[13] We should be fully conscious of the fact that we are theologising after *Lumen Gentium*, in which the Church is explicitly not presented as a source and origin of Gods salvation for the world, but is said to be 'like a sacrament', that is 'sign and instrument both of a very closely knit union with God and of the unity of the whole human race', which is the double result of our redemption in Jesus Christ.[14] We should be aware that we speak after *Gaudium et Spes*, that confesses to the world as created and sustained by its Maker's love, fallen indeed into the bondage of sin, yet emancipated now by Christ.[15] In this created and redeemed world, witnessing to its fallen state, but also to its restoration in Christ, the task of the Church is not simply to sustain and repeat the message once entrusted to her. The Church can only keep what is given to her by receiving it ever anew. In order to do that it has to scrutinise the 'signs of the times' and interpret them in the light of the Gospel, as the Pastoral Constitution on the Modern World states.[16] *Gaudium et Spes* explains further:

> Motivated by its faith that it is led by the Lord's Spirit, Who fills the earth, the People of God labours to decipher authentic signs of God's presence and purpose in the happenings, needs and desires in which this People has a part along with other men of our age. For faith throws a new light on everything, manifests God's design for man's total vocation, and thus directs the mind to solutions which are fully human.[17]

As French social activist and Catholic mystic Madeleine Delbrêl (1904–1964) explained already before Vatican II, this implies that the Spirit of God and his Christ can truly be met in the midst of ordinary life in the streets that make up our highly secularised cities.[18]

Taking this as a starting point means it is impossible to read Catholic Social Thought as a unique treasure of the Catholic Church of which it can distribute what is necessary to a passive, receiving world. In 1979 the French Dominican theologian Marie-Dominique Chenu, who was very much behind the concept of 'the signs of the times' as developed in the documents of Vatican II, published a book criticising what he called the ideological aspects of the Catholic Social Doctrine.[19] In Chenu's view the Social Doctrine of the Church actively hides how it is related to other views on what society is and on what a good society should be, thus suggesting that the Church comes up with solutions to contemporary problems from outside the historical situation. Its rhetoric suggests that problems produced by human history and its disturbing and destructive chaos, can only be solved by the Church that represents a Divine presence that is not historical. For Chenu, this is against the Christian message that, in Jesus Christ, God was truly incarnated in human history. Here I will not go into the debate whether the revival of Catholic Social Teaching starting in 1980 with John Paul II's encyclical *Laborem Exercens*, was an attempt to re-install the idea of the Church as a source of solutions the world itself is unable to come up with.[20] For now, it suffices to stress the importance of reading and developing Catholic Social Thought in line with *Gaudium et Spes*, that is to say as a fully contemporary way of thinking, closely connected to, responding to and living from the world to which God has revealed his presence in Jesus Christ and the Holy Spirit.

With this in mind, it is possible to read the principle of subsidiarity as a contribution to our contemporary debates. In 1931, in his encyclical *Quadragesimo Anno*, Pope Pius XI introduced the principle of subsidiarity in the official documents of the Church, writing:

> As history abundantly proves, it is true that on account of changed conditions many things which were done by small associations in former times cannot be done now save by large associations. Still, that most weighty principle, which cannot be set aside or changed, remains fixed and unshaken in social philosophy: Just as it is gravely wrong to take from individuals what they can accomplish by their own initiative and industry and give it to the community, so also it is an injustice and at the same time a grave evil and disturbance of right order to

> assign to a greater and higher association what lesser and subordinate organizations can do. For every social activity ought of its very nature to furnish help to the members of the body social, and never destroy and absorb them (QA 79).

Not seldom the principle of subsidiarity is presented as embodying a 'third way', occupying the middle ground between liberalism, that only recognizes individuals as actors in society and considers them even to be fully autonomous actors, and socialism, that focuses on the collective and the state. And indeed, the so called 'solidarism' of Pius XI—and that of bishop Wilhelm Emmanuel von Ketteler (1811–1877) who inspired Leo XIII as he wrote *Rerum Novarum*, and of economist and social philosopher Heinrich Pesch SJ (1854–1926) who inspired *Quadragesimo Anno*[21]—of which the principle of subsidiarity originally was part, intended to develop an alternative to both liberalism and socialism.

However, from the way John XXIII took up subsidiarity in 1961 in his encyclical *Mater et Magistra*, it becomes clear that its ultimate focus is a specific anthropology. John XXIII stated that the whole of Catholic Social Thought rests on one basic principle: 'individual human beings are the foundation, the cause and the end of every social institution. That is necessarily so, for men are by nature social beings'.[22]

Mater et Magistra deals with international relations, and taking the principle of subsidiarity as its foundation the encyclical argues that people should be seen and treated as responsible for their own development, including the development of their communities on a local, a regional, a national and a global level. It is an injustice when people are considered to be passive material, building stones for a social edifice designed and built by others—even if these others are the politicians they democratically elected. Instead, they should be treated as both builders and architects, responsible for and directed to the good life for themselves through the building of the common good. Thus they are seen as created truly in the image of God: Creator, Sustainer and Redeemer of the world.

Subsidiarity as the Possibility to Think Democratic Self-Rule

The principle of subsidiarity makes it possible to take into account that society is built by people acting towards what they see as the common good, from their particular place and from their particular viewpoint. They are not, as liberal theories of society have it, acting solely or mainly on individual self-interest. Even empirically their behaviour cannot be explained on these terms: there is a lot of spontaneous mutual support and dedication to the welfare of others in all societies. This is exactly why democratic self-rule is possible and will not necessarily end in a war of all against all, as Thomas Hobbes predicts in his Leviathan (1651). Where the defence of family as the oldest society independent of the state by Leo XIII in *Rerum Novarum* (RN 12) could easily be understood as a defence of static, 'natural' relations in the private sphere, John XXIII clarifies that what is ultimately at stake for the Church is the ability of people to know what in principle is good for themselves and their fellow-humans, and to act accordingly. They do not need the state or any political of civil doctrine to know what to do. This is a major counter-point to all who approach policy making as 'social engineering', ignoring the experiences of people participating in the system because their point of view is of a limited nature, which is supposed to make them incapable of seeing the common good. This approach, I argue, is a major source for populist resentment against politicians and policy makers. Many people feel that their leaders are not really interested in what happens to them. As far as these leaders see their tasks in terms of engineering and the emotions of the citizens as something they have to manage, they are making a major point.[23]

At the same time, thinking in terms of subsidiarity accounts for the fact that society is not simply one. There is no obvious centre were the important decisions are made, where the major policies could be formulated and from where they could be co-ordinated. Society is what comes into existence through the enactment of a diversity of people on a diversity of ideas, responsibilities and pro-grams, all directed to what they consider to be the common good. As Thomas Aquinas already stated in his commen-tary on Aristotle's *Politica*, society exists in a plurality of melodies sounding together in harmony.[24] However, this might still be too Mediaeval a view to be immediately convincing. We moderns are aware of the fact that with a multitude of perspectives, harmony is not something given. We know that we cannot just contribute to a given harmony, both because this harmony does not simply exist and because if it seems to exist, it often means that groups and their approaches are excluded. This implies that taking seriously the principle that 'individual human beings are the foundation, the cause and the end of every social institution', can mean that what seemed to be harmony to most, has to be disturbed in the name of the excluded in order to have them included.

This means that—to stick to the musical metaphor—that by contributing to and trying to be a community and build a society with all our differences, in and from all the different places where we are living and working, we are inventing and improvising new harmonies. Mediaeval polyphony then is no longer the leading image, but contem-porary free jazz. What we do not need and should not want is one composer-conductor, as if our societies only exist as they are designed, organised and led to make them one. What we need are virtuoso improvisers who hear melodies in the cacophonies our societies are unto the untrained ear, who can then play that melody and induce others to play along with them. Presenting our dissenting melodies and at the same time attempting to harmonise our views on the common good: that is what builds a society that is on its way to being really common and really good.[25]

Key in the subsidiary view on society is that the fundamental differences between people in their points of view and in their views, in what they see as the common good and in what they consider to be part of the common good, is not considered to be a social problem, but a social wealth. That our ideas of what is going on and what should be going on are different is not a threat for our community, but ultimately its very foundation. It makes it worthwhile and even essential for us to listen to one another; without others telling us what they think and what they know, we know less and are poorer, both as an individual and as a community. Not our explicit view on the common good, but our struggle to formulate a view that encompasses not simply my concern, but those of all others as well, is the foundation of our society. We will probably not succeed in doing that as long as we live our historical lives, but in our attempts to formulate a common, all-compassing view what we hope and strive for is present among us in a hidden manner, analogous to how Augustine presents the *civitas Dei* as present, but never fully realised in the *civitas terrena*. To have people complaining about their exclusion from the *civitas* by not being approached as co-constructors of it, as in my analysis they do in populism, then presents a call to action. Policies should be developed not to 'make them happy' and to make it possible to realise some of the idea they put forward, but to put them in the position of co-creators of society, again or for the first time.[26]

Do we need a common ground, then, a common philosophy, a common tradition of life or even a common faith? It is often argued that we do, both from religious points of view and from secular points of view. Populist ideologies suggest that we need a common identity as a people before any argument about the nature of our communities and society makes sense. My point here is, however, that the principle of subsidiarity, the principle that 'human beings are the foundation, the cause and the end of every social institution' because humans 'are by nature social beings', presents an alternative to the view that we are held together by a common tradition, a communal identity or a collective heritage. From a Christian point of view, we are not so much inheriting our communities and societies from the past, or possess it in the present. Instead, we are receiving it from the very that future we are building, and that we are receiving from God as we are building it.[27] As Psalm 127 (verse 1) says: 'Unless the Lord built the house, those who built it labour in vain'.

In the Wake of the Future

Among the important insights I learned from Edward Schillebeeckx, my theological mentor, is that the Christian tradition does not concentrate on the past, neither does it focus on the present. The Christian tradition is about the future God is granting us. Therefore, ethically speaking Christianity is about the future we grant one another. According to the Gospel we live from the new possibilities we find and create, the ever new horizon God's enduring presence brings us and gives us.[28] This, in Schillebeeckx's view, is the kind of life Jesus has made possible for us by preaching and witnessing to the message that the kingdom of God is at hand.[29] We live in the space and the time opened up for us by Gods kingdom in its coming presence and present coming. It is from this future that all people can be seen as contributing to the kingdom of God, that it is possible to take them seriously in both their joys and their hopes, and in their griefs and their anxieties. They are building Gods kingdom from their hopes and anxieties.[30] That is exactly what the principle of subsidiarity enables us to understand, in my reading of it.

As I said already at the beginning of this essay, this is in my view the answer to contemporary populism. It makes it possible that people in all their differences and diversities see themselves as important for the society of the future we are building in the present. Their views and their engagements are essential to our common life and our common good, and therefore it is not only out of compassion that we should care of what happens to them. There is nothing wrong with compassion, of doing something because it is good for the other. But we also should be taking their experiences and their fates seriously because that is from what our future is built, in the same way as we, in our experiences and fates are providing the building stones for their future. What is lost time and again in our Western societies is the awareness that we are one another's wealth, one another's inheritance, one another's gift of life; that, in Timothy Radcliffe's phrase, 'I am because we are'.[31] We are like the prodigal son because we cut ourselves off from what really keeps us alive, and we are not fully lost because we may leave the community by which we are sustained, but the One who is the centre and focus of that community never leaves us and connects and reconnects with us. If necessary, over and over again.

This is, of course, not simply the fulfilment of the desire that is at the roots of contemporary populism, the desire to be seen and recognised, to be valued and considered important. It is also a break with the desire to be in the centre of attention, to set the standard of what it right and good. To understand oneself in the light of the principle of subsidiarity means handing oneself over to the community that is our future—the community that is not simply given in the present, but hidden in the conflicts and struggles we are facing today. This requires a particular step which the French Catholic intellectual and social activist Frederic Ozanam (1813–1853), among other things the founder of the Saint Vincent de Paul Society, called 'to go over to the side of the barbarians'. We have to understand that outsiders and those we spontaneously view as our adversaries, are ultimately struggling for the same *bonum commune* as we are struggling for. Our ideas may be mutually exclusive, where they point at is inclusive of us both. The barbarians for Ozanam were the people supporting the revolution of 1848, turning against state and Church and actively hoping for a new society in freedom, equality and brotherhood. Catholics should not fight them because of the anti-clericalism and laicism, but they should see that they were in fact fighting for what Catholicism holds dear. Hence Ozanam's call to his fellow-Catholics: *passons au barbaires,* let us go over to the side of the barbarians! Catholics should not stick to their own and exclude what seems threatening, but recognize that their deepest desire can only be fulfilled if they joined in their longing with those they considered barbarians.[32]

The principle of subsidiarity helps us to explain why this is so: the community that is seeking what it means to become a community, is the community we seek. In our sincere seeking we are in the space of God's coming kingdom and therefore by seeking we are finding what we seek. But that does not make it an easy thing to do. Going over to the side of the barbarians means leaving behind what one is, in order to truly find it. This requires faith, and this faith can only be given to us by someone who goes over to us. Christians believe that in Jesus Christ, God 'went over to the barbarians', to us, in order to enable us to become truly members of a society focusing on and encompassed by the search for the common good. What we do not need is a common philosophy or religion as the foundation of our community. What we need are people willing 'to go over to the side of the barbarians', who are willing to become strangers in their own community in order to build a common home with strangers. 'Healthy people don't need a doctor, but sick people do', says Jesus in the Gospel in defence of his intimacy with tax collectors and sinners (Matthew 9:12; Mark 2:17; Luke 5:31). It would help tremendously is we saw one another and ourselves as both needful of healing and able to heal. It would express the necessary change from 'Who is my neighbour?' to 'Who was neighbour unto those who needed one?' (cf. Luke 10:29 and 10:36)

At this moment of history, therefore, the Church should not so much try to give foundation to given communities, be it national communities, ethnic communities, or even faith communities. Communities that are built on a common view are by necessity exclusive. Instead, the Church should embody a community of people that do not hold on to their identity as their property, but see it as its identity and mission to go over to the side of the barbarians as long as there are any barbarians left. And explain that they do this to trustfully and faithfully await the all-inclusive community that is promised to all of us and that, as the full realisation of the common good, will be our true happiness.

Notes

[1] Th. Sarrazin, *Deutschland schafft sich ab: Wie wir unser Land aufs Spiel setzen* (München: Deutsche Verlags-Anstalt 2010).

[2] Cf. esp. I. Buruma, *Taming the Gods: Religion and Democracy in Three Continents* (Princeton: Princeton University Press 2010), 85–126.

[3] Re-inventing subsidiarity is a project I am currently involved in, sponsored by Tilburg University and a number of Roman Catholic organisations and funds in the Netherlands.

[4] See W. S. P. Fortuyn, *De verweesde samenleving: Een religieus-sociologisch tractaat* (Utrecht: 1995) (The Orphaned Society; A Religio-Sociological Tract). For analyses of what came to light in Pim Fortuyn as a fenomenon, see my 'Presentie in een verweesde samenleving: De gebeurtenissen rond Pim Fortuyn als tekenen van de tijd', in: *Tijdschrift voor Theologie* 42 (2002), 233–242 (Presence in an Orphaned Society: The Occurrences Around Pim Fortuyn as Signs of the Time); P. J. Margry, 'The Murder of Pim Fortuyn and Collective Emotions. Hype, Hysteria, and Holiness in the Netherlands?', in *Etnofoor: Antropologisch tijdschrift* 16 (2003), 106–131 .

[5] For the Wilders ideology, see M. Bosma, *De schijn-élite van de valse munters* (Amsterdam: Bert Bakker 2010) (The Peudo-elite of the Forgers). For an analyses on what is at stake in Wilders as a phenomenon, see M. Fennema, *Geert Wilders: De tovenaarsleer-*

ling (Amsterdam: Bert Bakker, 2010) (Geert Wilders: The Sorcerer's Apprentice).

6   Cf. *None of the Above: Non-voters and the 2001 election*, A Hansard Society Briefing, Ed. S. Diplock, London: Hansard Society 2001 <www.ipsos-mori.com/Assets/Docs/Archive/Polls/hansard2.pdf>.

7   Vatican II, *Gaudium et Spes*, 1. Official document of the Catholic Church are quoted in the English version from the Vatican website.

8   As a background of what follows, see A. J. Hultgren, *The Parables of Jesus: A Commentary*, Grand Rapids: Eerdmans 2002, 70–91; K. R. Snodegrass, *Stories with Intent: A Comprehensive Guide to the Parables of Jesus* (Grand Rapids: Eerdmans, 2008), 117–144.

9   Cf. A. de Swaan, *In Care of the State: Health Care, Education and Welfare in Europe and the USA in the Modern Era* (New York/Cambridge: Oxford University Press/Polity Press, 1988).

10   Cf. Ch. Collins / M. Wright, *The Moral Measure of the Economy*, (Maryknoll: Orbis, 2007).

11   For the Netherlands this is shown in some detail in an analysis of the feelings and the ways of reasoning of chronically dissatisfied native citizens; cf. M. de Gruijter / E. Smits van Waesberghe/ H, Boutelier, *'Een vreemde in eigen land': Ontevreden autochtone burgers over nieuwe Nederlanders en de overheid* (Amsterdam: Aksant, 2010) ('A stranger in ones own country': Dissatisfied autochthon citizens one new compatriots and the government).

12   Cf. for the analysis of this logic, T. Radcliffe, *Why Go to Church?: The Drama of the Eucharist* (London: Continuum, 2009), 16–27.

13   Of course it is not easy to say what a 'post-Vatican II reading' of Catholic Social Thought, given the ongoing fundamental debate on the right 'hermeneutics' of the documents of council. In my view it is a matter of intellectual honesty to recognize that the documents are in marked discontinuity with important aspects of the official Church teaching in the period directly preceding it. But the claim was, is and should be that this restores a continuity on a deeper level that was threatened by certain tendencies in Catholic theology and Church teaching in the Modern era. Cf. my article 'Retrieving God's Contemporary Presence: The Future of Edward Schillebeeckx's Theology of Culture', in: L. Boeve / F. Depoortere / S. van Erp (ed.), *Edward Schillebeeckx and Contemporary Theology* (London: T & T Clark, 2010), 235–251.

14   Vatican II, *Lumen Gentium*, 1.

15   See Vatican II, *Gaudium et Spes*, 4.

[16]   See *ibid.*, 4.

[17]   *Ibid.*, 11.

[18]   Cf. M. Delbrêl, *Nous autres, gens des rues* (Paris: Seuil, 1966).

[19]   M.-D. Chenu, *La doctrine sociale de l'Église comme idéologie* (Paris: Cerf, 1979). For the role of Chenu at Vatican II, see G. Alberigo, 'Un concile à la dimension du monde: Marie-Dominique Chenu à Vatican II d'après son journal', in: Marie-Dominique Chenu, *Moyen-Age et modernité* (Paris: Cerf, 1997), 155–172; G. Turbanti, 'Il ruolo del P. D. Chenu nell'elaboratione della constituzione Gaudium et spes', in *Ibid.*, 173–209. Cf. Chenu's own commentary in M.-D. Chenu, *Peuple de Dieu dans le Monde* (Paris: Cerf 1966), 11–34: 'Une constitution pastorale de l'Église' (1965) ; 35–55 : 'Les signes du temps' (1965); Idem, 'Les signes des temps: Réflexion théologique', in: Y. Congar/M. Peuchaurd (ed.), *L'Église dans le monde de ce temps: Constitution pastorale 'Gaudium et spes'.* Tome II: *Commentaires* (Paris: Cerf 1967), 205–225.

[20]   For the importance of the revitalizing of Catholic Social Teaching in the program of Pope John Paul II, see G. Weigel, *Witness to Hope: The Biography of Pope John Paul II* (New York: HarperCollins, 1999).

[21]   See esp. H. Pesch, *Liberalismus, Sozialismus und christliche Gesells-chaftsauffassung*, 2 delen, Freiburg: Herder 1893 en 1900. For further background information, cf. K. Petersen, *'Ich höre den Ruf nach Freiheit': Wilhelm Emmanuel von Ketteler und die Freiheits-forderungen seiner Zeit—eine Studie zum Verhältnis von konserva-tivem Katholizismus und Moderne* (Paderborn: Schöningh, 2005); F. H. Müller, H. Pesch: *Sein Leben und seine Lehre* (Köln: J. P. Bachem Verlag, 1980).

[22]   Pope John XXIII, *Mater et Magister*, 219.

[23]   This implies that in my view the crisis of the Social Democratic parties in Europe originates in the social engineering approach that dominated their policies massively since the 1970s. This is not the place to develop this argument further.

[24]   St Thomas Aquinas, *Sententia libri Politicorum*, Liber 2, lectio 5.

[25]   Without explicitly relying on the principle of subsidiarity, this approach is developed theoretically in J. C. Alexander, *The Civil Sphere* (New York: Oxford University Press, 2006).

[26]   I have tried to convince executives and senior policy makers of Dutch civil society organisations of Roman Catholic and Protestant origin, that have often become highly bureaucratised and dependent on government subsidies, that they have a primal

responsibility here. See my '"Alles wat van mij is, is van jou":
lezing Christelijk Sociaal Congres, 26 augustus 2010'
<http://www.stichting-csc.nl/Downloads/Erik_Borgman_2010.pdf>
('All that is mine is yours' [Luke 15:31]: Lecture at the Christian
Social Congress, 26 August 2010).

27 Here I am particularly inspired by John Courtney Murray
(1904–1967); see his *We Hold These Truths: Catholic Reflections on
the American Position* (Lanham: AltaMira, 1960, 2005). For back-
ground, cf. T. P. Ferguson, *Catholic and American: The Political
Theology of John Courtney Murray* (Lanham: Sheed & Ward, 1993);
R. P. Hunt, 'The Quest for the Historical Murray', in: K. L. Grasso,
G.V. Bradley & R. P. Hunt (eds.), *Catholicism, Liberalism, and
Communitirianism: The Catholic Intellectual Tradition and the Moral
Foundations of Democracy* (Lanham: Rowman & Littlefield, 1995),
197–218.

28 See the title of a collection of essays of his: *God the Future of Man*
(London: Sheed and Ward, 1969).

29 See especially his *Jesus: An Experiment in Christology* (London:
Collins, 1979).

30 This is what Schillebeeckx mainly elaborates in the second half
of his Christ: *The Christian Experience in the Modern World* (London: SCM, 1980).

31 See T. Radcliffe, *What is the Point of Being a Christian* (London:
Burns & Oates, 2005), 129–142: 'I Am Because We Are'.

32 Cf. G. Cholvy, *Frédéric Ozanam: L'engagement d'un intellectuel
catholique au XIXe siècle* (Paris: Fayard, 2003). See for a program-
matic explication of what this may involve, see my *Overlopen naar
de barbaren: Het publieke belang van religie en christendom* (Kampen:
Klement, 2009) (To go over to the barbarians: The public interest
of religion and Christianity).

Global Justice as Participation: The Missing Link in the Dominant Secular Moral Philosophical Debate?

ELLEN VAN STICHEL

> *There are 'two women of justice', one with a scale and her eyes blinded, and the other, who proclaims: 'He has shown might with his arm, dispersed the arrogant of mind and heart. He has thrown down rulers from their thrones, but lifted up the lowly. The hungry he has filled with good things, the rich he has sent away empty.' (Lk 4)*

J. R. Donahue, 'Biblical perspectives on Justice', 1977.

A casual reader of the news is weekly, if not daily, reminded of huge atrocities that divide the affluent and poor countries: huge food prices resulting into structural hunger, suffering from easily curable diseases such as malaria, climate change that triggers uncertain living conditions and insecure future prospects, etc. all of which characterise our global world. The financial crisis made the situation even worse since there are the people living in the 'Two-Thirds World' who were hardest hit by the fallout even though they live far away from the origins of this crisis.

Faced with such huge inequalities and severe deprivation and under the impulse of the groundbreaking work *A Theory of Justice* by John Rawls, a debate has risen within moral philosophy on the responsibilities of the more affluent countries (or their citizens) toward the so-called 'distant poor'.[1] Besides the expected question of what must be done and how, the debate focuses on the more profound question of *whether* affluent people do indeed have any obligation toward these global poor. Hence, as David Hollenbach puts it, 'more basic than the arguments about the size of the slices is the one about who should be at the table in the first place.'[2]

Whether affluent people have an obligation to take care of global poverty and inequalities rests upon how one defines this obligation. Here, moral philosophy distinguishes charity,[3] justice and humanitarianism. Charity is supererogatory, transcending duty in the strictest sense (and is thus of a voluntary and individualistic nature), whereas justice refers to a strict obligation that also takes structural changes into account. In between there is the third option of humanitarianism which implies a moral argument to fulfil obligations while glossing over the need for structural and institutional reform. As such, 'it serves only to treat the symptoms of injustice rather than to tackle the underlying cause of it.'[4] Based on these distinctions, the debate on global duties has evolved around the question whether the obligation toward the distant poor is a matter of humanitarianism or of justice. Put differently, this debate's priority is to define justice in order to investigate whether it should apply globally.

This article's aim is to show that Catholic social thought has a specific contribution to make with regard to the question of global justice. This claim requires a careful analysis of different schools of thought within moral philosophy. In the first section of this chapter, I will consider those who are averse to a global application of justice. These adversaries reject the global application of justice because of the lack of either shared identity or institutions. In the second section, I will look at the proponents of an application of global justice who believe that moral equality fulfils the necessary conditions for an effective application of global justice. As this article will detail, the concept of justice expands while shifting from one conceptualization of justice to another. I, however, believe that even the most extended moral concept of justice is too limited to adequately grasp the notion of global justice and needs to be expanded. It is at this level that Catholic social thought can make a specific contribution, as the third section aims to show. Recent research into its contemporary tradition shows that the notion of justice as participation seems to be the missing link within this philosophical debate.

Adversaries of global justice

The most fervent critics of a possibility of global justice are the sceptics who argue against any possibility of justice whatsoever.[5] Since, they argue, justice is unachievable on the national level because of the multiculturalism that characterizes democratic societies, then the idea of global justice is hopeless. In addition to these sceptics, others do support justice within only a limited space because of the lack of a global application for the necessary relation for justice to apply. Two strands of thought can be distinguished based on how they define this relationship. Namely, the philosophers that focus on the shared identity as necessary and sufficient condition for justice and those that emphasize the existence of shared economic or political institutions.

The first of these philosophers are the so-called communitarians or nationalists. They depart from the idea that the self-understanding of a person, her morality in general, and her view on the good in particular have a 'social origin':[6] the community in which 'an individual' is born constitutes both her identity and morality (through the particular morality of the community). Charles Taylor speaks here of 'frameworks' that are given in the context in which someone is born; the question 'Who am I?' is answered within a horizon that enables human beings to determine what is important for them, because identity is 'defined by the commitments and identifications which provide the frame or horizons within which I can try to determine from case to case what is good, or valuable, or what ought to be done, or what I endorse or oppose.'[7]

The community one finds oneself in has a particularity which is reflected in Michael Walzer's notion of 'shared understandings': members of a community have shared understandings on 'the good' in general, and, derived from that, on what meaning particular goods have within their community. The latter goods are considered as 'social goods'[8]: their meaning is dependent upon the particular community in which they are produced and consumed. As a consequence, the content of moral principles is tied to the particularity of the community, such that 'what I learn as a guide to my actions and as a standard of evaluating them is never morality as such, but always the highly specific morality of some specific social order.'[9] Furthermore, communitarians limit the scope of morality to the particular community for two reasons. First, moral actions and their meanings and interpretations are not absolute norms but contextual, dependent on communal life and beliefs. Second, the nature of moral obligation depends on relations between the members of the community. Put differently: living in a community brings about special, partial obligations toward members that one does not have toward non-members.

The idea of global justice is thus rejected by communitarians. For there will be no universal agreement on the content of principles of justice. Since justice is considered as a human construction, 'it is doubtful that it can be made in only one way.'[10] Moreover, justice has to do with the division of goods, 'social goods', so that the criterion of their distribution is contingent, particular and partial.[11] As a result, the scope of justice must always be limited to the boundaries of a particular community. Consequently, I consider it to be the most limited conception of justice, since these theorists not only limit the scope of justice, but also its content. In fact, there is a causal relationship between both: it is because of the partiality of the content of principles of justice that the scope must be limited as well.

A second strain of secular theories that are in favour of a limited, partial scope of justice, but at the same time argue for impartial principles of justice within this scope seems more appropriate. Like communitarians, this set of theories limit the boundaries of moral obligations of justice to a certain context, namely the state. Unlike communitarians, however, this limitation is not based on a shared identity, but rather on shared institutions, be they economic or political.[12] Since discussing both theories is too elaborate for the scope of this chapter, I will focus on the first one as it is—as the trigger of the whole debate—a seminal contribution.

The most famous representative of this category is John Rawls. In his *A Theory of Justice*[13], he starts from the assumption that, in a state of nature, human beings will enter into a cooperative scheme since that is the most efficient thing to do. By cooperating, an economic surplus is created that can and must be divided among the contributors. However, when an agreement about the distribution of the surplus must be reached, problems will arise since the contributors will have different, maybe even opposite, views on both the good life in general and the distribution of the goods accordingly. Hence, institutions are needed to regulate the distribution based on impartial principles.

In order to decide on the content of these impartial principles, Rawls departs into a thought experiment that introduces the idea of the 'veil of ignorance': under a veil of ignorance the personal ideas and knowledge of individuals on the good life, their socio-economic position and status, their inheritance and so on are bracketed out. In other words, being able to distance themselves from these contingent factors, free and equal persons will, under the veil of ignorance, be able to decide on principles of justice without aiming to favour their own situation. This initial situation will lead to fair bargaining between the persons and, therefore, to fair principles of justice implying equal rights and liberties, equal opportunities and the famous difference principle whereby policy measures always have to be to the benefit of the least advantaged.[14]

Within the context of the global justice debate, the (possibility of the) global application of the difference principle has been an object of discussion ever since the publication of *A Theory of Justice*.[15] In 1999, Rawls presented his own view in *The Law of Peoples*[16] in which he seeks to formulate principles that must guide political relations between different peoples at the international level.[17] Besides the well-known guidelines of traditional law for peoples (such as non-intervention, self-defence, etc.) his duty of assistance is rather remarkable: stating that affluent peoples should help less advantaged peoples to reach a decent, or just, level of well-being.[18] The terminology is significant: it is a duty of *assistance*, not of *justice*: a global redistribution principle like the difference principle is not required. Indeed, the scope of the Rawlsian principles of justice, ensuring more equality between its members, is restricted to the national level. According to Rawls, one of the main reasons for this restriction is that the sufficient and necessary relations for justice to apply, namely shared (economic) institutions, do not exist at the global level. Consequently, global redistribution as the difference principle would require, is not appropriate.

The non-existence of a certain relationship, namely the lack of a shared identity or shared institutions, implies the rejection of a global application of justice for these set of theories. How do the proponents of global justice then define justice?

Proponents of global justice: the cosmopolitans

While the adversaries of global justice want to keep justice contained within individual states or communities, the so-called cosmopolitans plead for global justice on the basis of the human moral equality, founded upon their common humanity which implies that justice has no borders.[19] 'Everybody matters' is their key idea.[20] Consequently, contemplating on justice, one must take equally all human beings into account, irrespectively of boundaries and nationality which are considered to be contingent and arbitrary.[21] This cosmopolitan thought is in fact very old; it already existed in the Greek stoic tradition. However, it gained numerous adherents during the Enlightenment with its emphasis on the individual. Gaining relevance due to global poverty and inequality, cosmopolitanism nowadays appears to have become an umbrella term which covers very distinct theories.[22] These notions of cosmopolitanism can be distinguished as either 'conditional' or 'unconditional' cosmopolitanism. While the former assumes a special, causal, relationship between the wealth of a few nations versus the poverty of others as the sufficient and necessary condition for justice, the latter focuses on the idea of our common humanity in general to discern what justice implies—independently from the responsibility for poverty and inequalities as they exist.

First, I shall inquire about the conditional cosmopolitans. In contrast to Rawls' analysis of the international order, others have argued that in a globalised world like ours, there is indeed a global economic cooperative system that creates both a global surplus and inequalities. In our current world, states are not self-sufficient and self-contained, independent islands, but global enterprises. They have interactions and transactions of goods and money as well as travel opportunities, aid, foreign investment, cultural transference, and so on; all of which connect different places worldwide. For a global analogy with Rawls' theory, however, the international trade and investments organised by the global political and economic structures is the most relevant aspect of this globalisation process. Already in 1979, Beitz argued that global interdependencies give rise to both substantial benefits and costs and to the development of a global structure. Not only do global economic transactions generate a 'higher global rate of economic growth as well as greater productive efficiency',[23] but they also produce economic and political inequality within and between states. Furthermore, the rise of a global institutional structure has important 'distributive implications'[24]: the policies and decisions of economic institutions like the IMF, World Bank or OECD determine the level of wealth and growth in countries worldwide. As a result, the necessary conditions are fulfilled for principles of justice—even in terms of the Rawlsian difference principle—to be applied globally.

As conditional cosmopolitans, another strain of thought goes even further and looks into the nature of these institutions that are considered to be an unjust harm imposed on the 'distant poor'. Thomas Pogge's main argument is that our current global scheme violates the negative duty not to harm in several ways: global interactions prove indeed to be disadvantageous for less powerful poor countries, so that citizens in the affluent countries are (although maybe only indirectly) responsible for these deprivations. Therefore they need to correct this situation 'by shaping and enforcing the social conditions that foreseeably and avoidably cause the monumental suffering of global poverty, we are harming the global poor—or (...) we are active participants in the largest, though not the gravest crime against humanity ever committed.'[25]

Pogge refers to the global institutional structure as such that indirectly and directly harm the poor. For the indirect factors he refers to the problem of corruption involving multinational companies and statesmen of wealthy societies pressuring leaders in poor countries to support their products and factories[26] and gaining certain advantages such as 'borrowing' and 'resource' privileges.[27] These privileges are attributed to 'any group controlling a preponderance of the means of coercion within a country's territory and people— regardless of how that group came to power, of how it exercises power, and of the extent to which it may be supported or opposed by the population it rules.'[28] The former privilege creates space for corrupt and undemocratic leaders to take out loans that can burden their domestic societies for a long time. The second, resource privilege, includes the 'effective control over the natural resources of the country in question (… and …) the power to effect legally valid transfers of ownership rights in such resources.'[29] This explains why a resource-rich country is more likely to be overpowered by corrupt elites, resulting in a high poverty rate despite its natural wealth. More direct factors that maintain the injustice of the institutional order are, first, its bargaining structures. The international negotiations concerning global issues are mostly based on free bargaining under unequal power relations and thus vulnerability which sets the door wide open for inequalities to flourish uncontrollably and without limit: economic inequalities lead to 'democratic deficits' on the global level. Other direct factors are policies such as protectionist measures like export subsidies for agriculture or the intellectual property rights.

Both Beitz and Pogge start from Rawlsian premises. The claim for distributive justice arises when people cooperate within a common 'basic structure'. For Rawls, socio-economic advantages and burdens are generated by a basic structure that is mainly national. Beitz and Pogge too have good arguments to prove the existence of a global basic structure: global interdependencies give rise to special obligations between all people in the world. Despite the broadening of the scope within Beitz's and Pogge's theory, this view is, however, not unproblematic. Indeed, it gives the workers in poor countries a claim to a substantial share of the wealth they help to produce: it justifies the claims of South-African miners, Indian ICT-programmers or Tunisian textile workers. But what about all these innumerable marginalised persons, the shipwrecks of development, living in the slums of the 'megalopolis' of poor countries, who do not contribute to worldwide economic growth and who hardly participate to the creation of a global surplus? Do the wealthy have any obligation towards them? Or is that only a matter of charity? The Rawlsian argument referring to a basic structure within which people cooperate seems to be much too productivistic. Paradoxically, the conditional cosmopolitans' rationale is similar to the adversaries to global justice in viewing justice as the consequence of a special relation: a certain bond (e.g. through economic and political institutions) between the parties involved (e.g. the North and the South) establishes obligations of justice.

Consequently, unconditional cosmopolitans seem to do more justice to the basic assumption of cosmopolitans, namely the equal dignity of all human persons for it does not consider a specific relationship to be the necessary conditions for justice to apply. Examples are the capability approach like Martha Nussbaum's, or a basic rights theory like Henry Shue's. Both have listed things that people have a right to, so that they can live life in dignity. In this case, 'his or her due' is to ensure that every person has access to these capabilities or rights. Their account is 'prepolitical':[30] it considers what people have a right to on the basis of our common humanity, independent of mutual relationships. As such, the capabilities or rights refer to a minimum threshold: falling under this minimal level would jeopardise one's self-respect and, therefore, one's dignity.

Maybe the rights approach is the most self-evident cosmopolitan theory one can think of: since the notion of human rights implies intrinsically the universality of these rights, despite national borders or geographic distances, this approach is definitely cosmopolitan. Characteristic for human rights is that they reflect claims with regard to human beings' basic needs: their aim is to be a 'minimal protection against utter helplessness to those too weak to protect themselves.'[31] Their link with basic human needs grant human rights not only the necessary justification but also the normative force as convincing arguments in ethical discourse.[32] According to Shue, the two most basic human rights are the right to physical security and the right to subsistence or minimal economic security.[33]

Like the human rights approach, the capabilities approach wants to determine a minimum threshold for dignified human life.[34] Unlike the human rights theory, this minimum is much more demanding and its basic ideas are thoroughly different. According to Nussbaum, for example, every person has a right of access to ten capabilities, starting from a capability to live to a capability to play.[35] The specificity of the capabilities approach is the recognition that equal access to an equal distribution of goods through rights will appear insufficient: due to both external and internal factors (such as respectively the natural and social environmental factors like climate etc. and personal characteristics such as age, gender, physical and psychological capacities etc.) a more equal distribution of goods will not guarantee a better standard of living. Because of this interpersonal diversity, the 'conversion' of goods to capabilities, to function in order to realise the life freely as one wants to, varies between different people and thus requires unequal distribution of goods.[36] The aim of this approach goes further than merely realising well-being; the freedom to realise one's own well-being is crucial as well. Hence, rather than the distribution of goods as means to freedom, the capabilities reflect the freedom to choose for those functions that one values in life. Well-being is important not only at the end, but also during the process of reaching this goal.

The commonality of both unconditional cosmopolitan theories is that they both claim to give a universal account of their interpretation of human dignity, resulting in a cosmopolitanism with a concept of justice that is both impartial in content (since it takes an impartial standpoint to depart from) and in scope (since its implications has universal reach).

A 'reciprocity-based' concept of justice seems to be the overarching and most dominant model within moral philosophy: both the adversaries of global justice and the conditional cosmopolitans confirm the necessity of a special relationship as a condition *sine qua* non justice applies. In contrast, unconditional cosmopolitanism is different because of its 'subject-centred'[37] approach, starting from the needs and rights of the distant poor and as such have a teleological understanding of justice: one first determines what justice implies and then goes on to apply it to reality. The fact that these theories are mostly considered as too broad or as humanitarianism rather than justice shows that the dominant trend in moral philosophy is to emphasise reciprocity-based theories.

Global justice from a theological perspective: the specific contribution of Catholic Social Thought

When considering all this, it does not come as a surprise that Catholic theology will relate more to these cosmopolitan 'subject-centred' theories of justice. The universal love of God as expressed in the idea that human beings are *imago Dei* and as announced by the parables and deeds of Jesus Christ makes this religious tradition inherently cosmopolitan. Moreover, such a theological notion is also teleological: starting from a vision of how the world should be (expressed in the idea of the Reign of God), so that justice then is formulated as what is needed to achieve this world and thus paving the way for a commitment to start to work for the Reign of God.

Unlike the unconditional cosmopolitanism, however, the Catholic concept of justice is not impartial. The abovementioned universal love of God expresses a special care for the excluded and outcasts in the world, implying that this justice is always in a certain way partial, because of its attention for particularly these people. Hence, such a theological conception of justice will always be broader than the philosophical notion of justice *stricto sensu*. A second difference with this cosmopolitanism is the focus on the common good, a common good that due to globalization has become global as well—as Catholic social teaching, with the encyclical *Mater et magistra* (1961), has become aware of. Its conception of justice does not only focus on the rights and needs of every human person as an individual (as unconditional cosmopolitanism tends to do), but always takes the broader community and the interplay between human person and community into account as the notion of common good expresses. In other words: different anthropological assumptions will lead to different conceptions of justice. These differences rightly appoint characteristics of a concept of justice. Yet it does not yet define justice as such. What would such a definition entail?

It is not evident that a clear-cut definition of justice within Catholic social thought can be found. If it's discourse is even present. For it is not hard to see that justice was much more prominently present in the body of Catholic social teachings in the 1960s and 1970s, whereas recently a tendency seems to exist to remove it from the forefront due to the focus on solidarity and charity within the teachings of Pope John XXIII and Pope Benedict XVI, respectively.[38] Even a quick look at the recent history of papal teachings of the last five decades shows that the notion of justice is not univocally used in this tradition, as if there would exist a clear definition.

Might it then not be better to start from how injustice is described to learn more about its ideas on justice? Investigating the teachings on the relationship between the descriptions of injustice on the one hand, and the notion of justice on the other, reveals however a discrepancy between the analysis of problems conducted and the proposals for reform. Some examples will clarify this point. The promoter of the justice discourse within Catholic social teaching, namely Pope Paul VI, refers to injustice in his encyclical *Populorum progressio* as hunger, misery, diseases, and so forth[39] and thus speaks about absolute poverty in terms of lacking those means to lead a dignified life. At the same time he defines the structural implementation of inequality as injustice, implying that this absolute poverty has structural roots such as the unequal power relations at the global level that result in unequal trade agreements.[40] To reform this situation, Paul VI proposes as 'a matter of social justice' that these trade relations have to be improved.[41] Reducing justice merely to this aspect of trade relations appears, however, an unqualified limitation of justice in view of the structural analysis made earlier. A similar discrepancy is even more obvious in *Mater et magistra*, the encyclical of his predecessor pope John XXIII. This encyclical explicitly states that justice requires that something has to be done about huge international inequalities and thus takes not only absolute but also relative poverty into account — without, however, considering the structural aspects of this poverty.[42] When this pope starts to define the obligation of justice, however, he interprets it as the duty of aid[43] — and thus again shows a discrepancy between the analysis and the proposals. Lastly, pope John Paul II is very critical in his analysis of inequalities: he refers to the 'gap'[44] between the growing development of some and the deprivation of others as 'one of the greatest injustices in the contemporary world.'[45] His social teachings are known for his structural analysis of these 'mechanisms'[46] of 'sinful structures'[47] of current developments. Despite this analysis and the recognition of the need for global justice,[48] John Paul II focuses on the concept of solidarity for his recommendations: solidarity will solve these problems more accurately than justice[49] — another example of the discrepancy between analysis and suggestions.

Should these examples lead to pessimism about the use and delineation of justice within Catholic social teaching? This does not have to be the case, for there are remarkable suggestions on the implications of justice within these teachings if one takes the criteria of the common good and of the partiality in favour of the least advantaged into account. For example, paragraph 43 of the Apostolic Letter *Octogesima adveniens*, written after *Populorum progressio*, to introduce the theme of global justice for the Bishops' Synod of 1971 and thus in the midst of evolution taking place in Latin America under impulse of liberation theology. In this encyclical, Pope Paul VI states that it is 'the most important duty of justice' to ensure that each country is 'allowed to promote its own development, within the framework of a cooperation free from any spirit of domination, whether economic or political.' This pope suggested something similar in *Populorum progressio* — that people would become the creators of their own growth — but this was at that time still considered as a matter of solidarity, not justice.[50]

One of the most surprising passages of papal teachings, namely in *Centesimus annus*, even goes a step further. In here, John Paul II writes how love should manifest itself concretely in working for justice, implying that one does not only give of 'surplus goods' but enables marginalized and excluded people to become part of the 'economic and human development.'[51] An adequate interpretation of the common good means that everybody can enjoy the fruits this development and thus is included in the circle of these interdependencies.

It is these passages, and certainly the last one, that give a glimpse of the specific concept of justice the Catholic tradition can promote, namely 'justice as participation'. To fully grasp the meaning of this concept, one needs to look further than official Catholic social teaching as promulgated by the popes. A good starting point is the document *Iustitia in mundo* of the Bishops' synod in 1971: with the majority of the participants coming from the developing countries, a different perspective, that focuses on the situation of the distant poor and has been influenced by liberation theology, saw the light in Catholic social teaching. Although not using the term 'justice as participation' as such, the bishops do provide new insights on the meaning of global justice.

Through its analysis of the structural aspects of current injustices as reflected in the global 'network of dominance, oppression and abuses'[52] as well as socio-economic and political inequalities, the ideal of justice rises at the horizon. The document's focus on dominance and dependence shows that justice means realizing freedom, freedom from oppression in order to have freedom for taking up responsibility. Also it's ideal is that development is more than economic growth but also implies participation confirms this ideal.[53] This participation should enable these people to 'authentically manifest their own personalization.'[54] In comparison to the above-mentioned passage of *Octogesima adveniens* — that chronologically speaking came later — *Iustitia in Mundo* even adds a crucial extra aspect. Namely the link between participation and the global common good: the distant poor should not only participate to build up their own culture and prosperity; rather the bishops are convinced that they are enriching for the global common good. In other words: they have their own contribution to make to achieve this common good and this is what makes their participation both valuable and necessary.[55]

In the wake of upcoming liberation theology, these statements should not surprise us. *Iustitia in mundo* undoubtedly found its inspiration in the Latin American bishops' conference of 1968. In confrontation with massive inequalities and injustice, these bishops state that a new just global order is required; one in which each person's dignity is respected through the absence of need and dominance, in short so that 'persons are not objects but agents of their own history'.[56] Indeed, the expression borrowed from Gustavo Gutierrez 'agents of their own history' captures the idea of justice as participation in a very adequate manner. Added to that, the bishops argue that especially the 'lower classes' should be ensured to become 'active and receptive, creative and decisive' participants in the construction of this (re)new(ed) global society.[57] Hence, not only justice as participation but the partial perspective of justice is emphasized.

A final crucial document with regard to justice as participation being *Economic Justice for All* of the Bishops' Conference of the United States links this partial characteristic of biblical-grounded justice and participation in a specific manner. As the title of the letter reveals, the bishops reflect on justice for all, including the distant poor, while considering the privileged status the United States have in the global economy. Going back to the sources of the Catholic faith to reflect upon justice, the Bible shows how God measures the faith of God's community on the basis of their treatment of the lowest and the poorest people in society. Consequently, any Catholic conception of justice must necessarily link justice to the situation of the deprived and thus must be partial which gives this notion its specificity.[58] Policies should, for example, be judged on their consequences for the poorest—even at the global sphere. The bishops state explicitly that this conception of justice is different from a mere philosophical one because it is more concerned with the relationship of human persons to God through the community rather than with the strict definition of rights and duties.[59]

Reestablishing the community is central here, implying that one cannot speak of a community when exclusion and marginalization exists. As such, the relation with justice as participation is easily made: participation becomes the criterion to judge the level of (economic) justice of a community, and thus of the relationship between the community and God. From this perspective, the bishops do not only question 'what the economy does *for* people' or 'what it does *to* people', but also 'how people *participate* in it?'[60] Based the Thomistic framework, social justice is interpreted as 'contributive justice'[61]: against exclusion and marginalization –social phenomena that seems to suggest that certain people do not count and are not important for the establishment of the common good– persons have to be given the necessary means so that they can contribute to society and participate in establishing the society as they imagine it. At the global level this means that people have to be given the means in order that they can participate in the global economy and common good. The other side of the coin of contributive justice is that every human person has a duty to participate; that it is morally questionable for people to not bother about one's own responsibility but leaving others to do their part.

What this section shows is that Catholic tradition has a contribution to make to moral philosophy. However, the idea of justice as participation is highly debated and to a lesser or higher degree accepted. Treating it with the justice it deserves would imply that papal teachings would recognize its importance more explicitly. We should not merely reduce them to a side issue of past decades or of the 'lower', second-class tradition of regional Catholic social thought.

Conclusion

In this chapter I have examined whether and, if so, how, Catholic social thought has a specific contribution to make to the moral philosophical debate on global justice. Main stream philosophy argues that duties of justice are based on relationships and reciprocity: because people stand in a certain relationship to one another (be it based on identity or shared institutions) that people owe justice to each other. One exception, not taken very seriously by the dominant flows of thought, focus on a person's dignity to define principles of justice. Although this conception relates to theological accounts of justice because of its individualistic anthropology and thus lack of attention for the importance and role of community it is not yet sufficient. Inspired by its Biblical inheritance, Catholic theology has a specific contribution to make because its focus on the exclusion of the poor compels it to consider justice as exclusion's counterpart, namely justice as participation.

Within this context, the statement of Hollenbach seems even more relevant now: who sits at the table? Is it those with whom one already has a relationship (through a shared identity in a community or shared national or even global institutions)? Or is it those with whom one does not yet have a relationship, except the ontological one of being shaped as God's children and thus those who are excluded from everything? Moreover, who determines who sits at the table? For the starting point of the dominant debate is the question what do *we*, as more or less affluent citizens in affluent countries, owe to the distant poor? But to take the distant poor as the point of departure of the analysis implies reversing the question by asking what are *their* rights and how do we fulfil them. Moreover, the strength of Catholic social thought is that it even criticizes this reversal, for as the global common good shows to us: it is not *us* versus *them*, but we are all in this boat together. Or rather: we sit at the same unfinished table.

Notes

[1]   The concept of 'distant poor' is partly based on the book of Deen Chatterjee, *The Ethics of Distance. Morality and the Distant Needy.* I realize that the term is problematic and all but neutral. I use it here in its most literal sense, namely referring to spatial distance.

[2]   David Hollenbach, *Justice, Peace and Human Rights: American Catholic Social Ethic in a Pluralist Context* (New York: Crossroad, 1988), 80.

[3]   From a theological perspective, charity can refer to the supernatural virtue that by grace enables people to love God and to love their neighbour. Within this chapter, however, charity shall only be used in a philosophical sense, namely as referring to charitable works.

[4]   Kok-Chor Tan, *Justice Without borders: Cosmopolitanism, Nationalism and Patriotism* (Cambridge: Cambridge University Press, 2004) 68.

[5]   For an example, see Chandran Kukathas,'The Mirage of Global Justice', *Social Philosophy and Policy* 23 (2006), 1–28.

[6]   Stephen Mulhall & Adam Swift, *Liberals and Communitarians*

(Oxford: Blackwell Publishers, 1992), 112.

7   Charles Taylor, *Sources of the Self. The Making of Modern Identity* (Cambridge: Cambridge University Press, 1989), 27.

8   Michael Walzer, *Spheres of Justice: A Defense of Pluralism and Equality* (New York: Basic Books, 1983), 7.

9   Alasdair MacIntyre, 'Is Patriotism a Virtue?', in *Debates in Contemporary Political Philosophy: An Anthology*, eds. Derek Matravers & Jonathan Pike (London—New York: Routledge, 2003), 291.

10   Walzer, *Spheres of Justice*, 5.

11   See Walzer, *Spheres of Justice*, 8–9.

12   In the former case, it is argued that within a state people are gathered in a cooperative scheme, producing an economic surplus that must be divided among its contributors requiring principles of justice to do so. In the latter case, the fact that people are coerced under a common rule of law which they did not completely choose themselves freely, results in the need for principles of justice and care for fellow-members. The second, political interpretation refers to the writings of Thomas Nagel and Michael Blake: Thomas Nagel, 'The Problem of Global Justice', *Philosophy and Public Affairs* 33 (2005) 2, 113–147; Michael Blake, 'Distributive Justice, Coercion and Autonomy', *Philosophy and Public Affairs* 30 (2002) 3, 256–296.

13   John Rawls, *A Theory of Justice* (London: Oxford University, 1973).

14   *Ibid.*, p. 302. As we are only interested in how Rawls interprets this on the international level, I will not enter into detail on these principles, their consequences, or possible critiques.

15   Ever since its publication the Law of Peoples has been widely discussed. See for example Rex Martin & David Reidy (eds.), *Rawls's Law of Peoples. A Realistic Utopia?* (Malden (MA): Blackwell Publishing, 2006); Chris Brown, John Rawls, '"The Law of Peoples" and International Political Theory', *Ethics and International Affairs* 14 (2000), 125–132; Allan Buchanan, 'Rawls's Law of Peoples: Rules for a Vanished Westphalian World', *Ethics* 110 (2002) 4, 697–721; Andrew Kuper, 'Rawlsian Global Justice: Beyond the Law of Peoples to a Cosmopolitan Law of Persons', *Political Theory* 28 (2000) 5, 640–679; Samuel R. Freeman, *Rawls* (London: Routledge, 2007), especially chapter 10; Martha. C. Nussbaum, *Frontiers of Justice. Disability, Nationality, Species Membership* (Cambridge: Harvard University Press, 2006), especially chapters 1 and 4; Charles. R. Beitz, 'Social and Cosmopol-

itan Liberalism', *International Affairs* 75 (1999) 3, 515–529; Charles. R. Beitz, 'International Liberalism and Distributive Justice: A Survey of Recent Thought', *World Politics* 51 (1999) 2, 269–296; Charles R. Beitz, 'Rawls's Law of Peoples', *Ethics* 110 (2000) 4, 669–696; Simon Caney, 'Survey Article: Cosmopolitanism and the Law of Peoples', *The Journal of Political Philosophy* 10 (2002) 1, 95–123; Thomas Mertens, 'Defending Rawlsian League of Peoples: A Critical Comment on Tan', *Leiden Journal of International Law* 18 (2005). 4, 711–715; Thomas W. Pogge, *World Poverty and Human Rights: Cosmopolitan Responsibilities and Reforms* (Cambridge: Polity Press, 2002), especially chapter 4; Thomas W. Pogge , 'Egalitarian Law of Peoples', *Philosophy & Public Affairs* 23 (1994) 3, 195–224; Thomas W. Pogge, 'Critical Study: Rawls on International Justice', *The Philosophical Quarterly* 5 (2001) 203, 246–253; Kok-Chor Tan, *Justice Without borders: Cosmopolitanism, Nationalism and Patriotism* (Cambridge: Cambridge University Press, 2004); Kok-Chor Tan, 'International Toleration: Rawlsian versus Cosmopolitan', *Leiden Journal of International Law* 18 (2005) 4, 685–710.

[16] J. Rawls, *The Law of Peoples* (Cambridge—London: Harvard University Press, 1999).

[17] Notice the shift in words: from 'global' to 'international'. This is not unconsciously, but reflects the fact that Rawls considers the global scene as 'inter-national' as will become clear.

[18] Rawls, *The Law of Peoples* (1999), 37.

[19] See Tan, *Justice Without Borders*, 1.

[20] K. A. Appiah, *Cosmopolitanism. Ethics in a World of Strangers, Issues of Our Time* (New York, NY: Norton, 2006), 144.

[21] A. Kuper, 'More Than Charity: Cosmopolitan Alternatives to the "Singer Solution"', in *Ethics and International Affairs 16* (2002) no. 1, 107–120, 108; C. Jones, 'Institutions with Global Scope: Moral Cosmopolitanism and Political Practice', in D. Weinstock (ed.), *Global Justice, Global Institutions,* Canadian Journal of Philosophy. Supplementary volume, no. 31 (Calgary (Alta): University Of Calgary Press, 2007), 1–27: 1.

[22] Cf. P. Kleingeld & E. Brown, 'Cosmopolitanism', in Stanford Encyclopedia of Philosophy, 28 October 2006. http://plato.stanford.edu/entries/cosmopolitanism(accessed 19.12.2010).

[23] C. R. Beitz, *Political Theory and International Relations*, 2nd ed., (Princeton NJ: Princeton University Press, 1999), 145.

[24] Beitz, *Political Theory*, 149.

[25] T. W. Pogge, 'Real World Justice' in *The Journal of Ethics. An International Review* 9 (2005) nr. 1/2, 29–53, p. 33.

[26] Cf. T. W. Pogge, *An Egalitarian Law of Peoples*, p. 213–214. Idem, 'Priorities of Global Justice', in *Metaphilosophy* 32 (2001) 1/2, 6–24, 18–19.

[27] Cf. Idem, *World Poverty and Human Rights*, 112–115. Idem, 'Priorities of Global Justice', 20–21.

[28] T. W. Pogge., 'Priorities of Global Justice', 19–20.

[29] *Ibid.*, 20.

[30] Nussbaum, *Frontiers of Justice*, 285.

[31] H. Shue, *Basic Human Rights*, 18. See also Jones, *Global Justice*, 55.

[32] Jones, *Global Justice*, 58.

[33] H. Shue, *Basic Human Rights*, 23.

[34] M. C. Nussbaum, *Frontiers of Justice. Disability, Nationality, Species Membership* (Cambridge: Harvard University Press, 2006), 281: 'Our world is not a descent and minimally just world, unless we have secured the ten capabilities, up to an appropriate threshold level, to all the world's people.'

[35] The ten capabilities are: life; bodily health; bodily integrity; senses, imagination and thought; emotions; practical reason; affiliation; other species; play; control over one's environment.

[36] Cf. A. K. Sen, *Inequality Reexamined*, (New York, NY—Oxford: Russell Sage Foundation—Clarendon Press, 1992), 33.

[37] For this distinction between 'reciprocity-based' and 'subject-centred' approach of justice, see A. Buchanan, 'Justice as Reciprocity Versus Subject-Centered Justice', *Philosophy and Public Affairs* 19 (1990), no. 3, 227–252.

[38] See for example Johan Verstraeten, 'Justice Subordinated to Love? The Changing Agenda of Catholic Social Teaching since *Populorum Progressio*', in *Responsibility, God and Society: Theological Ethics in Dialogue: Festschrift Roger Burggraeve*, eds. Johan De Tavernier et al. (Leuven, Paris and Dudley: Leuven University Press, 2008), 389–405.

[39] Cf. *Populorum progressio*, 1.

[40] See *ibid*, 58.

[41] *Ibid.*, 44.

[42] Cf. *Mater et magistra*, 122; 161.

[43] *Ibid.*, 161.

44 *Sollicitudo rei socialis*, 14.

45 *Ibid.*, 28.

46 *Ibid.*, 16; 22; 35.

47 *Ibid.*, 40

48 See *ibid.*, 10.

49 See *ibid.*, 9; 38.

50 See *Populorum progressio*, 65.

51 *Centesimus annus*, 58

52 *Iustitia in mundo*, 3. On these structural dimensions of current injustice, see also 5; 16; 20.

53 See *ibid.*, 18.

54 *Ibid.*, 17.

55 See *ibid.*, 71.

56 Second General Conference of Latin American Bishops, *The Church in the Present-Day Transformation of Latin America in the Light of the Gospel: Document on Peace*, 13.

57 See United States Conference of Catholic Bishops, *A Decade after 'Economic Justice for All: Continuing Principles, Changing Context, New Challenges: A Pastoral Message of the National Conference of Catholic Bishops on the Tenth Anniversary Statement of the Economic Pastoral*, 17.

58 See *Economic Justice for All*, 16.

59 See *ibid.*, 39.

60 *Ibid.*, 1 (original italics).

61 *Ibid.*, 71.

Rehabilitating Personalism:
The Human Person and Human Rights

KEITH CHAPPELL

Rights and the Person

Few elements of social thought are as fraught with controversy as the notion of Human Rights, which seem to initiate strong responses whether discussed within a secular or a Church context. The relatively recent incorporation of the European Convention on Human Rights into UK law in the form of the Human Rights Act 1998, which came into force in 2000, and its subsequent interpretation through the courts has proved something of a *bête noire* for the British press. Issues such as the right to privacy for public figures, prisoner voting, provisions made for asylum seekers and the non-deportation of foreign nationals convicted of serious crimes have all incensed sections of the press and led to front page coverage. Much of the debate centres on what are deemed to be conflicting rights such as the right to privacy versus the freedom of the press, or the right of the individual not to be sent to a country where torture is likely versus the right of the public to be protected from potential harm. Often at the heart of the discussions is the idea that some action or choice made by an individual legitimises the forfeiting of their rights in some areas. A prisoner, for example, might be considered to have forfeited his rights to privacy and to enfranchisement along with the restriction of his liberty. Similarly, a celebrity or politician may be deemed to have lost any right to privacy due to their public status; the argument being that reporting their whole existence is now 'in the public interest' rather than simply being 'of interest' to the public. The revelations relating to the actions of the News International group in the UK and the subsequent fallout for the press, politicians, the police and even the Church have brought those assumptions into question.

The struggles surrounding the secular notion of human rights are perhaps due to attempts to reconcile seemingly incommensurable rights within a moral system essentially rooted in utilitarianism. The question of how the rights of the individual can stand in the face of the rights or needs of a much larger group are truly a thorny issue whatever your philosophical assumption. If you seek the 'greatest good' or 'greatest happiness' then simple arithmetic makes the rights of the individual almost nonsense in all circumstances other than those concerning decisions between two individuals. However, reservations relating to the notion of human rights are not limited to the popular press or secular utilitarians. It is by no means uncommon to encounter resistance to the notion of human rights in Catholic circles. This is rarely expressed in any official capacity and is usually done through the means of emphasising the importance of duties or responsibilities. This is, of course, a right and proper emphasis. Duties are essential if we are to talk about rights in any meaningful way. Indeed, they are essential if rights are to be observed and thus they act on a higher level of the ethical life. What does seem to occur at almost every public lecture I attend, or I read in the popular Catholic press or, increasingly, I find in student writing is a myth that is gaining ground and now appears to be received wisdom. This myth is that there is too much emphasis on the notion of rights and not enough talk about duties and responsibilities. This idea has gained so much ground that I recently marked a student essay in which the confident statement was made that 'Human rights are not a concept compatible with Catholic Social Teaching'. Needless to say, the student then proceeded to argue for a greater emphasis on duties and responsibilities. It is, of course, true that if all fulfilled their responsibilities and obligations towards one another then there would be no need for any notion of rights; but this is not the reality within which we live. Social thought, from whatever tradition, must be above all things practical in nature. Thought without praxis is simply navel gazing and worthless. We need look no further than the Gospel to see the social witness of Christ expressed through teaching, praxis and even outrage. This must be our guide.

At the heart of Catholic Social Teaching are four pillars or permanent principles:

- The dignity of the human person
- Solidarity
- Subsidiarity
- The Common Good[1]

The Church believes that these principles are the expression of 'the encounter of the Gospel message and of its demands summarised in the supreme commandment of love of God and neighbour in justice with the problems emanating from the life of society'.[2] This would seem fair as they have served as good principles in guiding social thought in the Church as it has developed over the last century or so. Indeed, the notion of Subsidiarity as put forward by Pius XI in *Quadragesimo anno* has found itself enshrined in European Union thought; providing a clear example of where Catholic social thinking can impact beyond its immediate bounds.

Of these principles, the Common Good is, in essence, the aim or the goal. It seeks conditions that 'allow people, either as groups or as individuals, to reach their fulfilment more fully and more easily'.[3] Solidarity and Subsidiarity are important principles in achieving this and are discussed more fully elsewhere in this book. The dignity of the

Human Person is the foundation of the other principles, and the whole of Catholic social thought.[4] It is especially, and most directly, associated with the concept of human rights as understood in the Catholic tradition. The dignity of the human person, and its bearing on the notion of human rights, that will be our primary concern here.

Created in the Image of God

'God created man in his own image, in the image of God He created him; male and female He created them' (Genesis 1:27).

In casual conversation or academic discussions it is by no means unusual to encounter reference to Leo XIII's 1891 encyclical *Rerum Novarum* as the foundational document of Catholic social doctrine, and in terms of modern social teaching it is certainly seminal. However, as Rodger Charles makes clear in the first volume of his two volume work *Christian Social Witness and Teaching*, we should start with Scripture and, more specifically, with Genesis.[5] Created in the image of God, humanity is created as a moral being and this must be our starting point for any notion of rights and responsibilities.

Being created in the image and likeness of God, the human possesses the dignity of personhood; not just a thing but a person. The human person is capable of self-knowledge, self-possession, free will and the ability to enter into communion with other humans but also with God Himself; mankind has a 'capacity for God'.[6] This is inherent in the very nature of humans and is not simply grafted on; nor can it ever be taken away from us as a species or as individuals. This means that humans have an inherently relational nature, rooted in their relationship with God. What is more, we cannot fully become what we are without being in relationship with others. Thus *Gaudium et spes* refers to man as '... a social being, and unless he relates himself to others he can neither live nor develop his potential.'[7]

We find this social and communitarian nature firstly in the fact, as it says in Genesis, that He created us as man and woman. Plants and animals were not enough. Adam needed to dialogue, to commune with one like himself. This is of course why a fundamental equality between men and women exists. Not simply that both are created in the image of God, as if that wasn't enough, but because of the relationship that exists between them as fellow humans, what the Catechism calls 'the dynamic reciprocity', gives them life and is itself an image of God.[8]

We are thus entrusted not only with responsibility for our own lives and wellbeing but also with the lives and wellbeing of others. So, we have the fifth commandment, 'Thou shalt not kill', and the positive commandment in Leviticus 19:18, 'You shall love your neighbour as yourself', which Jesus expands to make clear our obligation to tend to their needs in a very practical way in the parable of the Good Samaritan.

Sin

Now, this all sounds very cosy and it's hard to imagine why society doesn't just work perfectly, but the reality is we don't live in perfect communion with each other, with ourselves or with God. This is, of course, the result of what can rightly be called 'The Tragedy of Sin'.[9] Sin is not inherent in our nature as created by God, but it is part of the reality of our existence as heirs of Adam and Eve. We often tend to shy away from explicitly talking about the notion of sin but to do so is to deny this reality and to fail to address the core of many of the issues that scandalize us. Sin is at its core a separation from God and brings with it an alienation not only from God but from our own selves, from each other and from rest of creation. To ignore our fallen state is also to lose sight of who we are as we strive for our original unity and harmony as individuals and as a society. It is also to forget that many 'helps' are needed and granted along the way and amongst these, I would suggest, are our notions of responsibilities, duties and rights.

Every sin is both personal and social. Each sin is personal in that it is the act and choice of an individual which affects him and his relationship with God. It is also social as a result of the solidarity of all humanity and nothing that we do is without impact on others. Some sins are more clearly against our neighbour, but to try and convince ourselves that some of our sins are without impact on others is one of the great errors of the individualism that permeates much of modern social thought, ethics and politics. These impacts can spread far and wide, and down through the generations, through the creation and perpetuation of what John Paul II rightly calls 'structures of sin'.[10] We see these in our own society through systematic prejudice and privilege. Institutional racism and sexism as identified in many organisations, exemplify structural sin. Hiding behind 'the system' is not sufficient defence when we are perfectly aware of wrongdoing on an institutional scale. Such structural sin is perpetuated solely by the complicit actions of individuals as they choose to continue committing particular sins. Social sin is no defence against our personal choices. True, it can make it difficult and often it involves taking a risk or even facing martyrdom, but to fail to resist structures of sin is to be complicit with them. Such structures prevent the development of people and hinder each person in their calling to be all that they can be.

Sin is universal and as I have just said it is rightly called a tragedy. But, the story we are part of is not a simple tragedy like Oedipus or Macbeth in which the hero is destined to disaster through a character flaw. Our story with God is more of a romance, albeit with some tragic episodes. We are not left alone with our faults but instead we are saved, not by a knight in shining armour on his white steed, but by a carpenter on a cross. What this means is that the sin which surrounds us is eclipsed by the grace which permeates our life and transforms us into a new creation as adopted children of God. This New Covenant, if we choose to let it, also provides the source of all we need to meet the challenge of sin as expressed through inequality and injustice. Central to this is an understanding of the dignity of the human person, not only despite our fallen nature but because of our new status as sons and daughters of God.

The Dignity of the Human Person

Human beings thus have an intrinsic dignity rooted in their nature as created in the image of God; their social natures in which they are called to communion with each other and God, and as redeemed children of God.

Many notions of what it is to be human fail to take into account the fullness of what it means to be human by reducing our nature to one or two aspects. Indeed, the notion of Christian personalism that we just discussed is often mistaken for an individualistic vision of society in which we operate as separate units, only impacting incidentally on others in the society around us. Indeed, addressing this misconception was part of the role of Benedict XVI's encyclical letter *Caritas in veritate* in which the Pope emphasises the importance of what he calls 'integral human development'.[11] He devotes a good deal of space to the personal and social nature of what it is to be fully human.

The reality is, however, that our modern society is governed by individualistic notions of what it is to be human. This has permeated into popular thought and is central to the reservations that are often expressed about rights. It is fully understandable why many resist the notion of rights if their world view is governed by individualistic notions of what it is to be human. Indeed, rights make little or no sense if we are simply a society of competing individuals.

51

It is important that we should not think that there is a single notion of individualism. There are, in fact, many 'individual' types of individualism. In a recent paper the catholic sociologist Margaret Archer typifies three forms of individualism which permeate western societies and which prevent the common dignity of each person being recognised.[12] She calls the three individualistic concepts of the human person *Homo economicus, Homo sociologicus and Homo inconstantus*.

Homo economicus contributes nothing to the common good, unless by accident and his social relations are meaningless to him. He has one characteristic, the drive to maximise his choices and preferences, and in doing so to maximise benefit to himself. He is self-sufficient and contributes nothing unless there is a direct benefit to himself. He is essentially in competition with all other members of society in order to gain maximum benefit and has no bonds with those around him. This model puts services such as education, health and social care in the realm of unfettered competition and assumes that because each person will maximise benefit to themselves then the greatest overall good will be achieved. This of course runs counter to any notion of solidarity as it turns life into a competition. It also eliminates any sense of obligation to others and introduces only one right: the right to maximise personal benefit and wealth.

Homo sociologicus does not at first appear as individualistic. It is based upon the idea that each person occupies a particular social role and that this defines their abilities and responsibilities totally. Such people fulfil their roles but no more. Their full personalities are limited and they do not engage with others as fellow human beings, or persons, but solely as categories such as customer, applicant, patient or immigrant. There is no personal or moral investment in relationships and never any attempt to 'go beyond' or 'walk the extra mile'. It is this model which accepts the defence of hiding behind rules and procedures as a valid response to a query or appeal for help, or transforms local authorities from service organisations to law enforcement agencies. From a Christian perspective this model of humanity counters the notion of subsidiarity as it takes away from the individual any control over their life and centralises decisions and power into specific roles. Perhaps more worrying, and interesting in the context of the growing notion of Christian Stewardship, is that the Church's notion of human beings as 'gifted servants' is completely suppressed. Each person has talents (*munera*) and is called and willing to serve each other through fellowship. *Homo sociologicus* seeks to absorb such spontaneous service through regulation or incorporation into the State. Archer gives the example of when payment for blood donors was introduced in the US: both the numbers of donors and the quality of blood declined as what John Paul II called 'social love' was inhibited and reduced to a transaction.

Homo inconstantus feels freed from 'common values' and conformity and seeks to create his own 'culture'. He is the self-made man, creating his own life story divorced from history, culture and other people. Indeed, he may even live significant portions of his life through various avatars. Thus, with Margaret Thatcher, he agrees that there is 'no such thing as society' and that the only culture that matters is the one he creates for himself. Who he is can change at any point as it is entirely controlled by himself; he is always provisional and can change when the environment suits. He does not recognise the fraternity of others or any value in them beyond any direct implications they have for his identity.

The common problem with each of these is that they fail to countenance any notion of the dignity of each and every person. Indeed, no secular answer to the universal dignity of humans has ever fully succeeded. Arguments based on uniqueness simply point to uniqueness with no general right to dignity. Secular humanism promotes an anthropocentric approach which reduces the value of creation to that of mere utility to be harvested for human benefit; a view which, in my opinion, underpins the post-Enlightenment devastation of our environment. It does not contain any intrinsic protection for each person or a notion of equal value or rights to the goods of the earth. Similarly, modern secular sociology seems to have avoided the issue. The closest that it has come are ideas that give dignity to certain characteristics of being human such as suffering or thriving — but each of these ideas could be as true of animals as of humans.

It is in light of this signal failure of society to incorporate the notion of the human person as possessing a unique and universal dignity that it has become necessary to introduce the concept of 'rights' in order to provide protection for this dignity. However, such rights provide something of a challenge to individualistic concepts of the person and have not been accepted without resistance. Indeed, it is quite possible that the resistance observable from amongst some Christians is due to the appropriation of such individualistic concepts as Archer describes. It is, at least, a reflection of some form of distorted notion of the Person.

Human Rights

It is a tendency amongst ruling elites to restrict certain 'rights' for themselves. Thus, in this country, we have seen the right to vote being restricted on the basis of land ownership, income, race and gender. Indeed, voting remains a hot topic with the issue of whether rights to vote can legitimately be removed from convicted prisoners.

There is then a need to declare and defend certain rights as being universal and to this end both John Paul II and Benedict XVI have declared the UN Universal Declaration on Human Rights of 1948 as a significant contribution to the moral wellbeing of the planet.[13] However, whilst the Church welcomes the Human Rights declaration it is also clear to affirm that rights do not stem from human agency or in the powers of the State or other organisations. Human rights are founded in the dignity of the nature of humanity and in our Creator God.

There are three key aspects to all rights rooted in the dignity of humanity. First, they are universal because they are present in all human beings without exception of time, place or subject. Second, they are inviolable because they are inherent in the human person and human dignity. As Paul VI stated 'it would be in vain to proclaim rights, if at the same time everything were not done to ensure the duty of respecting them by all people, everywhere, and for all people'.[14] Third, they are inalienable in that to deprive someone of their Rights is to do violence against their very nature.

Human rights must then be defended, but not simply as individual rights. They form a coherent whole and to allow one to be transgressed is to damage them all as it is the dignity of human beings that is being harmed. This is the notion that rights are also indivisible. Thus the assertion of the rights of one group at the expense of another is unacceptable. A good example from our own society relates to children and parents. For many years we have asserted the rights of parents and ignored the corresponding rights of children. However, more recently we have moved to the assertion of children's rights and a complete disregard for any rights for parents[15]. There seems to be an inability to allow both to be held in balance. The reason? Because the rights enshrined in legislation are based on individualistic notions of power relations and not on any sense to the equal dignity of each member of the family. In such models achieving a balance is virtually impossible. This is why the current tendency of specific interest groups to declare their wishes, or privileges which are enjoyed for a period, as 'Rights' is not sustainable. We cannot simply create rights based on technological developments, shifts in political philosophy or the desires to fulfil individualistic ends. Even when these things are good things, such as certain medical treatments for example, we cannot simply make the leap to declaring them rights in any meaningful sense.

Duties

As stated above, rights are inextricably linked with duties, and in many ways it is more constructive to think of our duties toward each other rather than claiming our rights. Thus John XXIII says: 'in human society, to one man's right there corresponds a duty in all other persons: the duty, namely, of acknowledging and respecting the right in question'.[16] He then goes on to point out that those who claim rights but neglect their duties 'build with one hand and destroy with the other'.[17] It is fair to think that if we reach a point where a person, or a group, have to lay claim to rights then we have failed in our duties. If we observe our duties then rights will not be transgressed and, ideally, conditions should exist which go beyond the mere level of basic rights. This is particularly important with regard to vulnerable groups as they are less likely to have a voice with which to claim rights, and less likely to have knowledge of their entitlements.

In order to fully understand the role of duties and rights in Catholic social doctrine we would do well to look to the nature of the Covenant that we have with God. Before the Fall there was no Covenant, there was no need for a covenant in the Garden of Eden as we existed in a state of grace. Indeed, it would be a ridiculous notion. But humanity fell and to help us come back to Him, God gave us His Covenant and with it His Law. The Law was not simply a code of duties and responsibilities to ensure fidelity and justice amongst God's people. It was a source of divine guidance, and expression of God's love which was deserving of His people's love in return.[18] However, the Law was not observed and prophets were sent to remind the people of their duties and of God's love for them. In particular, their mission was often to remind the people of the need for justice for the weak, the widow and the orphan. Unsurprisingly, the prophets were met with abuse as they acted in this role, reminding the rich and powerful that the weak and poor were being ignored and that Israel was not fulfilling its obligations to them; and thus to God. It is easy to see a parallel with the notion of rights. Human rights act today like a thorn in the side of many who do not wish to be reminded of their duties and responsibilities to those with little or no voice. So to those who argue for greater emphasis on duties we must agree, but not if that means trying to silence the nagging prophets of rights which will act as a constant reminder of our obligations and of our fallen state. It is this fallen state which necessitates the need for Covenant, Law and prophets, and likewise for duties and rights. However, we are constantly called to something greater, not simply fulfilling obligations.

Civilization of Love

To achieve this we need to move beyond the notion of rights and duties, and to look deeper into the nature and dignity of each human being. The key to this is, of course, love. We are called to build what Benedict XVI calls a 'civilization of love'.[19] A society which recognises the beauty and dignity of each person and in which each person acknowledges and seeks to fulfil their duties to the other. This is not a vision that can thrive in the face of individualism but requires a deep understanding of our common humanity rooted in our creation in the image of God. It also requires an acknowledgement of our weakness, our sinful state, and thus our dependence on God and His Covenant. It is a vision achievable only as a result of the New Covenant in Christ in which our state has been elevated to that of Children of God. In seeking this we cannot afford to ignore the prophets that remind us of these things.

Notes

[1]   *Compendium of The Social Doctrine of the Church (CSD)*, 160.

[2]   Congregation for the Doctrine of the Faith, *Libertatis Conscientia*, 72.

[3]   Vatican II, *Gaudium et Spes*, 26.

[4]   Pope John XXIII, *Mater et Magistra*.

[5]   R. Charles, *Christian Social Witness and Teaching: The Catholic Tradition from Genesis to Centesimus Annus*, Vol 1 (Leominster: Gracewing, 1998).

[6]   Vatican II, *Gaudium et Spes*, 19.

[7]   *Ibid.*, 12.

[8]   *Catechism of the Catholic Church*, 371.

[9]   *CSD*, 115.

[10] Pope John Paul II *Sollicitudo Rei Socialis*, 36, 37.

[11] The term 'integral human development' forms part of the title of the encyclical and the theme is developed throughout the document.

[12] M. Archer, *International Journal of Public Theology* 5/3 (2011).

[13] John Paul II declared the Universal Declaration on Human Rights 'a true milestone on the path of humanity's moral progress' (2 October 1979 address to 34th General Assembly of the UN) and also as 'one of the highest expressions of the human conscience of our time' (5 October 1995 address to 50th General Assembly of the UN).

[14] Pope Paul VI, *Message to the international conference on Human Rights*, Teheran (15 April 1968) as found in *L'Osservatore Romano* (2 May 1968).

[15] For example, in a UK context, the Children's Act (1989) asserts the rights of children and responsibilities of parents but disregards the notion of rights with regard to parents.

[16] Pope John XXII, *Pacem in terris*.

[17] *Ibid.*

[18] See Psalm 119 (118).

[19] Pope Benedict XVI, *Caritas in veritate*, 33.

Did Catholics Learn From Marxism?
Some reflections from Eastern Europe

JOLANTA BABIUCH

When communist rule came to an end during the years 1989–1991, one of the many theories surrounding the sudden, comprehensive set of changes in Eastern Europe was penned by the US historian, Francis Fukuyama. His thesis about the 'end of history'—that the steady ascent of humanity towards the shining uplands of liberal democracy and global capitalism was now complete—gained much currency. It can be argued that the economic crisis of 2008–2009 finally put paid to such optimistic self-assurance. There may, indeed, be no better system than liberal democracy; but does that necessarily mean we should be satisfied with the current socio-economic order? There is, clearly, a need for holistic systemic analyses from a macro perspective, as well as for theoretical tools for critically dissecting and evaluating political and economic processes from the perspective of change.[1]

Systemic analytical tools and ideas of this kind were developed in Eastern Europe as a means of challenging and overcoming communist ideology and practice. Can modern Catholic social teaching learn from the intellectual debate which ensued? This chapter will look back at some of the ideas which characterised the debate, and especially at the dialogue between Marxism and Personalism—one coming from the atheist revolutionary programme, the other from Catholic social reformism. The story of this Marxist-Christian discussion is worth recalling, since it may help provide new ideas and perspectives for correcting and removing certain dysfunctions within the current capitalist system.

Personalism was, in its heyday, one of the most dynamic Catholic philosophical schools of the Twentieth Century. It made a significant contribution to the intellectual critique of communism, and played an important role in forging the coalition which overturned communist rule. Emerging in France in the 1930s, it represented the response of a group of Catholic intellectuals to crises provoked by the economic depression and the failings of democracy in the face of new totalitarian ideologies. As a worldview which placed the human person at the centre of events, Personalism helped liberate minds captivated by totalitarian thinking via peaceful metaphysical deductions. Its particular attraction lay in its specific concept of 'the person', which embodied a rejection of both individualism and collectivism.

In the post-War years, the influence of the Personalist tradition was evident among the founding fathers of the European Union, as well as the emerging schools of Christian Democracy and the Christian Left. It also had a profound impact, however, on Catholic social thinking under communist rule in Eastern Europe. Several architects of French Personalism proved influential in Poland and elsewhere, including Jacques Maritain (1882–1973), Emmanuel Mounier (1905–1950) and Gabriel Marcel (1889–1973), in tandem with other 'philosophers of dialogue' such as Paul Ricoeur (1913–2010), Martin Buber (1878–1965), Emmanuel Levinas (1906–1995) and Franz Rosenzweig (1886–1929). What all offered in common was an emphasis on human dignity and human rights, and the responsibility and duty of the person to engage in bringing about social justice.

Of course, the contexts were different. In pre-War Western Europe, totalitarian ideologies were asserting their power, whereas in communist-ruled Eastern Europe reflection focused on how to respond from a Christian perspective to the social and economic injustices which had existed before the war, and which communist ideology had exploited. This, in turn, required contrasting versions of Personalism. In Eastern Europe, it was interpreted and applied as a response to Marxism, and this made it distinct from the mainstream version predominating in Western Europe.

If we talk of a specific East European version of Personalism, it was, indeed, more a 'philosophy of life' than a school of thought, as given expression by movements such as the Workers Defence Committee (KOR) in Poland and Charter 77 in Czechoslovakia, in which Personalism forged an encounter during the 1970s with a predominantly secular human rights tradition. Let us start, however, with the first phase of Personalism in its encounter with Marxism. How did they relate to each other?

Personalism and Marxism

One common characteristic of the two philosophical schools was that they both generated a strong critique of capitalism, reacting to its dysfunctions and crises, but ending up with completely different conclusions and proposed solutions. In the mid-nineteenth Century, Karl Marx had unmasked and rejected the capitalist system from the perspective of social injustice, condemning it for its unjust, exploitative division of work and labour, and demonstrating how this led to alienation in human existence by treating people as commodities rather than assets. With some simplification, we can say both Marxism and Personalism offered practical philosophies of engagement and stressed the importance of individual social responsibility. In both intellectual perspectives, the person was called to act and bring about change; changing the system for better. Whereas the Marxist answer to social injustice was class struggle and social revolution, however, the Personalists of the 1930s proclaimed a moral and spiritual revolution.

Both philosophies, Personalism and Marxism, vigorously opposed liberal individualism, with its atomistic anthropology and derivatives in the logic of economic freedom and the market economy. Marxism was not interested, however, as a particular socio-economic system, in the personal perspective. Instead, it focused on aggregated groups—race, class, society—and viewed the human being as just a component of them. Its materialism assumed the human being was a social being, a product of nature and socio-economic relations with a life determined by the social and economic situation. The essence of man was his role in the collectivity: he needed only to participate in the project of a better society, which would always be more important than the individual.

Personalism, by contrast, stressed the person's nature as a social being. This person also never existed in isolation—the person found human perfection in communion with others. Yet Personalism also resisted the absorption of the individual into the collectivity and asserted the person's inherent worth. 'We are not individualists or collectivists—we are Personalists', the Personalist manifesto proclaimed. Individualism treats the self as an object, so the person is opposed to the individual. 'If the first condition of individualism is the centralisation of the individual in himself', explained Emmanuel Mounier, 'the first condition of Personalism is his decentralisation, in order to set him in the open perspectives of personal life'. While individualism sought personal realisation in the sphere of self-interest, Personalism asserted the need for openness to others as the very condition for that personal realisation.[2]

The Russian Personalist, Nikolai Berdyaev, was one of the religious and political philosophers who tried to find good elements in Marxism and incorporate them into Personalism. Berdyaev became a Marxist while studying law at Kiev University; but he later converted to Orthodox Christianity and was expelled from Soviet Russia in 1922. In a 1935 article, 'Marxism and Personalism', he concluded that Marxism was anti-Personalist in character, since it failed to provide a sufficient reflection on the person as an independent being. From the Personalist perspective, Berdyaev pointed out, the person was endowed with an independent inner core which was not determined by society. It was in the process of participating in society that the person was formed. Yet 'the realisation of the person is not just a natural or social process', Berdyaev argued, 'It is a heroic struggle for independence'.[3]

A just social system would thus take the form of a Personalist socialism, based 'not on the idea of equality or justice, but rather on the dignity of every human person, having the possibility to realise himself'. A Christian could be a socialist, Berdyaev insisted. Indeed, a Christian *ought* to be a socialist. 'But it is difficult for him to be a communist, since he cannot agree to accept the totalitarian world outlook of communism, into which materialism and atheism have entered.'[4]

Anti-Personalism was only one side of Marxism, Berdyaev pointed out. It had another side as well. Marx criticised the capitalist system from a Personalist and humanist perspective, seeing how it inflicted dehumanisation. He looked at the structures of economy from the perspective of human relations—an anti-materialist approach—and defined capital not as a tangible thing, but as a social relationship of people in the process of production. 'By this definition', Berdyaev observed, 'the centre of gravity of economic life was transferred to human activity and struggle'.[5] What Marxism needed was to incorporate a concept of the human person which acknowledged his self-worth and inherent depth. The human being could not be just a function of the social process.

Despite their contrasting conclusions and prescriptions, Marxism and Personalism had encountered each other in the pre-War years in a flourishing dialogue between religious believers and non-believers. People taking part in the discourse were often Marxists or socialists with searching minds who had converted to Christianity. While the Marxist and liberal intellectuals tended to be secular, most Personalists had religious or spiritual outlooks. It was not necessary, however, to be a religious believer to share the Personalist philosophy.

The Dialogue in Eastern Europe

The pre-War discourse between Marxism and Personalism continued in communist-ruled Eastern Europe, acquiring its own dynamic. In the aftermath of the Second World War, socialism was seen by many in the under-developed countries of Eastern Europe, for centuries under foreign domination, as a form of rapid modernisation. It promised a realm of emancipation, stability and prosperity, and elicited moral passion on the part of its supporters in a fight for social justice and commitment. For others, the War presented an alternative, a choice between fascism and communism. After such bitter experiences, many naturally concluded that the main enemy lay on the Right.

Much of the secular intellectual elite, raised and educated according to the Enlightenment tradition, identified Catholicism with regressive conservatism and nationalism. Personalism, by contrast, was viewed as a progressive Catholic alternative. It had been known before the War in Poland, where it had exerted an influence within the Catholic Odrodzenie (Renaissance) movement. Jerzy Turowicz, for example, editor of Poland's newest Catholic weekly, *Tygodnik Powszechny*, and a former Odrodzenie member, had had contacts with Mounier's *L'Esprit* review in the 1930s. Catholic intellectuals could thus study Personalism in the hope of finding answers and directions as to the best stance for Catholics in a secular communist-ruled country. In ideological terms, the immediate post-War period was idealistic and romantic, as the same Catholic intellectuals tried to find their place in the new system, referring to the Personalist principle that the person and community should be always together.

At *Tygodnik Powszechny*, Turowicz and his colleagues searched the neo-Thomist writings of Maritain for a means of opening themselves to the new world order and taking co-responsibility for rebuilding the Polish state without losing their Catholic identity. One key Personalist value which the weekly could propagate was universalism — which, in its Polish interpretation, rejected both narrow nationalism and the erosion of national identity associated with communism. Polish Catholic intellectuals were attracted by Maritain's philosophical realism, and its evident contrast with the idealistic Hegelian stream in philosophy, which had acquired negative connotations through its association with totalitarian thinking.[6]

For people like this, Personalist thought inspired both religious reflection on the need for openness in the Catholic Church, and political reflection on forms of social engagement which could constitute a coherent Christian answer to Marxism. 'Socialism, at least at the beginning, was Christianity's bad conscience', wrote Tadeusz Mazowiecki, who would later serve as first Prime Minister of a post-communist Poland. 'It was a guilty conscience which arose very clearly from social issues and undoubtedly unveiled the link between the Church and the class of owners.'[7] It was this first spark of rebellion against social injustice and prejudice which created an ethical space for dialogue between socialism and Christianity.

The Catholic Personalist movement embraced people from different philosophical traditions and political backgrounds in a shared belief in the values of pluralism and mutual respect. As such, it created a forum for dialogue between believers and non-believers, Christians and Marxists. In the 1950s, the new Catholic journals, *Znak* and *Wiez*, and the Catholic Intelligentsia Club network, permitted as a concession by the communist regime, became open to contributions by secular non-Catholic writers and thinkers.

For all the ideological pressure exerted by the regime, interesting ideas began to emerge from the dialogue between secular social radicalism and Catholic social teaching, as awareness grew of the destructive consequences of communism and the crimes and oppression perpetrated in the Stalinist period. After a Hungarian Uprising was crushed by Soviet intervention in 1956, and the 'Polish October' protests were quelled during the same autumn, Catholic intellectuals began to search in earnest for a response to the new injustice and oppression being generated in communist-ruled countries of Eastern Europe, and for ways of persuading the communist state to embrace a more humanistic and tolerant interpretation of socialism.

Theses and ideas, inspired by Personalism, emerged from the intellectual discourse through various manifestations in Eastern Europe. The notion of 'Living in Truth', a phrase coined by the Czech dissident playwright, Vaclav Havel, meant unmasking the crude techniques behind communism's ideological facade and creating 'little holes' or 'democratic spaces' within the system, in which a self-organising society might emerge. Havel's fellow-Czech, Vaclav Benda, called this a 'parallel polis'; and it was given its most dynamic expression by the August 1980 emergence of the independent Solidarity trade union movement in neighbouring Poland. The common aim was to act as if the citizens of the communist state were living in a free democracy. If a new revolution came, it must be a non-violent, spiritual revolution, creating change peacefully through pressure from a self-organising civil society and ensuring respect for the dignity of every human person, whatever their background and outlook. The Personalist perspective offered a metaphysical point of departure, a cornerstone, for defending the uniqueness of every human person which could be shared by religious believers and non-believers.[8]

The Significance of Karol Wojtyła

It was the future Pope John Paul II who provided one of many remarkable examples of this intellectual encounter. The then Karol Wojtyła wrote his doctoral thesis on Max Scheler's ethics of values, drawing on the Personalist school founded in Poland in the early 1940s by the Phenomenologist, Roman Ingarden (1893–1970). When presented in 1953, it embodied an interesting synthesis of Aristotelian and Thomist metaphysics and anthropology, based on Scheler's phenomenological approach. Wojtyła then became a professor of ethics at the Theological Faculty of Krakow and Lublin's Catholic University, where he helped build up the same Polish Personalist school.

Wojtyła's distinctive form of Personalism can be viewed as a response to his own experience of the Marxist-Leninist system. In a later 1994 work, *Crossing the Threshold of Hope*, he elaborated how the concern for the person and his inherent dignity became the main theme of the polemic against Marxism, forcing Marxists themselves to place the question of man at the centre of their arguments. Like the pre-War French Personalists, Wojtyła rejected the two extremes of individualism and collectivism:

> On the one hand, persons may easily place their own individual good above the common good of the collectivity, attempting to subordinate the collectivity to themselves and use it for their individual good. This is the error of individualism, which gave rise to liberalism in modern history and to capitalism in economics. On the other hand, society, in aiming at the alleged good of the whole, may attempt to subordinate persons to itself in such a way that the true good of persons is excluded and they themselves fall prey to the collectivity. This is the error of totalitarianism, which in modern times has borne the worst possible fruit.[9]

Long before, in his 1969 book, *The Acting Person* (in Polish, *Person and Act*), Wojtyła had drawn on the Personalist approach to show how people have a moral responsibility and obligation to act. It was a work which brought his thinking to international attention. He had, however, reached similar conclusions as a promising young priest in the early 1950s, in a much less known two-volume work, *Catholic Social Ethics*. This was produced secretly, with the approval of Wojtyła's archbishop, Cardinal Adam Sapieha of Krakow, and at the request of Catholic students, to fill the gap left by the suppression of other books on the Church's social doctrine by Poland's Stalinist rulers.

Today, this still-unpublished 511-page work is of considerable historical importance. It shows the future Pope was deeply read in Marxism by his early 30s and had already thought out a strategy for countering communism's ideological claims three decades before his Papal election. It also suggests he had radical, faith-inspired social sympathies—enough to provide a critical synthesis of Personalist thought which drew on a selective Marxist inspiration.

In his analysis, Wojtyła sought to bring the two approaches together: Marxism's critical theory of capitalism as a socio-economic system based on injustices, and Personalism's espousal of the uniqueness and dignity of every human being. In his hands, the aim of Catholic social teaching was to integrate the common good with the good of the person. 'The main task of the Catholic social ethic', Wojtyła wrote, 'is to introduce the principles of justice and love to social life'. It stipulates the rights and duties of citizens towards legitimate and illegitimate, just and unjust, power; and since co-operation for the common good is a 'supreme ethical duty', it accepts that 'struggle is, in many instances, the way to realise this', insofar as it aims at 'introducing social justice' and does not 'stand in contradiction to the love proclaimed by the Gospel'. There are certain points at least in which Catholic social teaching concurs with the powerful concepts associated with Marxism, such as the right to live in just society, the duty to struggle against work alienation and the need to elevate the sense of work far beyond the economic sphere. Both Marxism and Catholic social teaching stress that work must have a humanising value and retain primacy over capital. 'Human labour, which in various respects is a human duty, cannot be treated as a commodity', the future Pope explained, 'since it carries within itself the characteristics of an activity of free will'.[10]

John Paul II would fine-tune this Personalist argument about the dignity of work in his 1981 encyclical, *Laborem Exercens*. In *Catholic Social Ethics*, however, he was already listing the ethical requirements for a proper use of capital, and for the producer to fulfil his duty to society. An economic enterprise based on capital, insofar as it is ethically justified, serves the development of social prosperity; but if its main or sole aim is multiplication of the capitalist's profit, then it is ethically wrong. 'Social duties and the rights of capital should be defined according to this principle', Wojtyła contended. 'Society should lavish special care on those members who are in a state of material misery. Church and state have individual roles to play in this'.[11] Private property suits human nature; so it is necessary only to aim at a state of affairs in which reforms leading to the realisation of social justice can take place within the framework of an economic system based on private property.

More than three decades later, in *Sollicitudo Rei Socialis* (1987), the Pope would reaffirm that the right to private property was 'valid and necessary'. But it was also subject to a 'social mortgage' and had 'an intrinsically social function', since Christian doctrine taught that the goods of the world were 'originally meant for all'. Was it really possible, however, to create a social system without injustice and work alienation? Despite all the social projects attempted which during the Twentieth Century, that fundamental question was still open. For Marx, the total destruction brought by revolution was a value in itself, since it prepared the ground for a just society in which man was reconciled to the fruits of his labour. The precondition, however, had to be the destruction of private property. For Wojtyła, by contrast, such destruction was not an imperative. Profound changes were indeed necessary if social justice was ever to be realised; but they could be arrived at via reforms 'within the framework of an economic system based on private property'. It should be possible to build a just society in such a way that private property was made to serve the common good.[12]

Like Marx, Wojtyła saw that it was conflict, rather than consensus, which lay at the heart of modern social structures. He stressed the ethical primacy of co-operation; but he also acknowledged the need for certain forms of class pressure to force through change and contribute to the elimination of social and moral harm.

The Personalist duty to act with sensitivity and disapproval against social injustice remained actual and inalienable. So was the obligation to make social life fairer and better. The Church saw clearly and proclaimed the need for reform in the economic and social system. From its standpoint, it was a question of ensuring, by means of economic-structural changes, just participation by all members of society, and especially people of work, in possessing sufficient disposable assets and participating to some extent in the production process. In his lectures, Wojtyła linked the capitalist system with materialism. 'The Church, for its part, is aware that the bourgeois mentality and capitalism as a whole, with its materialist spirit, stand in glaring contradiction to the Gospel'.[13]

The duty of active resistance—against an unjust power inflicting dehumanisation on people—was shared and upheld by both Marxism and Personalism. 'Of course, from the viewpoint of the Gospel's ethical assumptions, such a struggle is a *malum necessarium* [necessary evil], as is every struggle or war between people', Wojtyła wrote. 'The Gospel postulates that love is the height of perfection in the ethical order. Yet it also demonstrates that struggle need not be the opposite of love. The opposite of love is mere hatred, whereas struggle in a concrete case does not have to arise from hatred. If it results from social and material harm, and aims at restoring a just distribution of goods, then such a struggle is not the complete antithesis of love... We know that justice is an indispensable condition for realising love; so social justice is a necessary condition for realising love in social life'.[14] In this way, a struggle aimed at introducing social justice did not stand in contradiction to the love proclaimed by the Gospel. Nor did it have to be an act of hatred.

Some lessons for today

When communist rule collapsed, it was natural that most East Europeans experienced an allergic reaction to ideas from the Left, as many had done to ideas from the Right half a century earlier. Marxism was totally discredited in Eastern Europe, communism a failed ideal; but there was still some lingering attraction to socialist ideas, and a continuing readiness to look to Christianity for the appropriate inspiration. As the transformation to a capitalist system gathered pace, however, Personalism lost its impact. The Church, for its part, was worried that Personalism, given its legacy of openness to secular humanist intellectuals, could lead to a blurring of the Christian identity. How could such faith-inspired social radicalism propose a model for practical, consistent application in such rapidly changing circumstances?

Yet it could be argued that both Personalism and Marxism still offered tools of critical analysis which could be developed and applied to the evolving political and economic order and its inherent power structures. Since the 1930s, philosophers such as Maritain and Mounier had been using the Personalist view of man to seek out a 'third way' between individualistic capitalism and state-sponsored socialism. This had rarely produced any developed economic thought. It had, however, generated some fruitful ideas in the area of civil society, non-governmental activity and human rights. Under pressure of external conditions, post-communist Eastern Europe quickly came under the domination of a liberalism based on rational self-interest—a laissez-faire philosophy which justified the choices made by strong, self-confident individuals. Certainly, this kind of liberalism had the capacity to strengthen human dignity. Yet for the ordinary people losing out because of the changes, it was hardly a forceful or appealing proposition.

Today, Personalism still has its exponents and supporters. In 1998, the Indian economist, Amartya Sen, was awarded the Nobel Prize for his Personalist contributions to welfare economics and social choice theory, suggesting the quest is still continuing for coherent alternatives and options. Can Catholic social teaching still learn something from ideas which emerged from the encounter with Marxism? Is Personalism still a fruitful tradition for such teaching to draw on?

I argue that while Personalism, like Marxism, is finished in its pure form, there is indeed a strong case for a modern version of Personalism, drawing on the spirit which still survives in the ideas and practices of civil society, and in the opposition to injustices. The radicalism shared by Personalism and Marxism, and the dialogue between them, enumerated important values in capitalist democracies, which may still evolve, as it evolved in Eastern Europe, in confrontation with contemporary challenges. The discourse between Personalism and Marxism could still contribute to developments in the capitalist system.

The Czech Vaclav Havel, for one, drew a distinction between 'procedural' and 'substantial' democracy. The communist-era opposition movement had no ambition to create a political party in the Western sense, he argued; rather, it aimed at the establishment of 'post-democracy'. How did this 'post-democracy' differ from parliamentary democracy? Parliamentary democracy, Havel observed, rested on the logic of power competition and electoral majority—for this reason, it could never develop a 'life in truth' by itself. Post-democracy, by contrast, without rejecting parliamentary democracy, sought its foundation in a people's openness to moral values.[15]

The Personalist 'philosophy of life' enumerated important values: human dignity, transparency, integrity, solidarity, good governance. Against a new backdrop of consumerism and materialism, it can still play an important role in fostering solidarity with the needy and powerless, and an impulse for resolving problems of hopelessness and incapacity. Its radical openness, as Levinas put it, can give the person a historical and transcendent dynamic which prevents encapsulation into existing power relations and structures. The Personalist-Marxist discourse, in short, still has value; and its spirit should survive at the level of ideas and practices. In the contemporary context, this means recreating and building up an intellectual dialogue between religious believers and unbelievers, based not just on the defence of one's own rights, but on the will to find shared answers to current world challenges.

It also means recreating and building up the kind of common ground which existed under communist rule—this time for a critical analysis of the current capitalist system, where economics still predominates over humanity in the materialism of a consumer society, and the worth of the person is still largely evaluated by his material function in the production process. There is still a fundamental need for a deeper anthropology; and this can come from Catholic social teaching—and particularly from the defence of spiritual existence in opposition to the prevalent materialism. In the current bonus culture and casino economy, much economic activity has been reduced to a technical process, rather than a means of improving wellbeing, and public debate degraded to the pragmatic power relations shaping the formation of institutions and methods of governance. By contrast, Personalism upholds the primacy of the ethical and moral realm. It ensures that what we owe to others takes precedence over the utility of impersonal systems, structures and processes, and that the moral life remains irreducible. It emphasises the possibility and duty to be engaged, react against injustice and make changes in our world.

In his June 2009 encyclical, *Caritas in Veritate*, Pope Benedict XVI invoked the Personalist tradition by recalling that the mode of being and acting of the person directly relates to his vocation of self-possession and self-giving. These are, in their way, an achievement of capitalism—far from being a slave, the person can act freely in selling his labour. In reality, however, he has little choice. Both the Pope and Amartya Sen have stressed this need for a capacity to choose; and in the logic of the liberal market economy, the freedom of choice is indeed a key value. Yet the ability to choose is often absent. The disadvantaged and vulnerable have little if any choice. Nor can the poor be free.

Instead, *Caritas in Veritate* develops the idea of 'charity in truth' and 'gratuitousness', which are ever-present, expressing humanity's transcendent dimension, but often 'unrecognized because of a purely consumerist and utilitarian view of life'. They need to be remain present if political, economic and social development is to be 'authentically human'. The idea of humanity's self-sufficiency, Benedict XVI points out, has led people to 'confuse happiness and salvation with immanent forms of material prosperity and social action'—and to a conviction that the economy must be autonomous and 'shielded from influences of a moral character'. Such notions have led to 'economic, social and political systems that trample upon personal and social freedom, and are therefore unable to deliver the justice that they promise'. Instead, the Church's social doctrine highlights the importance of social justice in the market economy as a means of ensuring the social cohesion it needs to function well. Without 'internal forms of solidarity and mutual trust', the market cannot do this. 'The economic sphere is neither ethically neutral, nor inherently inhuman and opposed to society', the encyclical argues. 'It is part and parcel of human activity and precisely because it is human, it must be structured and governed in an ethical manner'.[16]

Such ideas owe much to the Personalist tradition, and to the dialogue about ethical priorities which helped bring an end to communist rule—and which created an enduring hope that communist-era injustices would not be replicated in the new liberal capitalist system which followed. Only those who possess and govern themselves can act disinterestedly and charitably, in a process of self-realisation which ultimately makes human beings truly human and fully able to discover and realise their true self in relationship with others.

Notes

1   F. Fukuyama, *The End of History and the Last Man* (New York: Free Press, 1992). The thesis was first published as an essay in *The National Interest*, Summer 1989.

2   E. Mounier, *A Personalist Manifesto* (New York: Longmans, Green and Co., 1938).

3   N. Berdyaev, 'Personalism and Marxism', in *Put* Journal, No. 48, July–Sept. 1935, 3–19.

4   *Ibid.*

5   *Ibid.*

6   J. Żakowski, *Trzy ćwiartki wieku: Rozmowy z Jerzym Turowiczem* (Znak: Krakow, 1990), 55.

7   W. Wesołowski, ed., *Losy Idei socjalistycznych i wyzwania współczesności* (Warsaw: Polskie Towarzystwo Współpracy, 1990), 46.

8   V. Havel, 'Politics and Conscience', in *Open Letters: Selected Writings 1965–1900* (Vintage Books, New York, 1992). Vaclav Benda presented his concept of the 'parallel polis' in short seminal underground tract called, translated into English in 1978.

9   K. Wojtyła, *Personalizm tomistyczny* (Krakow: Znak 1961), 664–675. English edition: *Thomistic Personalism: Person and Community*, in Andrew Woznicki, ed., *Selected Essays* (New York: Peter Lang, 1993), 174.

10   K. Wojtyła, *Katolicka Etyka Społeczna*, 2 volumes of unpublished bound essays (Krakow:1952), 51. J. Luxmoore and J. Babiuch, 'John Paul's debt to Marxism' in *The Tablet*, 14 January 2006.

11   Wojtyła, *Katolicka Etyka Społeczna*, 176.

12   *Ibid.*, p. 67. John Paul II, encyclical letter, *Sollicitudo Rei Socialis*, 42.

13   Wojtyła, *Katolicka Etyka Społeczna*, 57.

14   *Ibid.*, 114. J. Luxmoore and J. Babiuch, *The Vatican and the Red Flag* (Geoffrey Chapman: London, 1999), 87–91.

15   G. van Heeswijck, *On Human Rights: The philosophical background to Vaclav Havel's thought* (Leuven: Ethical Perspectives 1999), 6.

16   Pope Benedict XVI, *Caritas in Veritate*, 34.

Part 2:
The Catholic Experience

Reflections on Persecution, Memory and Hope in Ukrainian Society

In a former life I was a prisoner of conscience (as Amnesty International puts it), imprisoned from 1977 to 1987 for human rights activities in the former Soviet Union. What I came to recognize from that experience is that, aside from cemeteries, nothing leads a person more effectively to reflect on eternal truths than prison. The time in the Soviet GULAG happened to be the most difficult, but, at the same time, the most spiritually rewarding in my life. Let me recall one interesting moment. It was in 1980 that a group of prisoners were punished by the administration for celebrating Easter. Suffering in the name of Christ has always been an honour for a Christian and we served our punishment with a peaceful heart. Nevertheless, we sent a secret letter to the Holy Father, John Paul II, informing him about this fact. The letter concluded with an interesting remark: 'We wish that Christians, and together with them the entire human race, can live in peace, goodness and truth, but not at the price of disregarding the most sublime blessing — our God-given soul.'

It seems to me that the world is still searching for a solution to this dilemma. More and more, people are concerned with saving their lives; less and less are they able to comprehend the meaning of losing their lives for Christ to finally find them (cf. Matthew 16:25). Safety versus Values is still the issue for mankind. Ukraine happens to find itself in the very centre of this controversy. I will try to demonstrate this in two fields: (1) European security and the memory of communist crimes, and (2) the building of a value-oriented society. The two issues are, of course, interconnected; both are at the very core of Catholic social teaching.

European Security and the Memory of Communist Crimes

Undoing the mental and moral degradation brought about by communism has turned out to be a much more difficult task than dismantling the Soviet Union. Unfortunately, desiring to live a civilized life is not the same as knowing how to do that. The habit of living under a paternalistic government has interfered with the formation of citizens used to taking responsibility for their own actions. In addition, over the last twenty years a certain irony of fate has become apparent. If communism preyed upon the ethical heritage of ages past while breaking and destroying those who were raised according to traditional ethical standards, today's independent Ukraine (and not Ukraine alone) must deal with Homo soveticus—a peculiar type of human being created under the ideological norms of communism. For this reason I am frequently led to conclude, with great pain in my heart, that the worst victims of communism are not those who were killed but those who survived.

In such conditions, the task of establishing the rule of law is very difficult. Twenty years ago, dissidents and political prisoners who came out of prisons and camps did not strive to have their persecutors put on trial. The desire to 'turn a new page' was overwhelming: we leave you alone, you forget about your past and help us build democracy. But it turns out that an evil deed becomes part of the past only when it has been condemned and repented of. Unrepented wrongdoing inevitably serves as a source of new problems. The most obvious example of this is the glorification of Stalin currently taking place in Russia; Ukraine has encountered many similar tendencies. In the early 1990s, the communist elite changed its flag but not its essence. The lack of condemnation and repentance for the evils committed led to further evils during the next presidencies. All of this has had a profoundly destructive effect on the Ukrainian people's faith in the possibility of the establishment and rule of justice.

At the same time, in condemnation of the communist past, our Western partners were also inconsistent. For instance, while Germany did not hesitate to make Honecker pay for his crimes, Ukraine heard little from the West besides warnings against starting a 'second Nuremberg' and putting the leaders of communist regime on trial. Why? Because Europe did not want to have more problems with Russia. When Ukraine brought back to light the terrors of Holodomor (the manmade famine of 1932–1933), not a few of our Western partners, disturbed by Russia's protests, condemned our supposedly excessive politization of the issue.

Thus it becomes clear that coping with the evils committed by communist regimes is a problem not only for the former satellite nations, but for the world as a whole. The security system currently protecting the entire world was developed in Yalta under the motto that Nazism is absolute evil, while Communism, which has conquered that evil, is less evil. The idea is not so bad, but simply misinterpreted by the East. Twenty years ago it seemed that the Yalta era had come to an end; but today it is apparent that plenty of people would like the world order to remain within the boundaries of that familiar status quo.

Politicians seem to have once again occupied themselves with remaking the world; naturally, they think they are busy trying to create a more just world order. The altruism of annus mirabilis—the year of wonders, that is 1989,—is increasingly replaced with the egoism of national security systems. Russia's wounded honour is increasingly reminiscent of the wounded order of Nazi Germany, humiliated by the Treaty of Versailles. The old Nazi doctrine of 'protecting our citizens in foreign lands' is gaining power in Moscow. Old Europe, today as in the past, does not wish to sacrifice its well-being at the altar of defending international values. In almost every European nation, political forces are coming to the fore who want an end to multiculturalism, pluralism, and civil liberties. Very often, they are once again drunk on the cult of force. Perhaps a viewing of the splendid tail of Halley's Comet is all that would be needed right now for mankind to become convinced that it is standing on the verge of new and tragic tribulations.

The conclusion is clear: by now, the spiritual heritage of post-war Europe has been almost exhausted, and new cracks continue to appear in the world order that has relied on that heritage. Will Europe grasp that consensus in questions of military and energy security cannot be reached until there is a consensus with respect to historical memory and justice?

The Yalta plan for security ignored the fact that there were two participants in the mad dance of September 1939–Hitler's Germany and Stalin's USSR. The terrors of Auschwitz, Treblinka, and Buchenwald have been preserved in the collective memory of mankind, while those of the GULAG and Holodomor, Solovki and Katyn have been concealed under the victor's purple robe. Apocalyptic evil assumed the appearance of salvific good. Now, this unrecognised evil is turning into the seed of a new worldwide conflict.

Today, thanks to the entry of the peoples of central Europe into the European Union, there exists the possibility of considering the problem realistically. The forgotten evils of communism dwell in the European consciousness, and for as long as they have not been admitted and repented of, any hopes of mutual understanding among Europe's people are futile. On the contrary, we must fear that attempts to bring about such understanding can worsen relations and decrease trust all across the European continent. This is why reevaluating Europe's historical memory is a sine qua non for the successful realization of any civilization-wide projects.

I see the following solution to this situation. First of all, the evils of communism naturally call for a trial; however, the most important outcome of this trial would not be for the evildoers to be punished, but for the nature of the evil to be brought to light and clarified. No judge can condemn the criminals of communist regimes to greater punishment than that to which they have already condemned themselves. The illusions and temptations that lead to the sin of communism must be understood, the way that this has been done with respect to the sin of Nazism. In addition, the question of who must play the roles of defendant and judge, respectively, must be given serious thought. I am not aware of any people that has the moral right to wear the judge's robe: the temptation to communism has been a disease of the entire human civilization. On the other hand, I see many peoples, including the Ukrainians, who could keep Russia company on the defendant's bench. And we cannot hide from the ethnic aspects of the issue: Nazi criminals were not the only ones to have a nationality.

Responsibility for the evils of communism

But to stop here would be once again to lose touch with history. For the line between good and evil does not pass between ideological or national affiliations. As every Christian knows, it passes through the human heart (see, for instance, Matthew 15: 16-20), which is home both to sin and to the only cure for sin–repentance and forgiveness.

Forgiveness, however, is not easy to come by in the world in which we live. It has long been noted that a distinct characteristic of the post-communist space is the fact that all the peoples inhabiting it see themselves as the victims, not the perpetrators, of communism, and therefore do not see the need for repentance. Many former Soviet republics have developed the formula that they are victims of occupation, and someone else is the oppressor. The role of oppressor is usually played by 'Communist Moscow' or 'Bolshevik Russia.' Indeed, the blame that may be placed on the various peoples occupied by Russia cannot be compared with the guilt of Russia itself. Communist ideology served Russia's imperialist interests in the same way that today they are served by its dominance in oil and natural gas.

There was, however, another side to the communist 'coin.' Communist 'demons' have been found among all the peoples of the Russian empire; the blame for the evils of communism truly falls on them all. From this point of view, Russia is no less a victim of communism than other peoples, and the cruelty with which the Bolsheviks robbed her nobles and raped her nuns was no less apocalyptic. On the other hand, being a victim does not automatically absolve one of guilt; the German people were one of the greatest victims of Nazism, but accepted the blame and were forgiven and cleansed.

The conflicting diversity of historical memories has led to confusion in all international and inter-ethnic relations in Europe. I am convinced that this diversity has not only a political and ideological, but primarily an ethical nature, and is deeply connected to lack of repentance for the evils of communism. That all the groups involved see themselves as the victims and not the perpetrators of communism is a reality that must be taken into account. But do these groups understand correctly the rights and responsibilities of being a victim? I would consider it a great victory over evil if all the peoples of the world fully and finally condemned communism as a sin against humankind. But to issue an accusing verdict against communism is only half the battle. As the fourth secretary general of the World Council of Churches, Emilio Castro, has reminded us, 'the victim is not only a recipient of restitution. The victim is also the one who has the key to a real and fundamental reconciliation, because it is in the victim that Jesus Christ is present.'[1] Only the victim can forgive; the perpetrator by definition cannot do that. That is a great moral responsibility, without which there can be no true reconciliation. The peoples of Eastern Europe were quick to present themselves as victims in order to win the right to accuse; will they show themselves worthy of the status of victim by forgiving?

This is why the only spiritual solution to the problem of assigning responsibility for the evils of communism is a joint confession by all the former Soviet nations of their guilt in worshipping the communist beast (in Russia's case, also for using the communist doctrine to promote its imperial interests), as well as a joint forgiveness of one another for all wrongs done. Western Europe too must undergo a cathartic experience of this nature, as its fascination with communism nourished and legitimized the apocalyptic beast in the eastern nations.

Building a society oriented towards values

Merely twenty years ago we lived in an understandable and predictable world in which good and evil, black and white, were clearly distinguished. There was the 'evil empire,' with the ideological and power structures that sustained a system of wrongdoing. And there was a small yet coura- geous opposition, which located the source of goodness in the human person and directed movement towards it.

Today, we can say about that world that it is truly 'gone with the wind.' Good and evil have been mixed together, and separating them is almost impossible. The black-and- white world of communism and resistance to communism turned into a chaotic mixture of shades of grey that colours everything: political parties, civil organizations, and, at the end of the day, the independent republic for which we have all so longed. It is no wonder that many people have lost their orientation and sense of perspective.

The Orange Revolution in Ukraine restored this moral paradigm for one historical moment, and we were all drunk with the healing power of a communal catharsis. What happened after that can best be understood through a biblical metaphor: we doubted that it is possible to walk on water, and therefore, like the apostle Peter, began to sink.

Everything depends first of all on us—but also not only on us. There are powerful institutions in today's world that work consciously and hard, and get paid a lot of money, to confuse good and evil in our minds. As soon as a promising phenomenon arises within a society, the forces of evil immediately discredit it through the media or by creating an evil twin to it which serves to confuse and disorient people. Our times can be called the era of evil's revenge. But if everything is in fact a mix of good and evil, which good must we fight for? And on whom can we rely?

Recognizing the critical consequences of ignoring the ethical realm is ongoing today in most European and American nations, as the financial crisis has powerfully illustrated. Among other aspects, the conviction of the West that its energy security is more strategically important than protection of the values on which European civilization was founded now seems clearly mistaken. The victims of this misguided attitude include not only energy security itself, which can hardly be said to be greater today than it had been yesterday, but also the moral power of Western civilization. Indeed, Mr Putin need not strain his memory very much to be able to respond to Western politicians' dutifully delivered lectures of morality by rubbing their faces in their own moral errors.

It will not be easy to exit today's societal and political crisis. Nevertheless, I belong to those who are convinced of the primacy of spiritual processes over those that are purely political or economic. And I am certain that no consensus in matters of political, military, or energy security is possible until a consensus is reached on questions of social morality. In other words, the rapid progress of technology and information of the recent decades has not been accompanied by moral progress; on the contrary, moral relativism has been established as a dominant ideology around the world. Is this not a reason why the world worries about military and energy security, but continues to ignore the security of our souls?

An observant person will note that the struggles to fulfil the two great needs evident today—to protect Europe's overall security and to care for its spiritual safety—indeed support and reinforce one another. To reliably protect European security, the evils of communism must be properly understood. That task, in turn, requires recognizing the essential role of ethics and the primacy of spirit over matter. And the ability to look at the moral dimension of things and to recognize the law of God cannot be attained without recognizing and repenting of one's own guilt.

In conclusion, I wish to point out the following. Toward the end of the 1980s, the West expected that Eastern Europe, released from underneath the yoke of communism, would speak to the world in a new and authentic way. Unfortunately, so far the East has shown the West only the same old views and habits being quite distorted. Yet, by continuing to hold up the image of the past, the East may simultaneously be posing questions which both the East and the West must urgently address.

Notes

[1] Michael Kinnamon, Brian E. Cope, *The ecumenical movement: an anthology of key texts and voices*. (Geneva: WCC Publications, 1997), 67.

Catholic Social Teaching in the Context of a Post-Communist Country

LÁSZLÓ LUKÁCS

From the Gospel to Catholic Social Teaching

The mission of Jesus Christ is summarised by the Gospels in the following sentence: 'He went round the whole of Galilee teaching in the synagogues, proclaiming the news of the kingdom...' Matthew, however, adds: 'and curing all kinds of disease and illness among the people' (Mt 4:23). Jesus invited all people to the eternal life of salvation, yet the Kingdom of Heaven, the 'life beyond' was not his only concern: he sympathised with all people in trouble and went out to help them to have a better life here on earth too. What is more, far beyond the individual needs and miseries, he condemned all types of social injustice and the oppression and exploitation of the poor. He proclaimed his Father to be the God of justice and mercy. The foundation of a sane society is justice: 'Every kind of wickedness is sin' (1 Jn 5:17). 'The Lord is the upright judge' (2 Tim 4:2). Nobody can be exempted from the law of justice in a society.

Following the example of its founder the Church serves the eternal salvation of humankind but at the same time tries to assist human development. The role of the Church is to proclaim the Gospel and to promote human development. It is to serve 'man's temporal welfare and his eternal welfare', as Pope John Paul II put it. Or as Cardinal Basil Hume remarked: 'The Church advocates a just social order in which the human dignity of all is fostered, and protests when it is in any way threatened'.

The twofold task of the Church was solemnly declared by the Second Vatican Council. Christians have to be engaged in human development: 'The joys and the hopes, the griefs and the anxieties of the men of this age, especially those who are poor or in any way afflicted, these are the joys and hopes, the griefs and anxieties of the followers of Christ.'[1] 'This council exhorts Christians, as citizens of two cities, to strive to discharge their earthly duties conscientiously and in response to the Gospel spirit. They are mistaken who, knowing that we have here no abiding city but seek one which is to come, think that they may therefore shirk their earthly responsibilities. For they are forgetting that by the faith itself they are more obliged than ever to measure up to these duties, each according to his proper vocation.'[2] 'The Church believes she can contribute greatly toward making the family of man and its history more human.'[3]

Moral theology examines first of all questions of personal responsibility, the good or bad actions of the individual. Throughout the centuries the Church made some moral statements concerning social and public affairs as well; yet a systematic, all-round social doctrine was developed only in the past century. The popes starting with Leo XIII issued encyclicals about social and economic issues. The contribution of the church to the common good is apparent in the development of the Catholic Social Teaching (CST) in the past 120 years. Papal encyclicals from *Rerum novarum* (1891) by Leo XIII to *Caritas in veritate* (2009) by Benedict XVI prove the special concern of the church calling for social justice and the common good for all, for solidarity and subsidiarity and the dignity of the person, protesting against all types of discrimination and exploitation.

CST is not restricted to the highest Magisterium of the Church, it is elaborated on regional and national levels, too. 'The option for the poor' is put into practice in various ways in different parts of the world. The general principles of CST were applied and concretised in the social-economic context of a particular country or a continent by social pastoral letters published by bishops' conferences (USA: 1986; England and Wales: 1996; Hungary: 1996; Germany 1997). The most powerful voice was that of the Latin-American Bishops' Conference (CELAM) with its famous documents (first of all Medellín in 1968 and then Puebla in 1979).

The Development of CST

In the past 200 years the social-economic situation of the world has dramatically changed. It is more than natural that there is an enormous development in the social teaching of the magisterial documents, too. Three fundamental phases can be distinguished in the development of the social teaching. The first step was taken by Pope Leo XIII, who in his encyclical forcefully criticised the exploitation of the working class and the social injustices caused by the industrial revolution. He declared that workers have the right to defend themselves by forming trade unions and other interest groups. On the other side, however, he defended private property as belonging to the fundamental rights of all human persons.

A turning point in the row of encyclicals was brought by Pope Paul VI's Encyclical *Populorum Progressio*. He went a great step further than his predecessors, adjusting his views to the changing world he lived in. He took into consideration the whole of humanity and each and every human person. The pope claimed for a just world order on a global level and the right of each human being to lead a full human life:

'Today no one can be unaware of the fact that on some continents countless men and women are ravished by hunger and countless children are undernourished. Many children die at an early age; many more of them find their physical and mental growth retarded. Thus whole populations are immersed in pitiable circumstances and lose heart.' The church 'must foster the development of each man and of the whole man'.[4]

Social problems cannot be resolved only by legislation and economic measures: they have a deep moral root as well: 'The Church has never failed to foster the human progress of the nations to which she brings faith in Christ.'[5] The pope pleaded for 'a new humanism' for all peoples and individuals: 'This is what will guarantee man's authentic development—his transition from less than human conditions to truly human ones.'[6] 'We must make haste. Too many people are suffering. While some make progress, others stand still or move backwards; and the gap between them is widening.'[7]

The Pope wanted to put into practice the principles given in the encyclical. For that purpose he created the Pontifical Council for Justice and Peace in the same year to follow the rapidly changing economic and social life.

By that time the fundamental principles of CST had crystallised: the dignity of the human person, solidarity and subsidiarity. These principles were proclaimed as valid for all people and states, for all political and social situations – without being committed to any economic theory or political system. Consequently, none of the ideologies or political-economical systems could appropriate them as their own. It is a moral teaching and by no means a political or economic program. It does not want to give concrete proposals, but interpret social and economic phenomena in the light of Christian faith and morality.

Most recently the Compendium of the Social Doctrine of the Church (2004) offers a complete overview of the doctrinal corpus of Catholic social teaching. It presents 'in a complete and systematic manner, the Church's social teaching, which is the expression of the Church's constant commitment to the grace of salvation and in loving concern for humanity's destiny'. The basic insights can be summed up in four points:

1. The Church opposes totalitarianism because it oppresses people and deprives them of their freedom.

2. While recognising the importance of wealth and the right for private property the Church denounces any abuses of economic power such as those which deprive employees of what is needed for a decent standard of living.

3. The Church also rejects the view that human happiness consists only of material wellbeing, and states that achieving material welfare alone cannot be the goal of any government.

4. If a government pays too much attention to material welfare at the expense of other values, it may advocate policies which reduce people to a passive state of dependency on welfare. Equally, if a government gives too little priority to tackling poverty, ill-health, poor housing and other social ills, the human dignity of those who suffer these afflictions is denied.

In every society respect for human dignity requires that, as far as possible, basic human needs are met. The systematic denial of compassion by individuals or public authorities can never be a morally justified political option.

In the middle of the twentieth century, during the time of the cold war, two dominating economic theories were put into practice by the two superpowers of the world. On one side (in the 'West') liberal capitalism was based on free market economy with its self-regulating function ('the invisible hand'), where the state has only a very limited role; on the other side (in the 'East') the Soviet model with a strictly centralised and planned state economy. The

Church's social doctrine adopted a critical attitude towards both liberal capitalism and Soviet-Marxist collectivism. In its own way each of the two blocs tended to a kind of 'imperialism', or to some form of neo-colonialism: an easy temptation to which they frequently succumbed, as history, including recent history, shows.

The cold war ended with the victory of Western capitalism and the collapse of the Soviet Union. Yet the theoretical (and in many respects practical) debate has continued ever since by protagonists of the two economic theories. In its extreme formulation: either a free-market without government control or a strong government regulating economic life. Naturally most countries seek some type of balance between the two extremes, and due to the present economic crisis a remarkable shift is to be observed between the two poles.

Hungary, as one of the satellite states under Soviet oppression was forced to adopt the planned state economy for 40 years (1948-1989). After the political changes in 1989-1990, freshly gained political independence, the transition from dictatorship to free democracy was followed by the introduction of the market economy almost overnight. At first a false euphoria reigned with most people expecting a quick improvement in their living standards. The myth of freedom and of free market was followed by bitter disillusion. Twenty years have passed since the political and economic changes: it is time to create a balance of the two systems and draw the conclusions. Hungary thus could serve as a type of experiment, a public laboratory where both systems can be examined in the light of CST. How do they fulfil the exigencies of CST? In the following an attempt is made to answer this question enumerating eight key principles of CST and examining their realisation both in the 40 years of communism and in the 20 years of capitalism.

The following list is by its nature simplified and, as a result, distorted in some places. Yet, it can give a glimpse into the actual system of both a totalitarian regime and a capitalist free market economy.

Key Principles of CST examined in the Hungarian 'laboratory'

Human dignity

The principle:

Each person is made in the image of God with inherent dignity. Human life is sacred. Everybody should have equal rights to life, to freedom, to food, shelter, employment, health care and education. Protection and promotion of the dignity of every person. But also: duties and responsibilities to one another, to our families, and to the larger society, the common good of all. Human dignity can be protected and a healthy community can be achieved only if human rights are protected and responsibilities are met.

Its communist implementation:

Brutal oppression of individual citizens by the communist state, basic human rights neglected or denied. Great numbers of people were deprived of their freedom in different ways, and were imprisoned or taken into labour camps. Private property (land, enterprises, factories etc.) was confiscated to make the party-state the sole owner of the whole country.

Its free-market implementation:

Human life is threatened by abortion, assisted suicide, euthanasia, cloning, the death penalty, gender ideology. In a consumer society the very core of the human personality is in danger. Excessive individualism ignores the common good, the good of other persons.

Solidarity and the Common Good

The principle:

Human beings are social by nature: they are not only individuals but persons living in community, linked to one another by a whole network of relationships. Everybody has a responsibility to contribute to the common good, to the good of the whole society. Marriage and family are the central social institutions that must be supported and strengthened, not undermined. People have a right and a duty to participate in society, seeking together the common good and the well-being of all, especially of the poor and vulnerable. The obligation to 'love our neighbour' has an individual dimension, but it also requires a broader social commitment.

Its communist implementation:

Collectivism was forced by the dictatorial government. Education was centralised, children were to be raised by the state to become a 'homo sovieticus'. No free civil associations were allowed to exist, the Communist Party ruled the whole society. Obedience to the Party was required instead of free individual responsibility.

Its free-market implementation:

Excessive individualism is widespread, private interests suppress the responsibility for others and for the common good, family bonds have been weakened (growing divorce rate, being single as the modern way of life, same-sex partnerships). Consumerist thinking gains strength together with an overwhelming profit oriented market.

Subsidiarity

The principle:

Society is based on organisations or communities ranging from small groups to national and international institutions. Individuals and smaller social groups have the right and duty to make their own decisions and accomplish what they can by their own initiative. A higher level of community or authority should only interfere in order to support them in cases of need, and to coordinate their activities with the rest of society with a view of the common good.

Its communist implementation:

The 'patron state' suppressed the notion of subsidiarity by providing all the necessary goods for everybody. Yet a certain freedom was maintained in small groups: families and friends' groups practiced a type of spontaneous subsidiarity, though with scant regard to the interests of society at large.

Its free-market implementation:

Overwhelming globalisation weakens or destroys local or even national initiatives. Multinational mega-companies oppress individual initiatives, ruin small enterprises. Local communities are gradually dissolved, more and more people are moving to big cities, losing their individual and group identity.

Constructive role of the government and economic justice

The principle:

The purpose of the government is to promote the common good, to ensure human rights, social justice and equality. 'There are needs and common goods that cannot be satisfied by the market system. It is the task of the state and of all society to defend them. An idolatry of the market alone cannot do all that should be done' (John Paul II). CST rejects the idea that a free market automatically safeguards justice. Competition and free markets are useful elements of economic systems. However, markets must be kept within limits, because there are many needs and goods that cannot be satisfied by the market system.

Its communist implementation:

The party-state was the only proprietor and effective power in the country. In its planned economy the government controlled and regulated the whole of economic (and political) life: the production, distribution and price of goods. The totalitarian system with its government-controlled economy was doomed to failure and necessarily led to the collapse of the system in the Soviet Union and in the Soviet Bloc countries.

Its free-market implementation:

The transition to the free-market system went on without any proper regulation or former experience. The process of privatisation was directed by the former party leaders and foreign investors. The party leaders changed their political influence into economic advantages: big properties (factories, real estates, enterprises) were bought up by them at very low prices, often with the help of foreign investors. Due to the lack of proper legislation corruption and fraud were present in many commercial transactions. As a consequence, a small group of new capitalists became billionaires within a few years, while the majority of the population were impoverished: the gap between the rich and the poor increased.

The Dignity of Work and the Rights of Workers

The principle:

Economy must serve people, not the other way around. Work is more than a way to make a living; it is a form of continuing participation in God's creation. If the dignity of work is to be protected, then the basic rights of workers must be respected – the right to productive work, to decent and fair wages, to the organization and joining of unions, to private property, and to economic initiative.

Its communist implementation:

According to the official propaganda the working class was the owner of all goods and the leading force of the country. In actual fact the party and its leaders were the only authority to make decisions. The 'working class' had no real rights or freedom; trade unions functioned as allies to the party instead of defending the rights of the workers. 'Unemployment within the walls': most people had a job, but without any real productive work. Wages and salaries were low but provided a small income for most people.

Its free-market implementation:

Rapidly growing unemployment: due to the reorganisation and modernisation of production great masses of unskilled workers have lost their jobs. Immense riches have been achieved via the black market and corruption. The wealth of the country is sold out to foreign investors and former party leaders. The average income of the average citizen is about one seventh of the European standard. More and more professionals migrate to find a job in Western Europe or the USA.

Option for the poor and vulnerable

The principle:

In a society with deep divisions between rich and poor the Gospel instructs us to put the needs of the poor and vulnerable first. CST proclaims that the moral test of a society is how it treats its most vulnerable members. This calls us to look at public policy decisions in terms of how they affect the poor. Presently a minority of 20% of the people control more than 80% of the world's resources, leaving few resources to be shared by the majority of the people, a major stimulus for liberation theology.

Its communist implementation:

In the first years of communist rule all properties were confiscated, from the big land properties to the small farmers. Great masses lost all their incomes. The new wealthy group of the society is the party-elite. According to the official propaganda 'flourishing socialism' defeats 'decaying capitalism', there is no need, no misery, no poverty in the country.

Its free-market implementation:

There is a growing gap between the rich and the poor on a global level. A relatively large part of the society is unemployed (10–14% unemployment rate), the number of homeless people is growing, along with growing delinquency, violence, drug addiction and alcoholism. According to recent statistics, around 25–30% of the Hungarian population is below the poverty line (2,8 million of a population of 10 million); 30% of the children live in poverty.

Care for the created world

The principle:

Entrusted with the stewardship of creation we are called to protect the planet and its inhabitants. This environmental challenge has fundamental moral and ethical dimensions. We have a responsibility to care for nature and the world's goods as stewards and trustees, not as mere consumers and users. Natural resources are limited and only partially renewable. Using them as if they were inexhaustible seriously endangers the planet Earth and with it human life today, but especially in the future.

Its communist implementation:

Ecological awareness was practically unknown, there was hardly any protection of the environment in industrial production, housing or agriculture, partly due to ignorance, partly because of the expenses of protecting the environment. As a consequence, the legacy of pollution is a large scale problem in many parts of the country.

Its free-market implementation:

Not long after the political changes the whole structure of production was changed: factories of heavy industry, mines etc. were closed. Foreign investors and the new post-communist elite launched, however, huge projects without taking into consideration the protection of the environment. A new boom of building plazas and hypermarkets and also luxurious housing estates destroyed precious natural environments. Profit hunting frequently defeats ecological priorities.

Promotion of peace

The principle:

Since the encyclical *Pacem in terris* by Pope John XXIII in 1963 the promotion of peace belonged to one of the main concerns in CST. The Second Vatican Council solemnly declared: 'Peace is not merely the absence of war. Nor can it be reduced solely to the maintenance of a balance of power between enemies. Nor is it brought about by dictatorship. Instead, it is rightly and appropriately called 'an enterprise of justice' (Is 32:7).'[8] Pope Paul VI declared January 1st the 'World Day of Peace' in 1968 and since then a papal message calling for peace has been issued every year inviting all people of good will to join their efforts for peace in the world.

Its communist implementation:

In the time of cold war and the arms race official propaganda insisted that communist countries 'safeguarded peace'. The slogan 'peace' was used for any possible purposes. For example the clergy loyal to the communist government was forced to organise a pro-government 'Peace Movement of the Catholic Clergy' (a movement that had absolutely nothing to do with the international Pax Christi movement).

Its free-market implementation:

Armed conflicts including local or regional wars, civil wars, revolutions and revolts, rebellions, secessions, coups, acts of genocide, ethnic and political violence have been continuing up till now. A new phenomenon is worldwide terrorism of which 9/11 has become a symbol. Now there is an almost continuous state of emergency in Western countries, not to speak about the frightening death toll in the Middle East.

Is there a way-out? The astonishing answer of Pope Benedict XVI

Hungary and the post-communist countries changed their centrally planned economic system, introduced free-market economies and started the privatisation of state-capital at a time when the market economy had its boom. (The words of Margaret Thatcher are well-known: 'TINA = There is no alternative'.) Yet more than once, especially in the recent past the most developed countries had to realise that the state cannot be completely eliminated without serious dangers in the functioning of the society and even of the economy. This led to the 'Soziale Marktwirkschaft' (social free-market economy) in Germany and then in other countries that try to find a balance between free-market and state following the principle: 'as much liberty as possible, as much state as necessary'. The market regulates itself through supply and demand and free competition. The state however, intervenes, in order to eliminate negative economic consequences, to create social equality and to support those who are socially weaker.

Pope Benedict XVI in his Encyclical *Caritas in veritate* (2009) proposed an amazing new way in the dilemma of the free-market versus the state. He invited a third actor to play an important role in economy: 'civil economy' and the 'economy of communion'. 'The continuing hegemony of the binary model of market-plus-State' has to be complemented with 'civil economy'. The commutative justice and the commercial logic of the market 'needs to make room for the principle of gratuitousness as an expression of fraternity'.[9] The Pope's conclusion: 'The market of gratuitousness does not exist, and attitudes of gratuitousness cannot be established by law. Yet both the market and politics need individuals who are open to reciprocal gift'.[10]

This vision of the pope opened new horizons for CST. Up until recent times papal encyclicals pleaded first of all for social justice. Pope Benedict XVI, however, at the very beginning of his encyclical declares: 'Charity is at the heart of the Church's social doctrine. It is the principle not only of micro-relationships (with friends, with family members or within small groups) but also of macro-relationships (social, economic and political ones)'.[11]

This amazing new aspect of CST, however astonishing it may sound, is not without antecedents in papal documents. Pope John Paul II urged people to create the 'civilisation of love', as the only alternative for the 'civilisation of death'. The phrase 'civilisation of love' had already been used by Pope Paul VI; Pius XI had spoken about 'social charity', Leo XIII about fraternity in society. The *Compendium of the Social Doctrine of the Church* repeatedly stresses the role of charity as the highest form of human action in political, economic and cultural life. Justice in itself is insufficient: 'humankind desperately needs the rule of the civilisation of love'.

The idea of an 'economy of love' has its traces in the development of Joseph Ratzinger's theology. Suffice to refer to his first encyclical *Deus caritas est* which can be taken as the summary of his immense theological oeuvre. Having examined the divine origin of love the Pope draws the conclusion: 'The ecclesial community becomes a witness before the world to the love of the Father, who wishes to make humanity a single family in his Son. The entire activity of the Church is an expression of a love that seeks the integral good of man'.[12] Comparing the role of the state and of the church he declares: 'The just ordering of society and the State is a central responsibility of politics.' 'Love – caritas – will always prove necessary, even in the most just society. There is no ordering of the State so just that it can eliminate the need for a service of love'.[13] His conclusion: 'The Church can never be exempted from practising charity as an organized activity of believers, and on the other hand, there will never be a situation where the charity of each individual Christian is unnecessary, because in addition to justice man needs, and will always need, love'.[14]

The Pope opens the immense transcendental horizon of humankind in the loving communion of the Holy Trinity, declaring that all real human community has its source and goal in the community of divine love. – Reading his encyclical one cannot avoid the question: are his views only a type of wishful thinking, majestic and pious homily of a churchman without any sense of reality? Is justice really insufficient in itself without love? What is more: can love really excel justice? Is love the only possible fulfilment of justice? The Pope makes a straightforward statement in *Caritas in veritate*: 'Truth needs to be sought, found and expressed within the 'economy' of charity, but charity in turn needs to be understood, confirmed and practised in the light of truth'.[15]

Doubts and objections might appear to be well founded, yet two considerations can help us to assert a positive answer to the above questions. The first step is the predominance of solidarity in the life of each society and in the global village. Though solidarity is hardly known and acceptable in extreme forms of free-market systems where the highest possible profit margins are the only goal. The sphere of social security is excluded from economy. The poor and marginalised – for whatever reasons they are in this miserable situation – are left alone or at best can be aided by a redistribution system operated by the state or by charity organisations. According to the encyclical the common good, integral and authentic human development, has to be respected and desired by all actors of a society: 'progress of a merely economic and technological kind is insufficient'.[16] The 'structures of sin' have to be changed into the 'structures of solidarity'. All and each of us are responsible for the common good and for one another. As UN General Secretary, Ban Ki-Moon, stated at a conference in Morocco in October 2010: 'Whatever else we learn from the crisis, this much is clear: global economic management can no longer afford to neglect the most vulnerable or the disadvantaged.'

Solidarity is a universal human requirement of all societies, but it is strongly recommended by CST, too. As the *Catechism of the Catholic Church* states: 'Socio-economic problems can be resolved only with the help of all the forms of solidarity: solidarity of the poor among themselves, between rich and poor, of workers among themselves, between employers and employees in business, solidarity among nations and peoples. International solidarity is a requirement of the moral order; world peace depends in part upon this'.[17]

Without the sense and practice of solidarity, both social and economic life can be destroyed in the long run: therefore solidarity belongs to a rightly interpreted self-interest. A second aspect, however, is added by CST, the relatively new aspect so strongly emphasized by both Pope Benedict XVI and Pope John Paul II: that of charity. It is not just an individual and personal attitude limited to one's circle of friends and relatives, but a universal guiding principle that ought to order society at large; it is also far more than a philanthropic attitude. The popes plead for a 'person-based and community-oriented cultural process of world-wide integration', they want 'to steer the globalisation of humanity in relational terms, in terms of communion and the sharing of goods'.[18]

Centrally planned economies can only be found in a few countries of the world now; the weakness and fragility of the globalised world economy has become apparent, among others, in the recent economic crisis. The experience of Hungary is testimony to the evil consequences of both systems that are in contrast with Catholic Social Teaching. Pope Benedict XVI has opened a new horizon by stressing the importance of gratuitousness and love in all dimensions of social and economic life. Will and can it be accepted by the actors of the contemporary political and economic life? Are they 'open to reciprocal gift', to solidarity and charity?

Notes

1   Vatican II, *Gaudium et spes*, 1.

2   *Ibid.*, 43.

3   *Ibid.*, 40.

4   Vatican II, *Populorum progressio*, 45.

5   *Ibid.*, 12.

6   *Ibid.*, 20.

7   *Ibid.*, 29.

8   Vatican II, *Gaudium et spes*, 78.

9   Pope Benedict XVI, *Caritas in veritate*, 35–46.

10   *Ibid.*, 39.

11   *Ibid.*, 32.

12   Pope Benedict XVI, *Deus caritas est*, 19.

13 *Ibid.*, 28.
14 *Ibid.*,29.
15 Pope Benedict XVI, *Caritas in veritate*, 2.
16 *Ibid.*, 23.
17 *Catechism of the Catholic Church*, 1940.
18 Pope Benedict XVI, *Caritas in veritate*, 42.

Blessed Are The Rich?
Uses and Misuses of Catholic Social Teaching in a Time of Transition

JONATHAN LUXMOORE

When the Christians of Eastern and Central Europe commemorate the collapse of communism each autumn, they have much to be proud of. In countries previously under one-party rule, democracy is now functioning, along with stable institutions, accountable governments, reliable judicial systems and productive economies. With the Iron Curtain now a distant memory, furthermore, the region's churches can celebrate, too.

Yet there has been another side to the story, which is less often told—of hardships and frustrations, injustices and inequalities which are far from being addressed. In what follows, I will look at the case of Poland, a country often hailed as a showcase of Catholic piety combined with free market prosperity, and ask critical questions about how the Church's social teaching—with its emphasis on human dignity, the common good, subsidiarity and solidarity—has been interpreted and applied in the two decades since communist rule.

In an August 2009 report, Poland's Roman Catholic Church deplored the 'savage capitalism' dominating national life, and demanded 'real, not propagandist actions' to stem the country's social and demographic decline.[1] But some Poles think the Church has been confused about its own values and failed to reaffirm a preferential option for the poor. Some believe it must share the blame for an often misplaced liberalism which has long denied help and support to the disadvantaged and vulnerable.

When Eastern and Central Europe were liberated from communist rule in 1989, there were hopes of a participatory democracy and social market economy, in which human rights were protected and a dignified existence guaranteed for all. There had been little serious thinking, however, as to how these ideals would be applied in practice. Today, with ten post-communist countries now members of the European Union and a dozen belonging to NATO, no one would deny the progress achieved at macro-institutional level. All have Gross Domestic Product per capita of half to two-thirds of the EU average, while rates of inflation and unemployment, with few exceptions, are close to the EU norm. The post-communist transition, not surprisingly, is usually presented as a triumph for prosperity and freedom.

Yet while the economic and political achievements have brought benefits and advantages for many, they have brought despair and hopelessness for others. Perhaps the very emphasis on negotiation and compromise back in 1989 was itself to blame, in enabling elite groups to seize the upper hand and private interests to gain primacy over collective values. When the thirtieth anniversary of Solidarity was marked in August 2010, members of a Church-government joint commission deplored their country's failure to honour the movement's legacy by offering help to the poor. Besides freedom of speech and association, they recalled, the movement's 21 demands had included minimum living standards. The economic and social aspects of its humanitarian programme, however, appeared to have been forgotten. 'Those who demanded free trade unions and struggled for our freedom also wanted a dignified life', noted the commission. 'Assurances that we are remembering the call of August 1980 are not credible if we forget how strong were the demands for an improvement in Polish family life, especially when these questions are still not resolved.'[2]

What happened to the 'ethics of solidarity' which were so much talked about at the time, and to the 'moral revolution' said to have been initiated by the fall of communism? What happened to the work for social justice and solidarity with the poor which the Polish Pope John Paul II prescribed for the Church as 'her mission, her service, a proof of her fidelity to Christ'?[3] How well have the state and its agencies understood their tasks? How adequately has Poland's predominant Church understood its role? These questions deserve to be asked in a critical spirit today.

In a 2009 report, the country's Main Statistics Office welcomed the modest but sound achievements occurring in a range of areas, from education and healthcare, to environmental protection and waste reduction. Average household incomes, it noted, had grown in the previous two years by 15 percent in Poland, which had been the only EU country maintaining slight but positive GDP growth during the economic recession.

Yet there was also 'another Poland', the Statistics Office cautioned, away from the smart office blocks and shopping malls of Warsaw, Gdańsk and Kraków. This was the Poland which was home to four of Europe's most depressed regions, a Poland in which fewer than three percent of rural inhabitants had higher education and one in five had no telephones or running water, where EU targets for reducing poverty and exclusion had been persistently ignored.[4]

Although boasting Europe's seventh largest car market, Poland still has only 400 miles of motorway and poor rail and bus connections. The lack of social and economic mobility has impeded access to the cities and reduced the life chances of those away from the labour market. Although funds are available from the EU, public infrastructural development has been negligible. Instead, Poland has spent more than GBP 20 billion on four state-of-the-art football stadiums to host the 2012 UEFA football championship.

Some social surveys have painted a damning picture of the new-look Poland. In January 2010, Eurostat found a third of Poles living in poverty, a proportion put by some sources at 16 million, or 43 percent of the population. One in five lacked the means to heat their homes in the Eurostat survey, and two-thirds were unable to take a week's annual holiday.[5]

Levels of material deprivation are worse in Bulgaria, Hungary, Latvia and Romania; but Poland has the highest levels of child poverty in the developed world after Turkey and Mexico, according to the Organisation for Economic Co-operation and Development. It also has one of the lowest birthrates, and some of the highest incidences of temporary employment on low pay without benefits, and of 'working poor' — those employed but paid so little that they cannot feed and clothe their children.[6]

Although joblessness has risen to 12 percent, after dipping during the mass migration which followed Poland's May 2004 accession to the EU, unemployment benefit is paid for six months only, and the majority of unemployed are ineligible for retraining schemes. Whereas some groups, such as miners, nurses and pensioners, have done relatively well, those without political support and organisation have been pushed aside, leaving many far worse off in relative terms than they were under communist rule.

Not surprisingly, mass migration has become a key feature of the past decade, just as it was historically in periods of hostile domination and repression. Up to two million Poles, some six percent of the population, went abroad following EU accession, fleeing unemployment and exclusion, according to EU data, of whom up to half travelled to Britain and Ireland. Departures rose consistently until 2008, according to the Statistics Office, when they dipped during the economic crisis. Large numbers of Poles are still migrating, however, leaving broken families and a shortage of skills in their wake.[7] Until conditions improve,

Polish government schemes to lure migrants home will remain ineffective. The poor and disadvantaged will continue, out of necessity, to vote with their feet.

In 1993, a pro-life law tightly restricted abortion with the sanction of fines and prison sentences, but also committed the state and local governments to provide 'all necessary material, legal and medical help' for pregnant women and single mothers. The measure was lauded as an expression of Poland's Catholic values, and as the first attempt by a developed country to restrict rather than relax access to abortion. Yet the second part of the law was quietly ignored. Today, with means-tested child benefit less than a quarter of the rate in Britain, Catholic Poland spends less than any other EU country on family support programmes—below one percent of GDP, compared to an EU average of 2.1 percent. Family supplements have been frozen for the past six years at 504 zloties (GBP 120) monthly, leaving half as many families receiving it now as in 2004. While up to half a million children fall below the qualifying level each year, 45 percent of large families, representing a third of all children, currently live below the poverty line, a figure much higher than in 1989, with many of the neediest failing to understand or trust the system. Unless priorities change, the Statistics Office report warned, Poland's population will plummet by a fifth over the next 25 years.[8]

Around 100,000 children with still-living parents are currently in care or under adoption, a figure much higher than two decades ago, when the birthrate was a lot higher. Antoni Szymański, a sociologist from the Church-government commission, thinks this telling statistic reflects the failure of the state to provide adequate family support. Whereas any changes in the welfare system would be carefully scrutinised in neighbouring Germany, and strongly resisted if deemed unjust, the record of state neglect and failure in Poland has been met with virtual silence, leaving a generation of children deprived of decent standards of living, health, education and family life.

'Families should fulfil their functions with all their might, struggling to improve their situation and their rights. But the state should also support the family where essential', Szymański argues. 'Even allowing for the economic difficulties facing our country, investing in our children is essential, and not solely in a financial sense. To make further savings on them will damage the fundamental interests of children and families—and, in effect, of our country'.[9]

Some experts say post-communist governments concentrated solely on the economic and political aspects of transition, and failed to grasp the importance of social trends for national stability and sustainability. When communist rule collapsed, a premium was placed on 'shock-therapy reforms' and rapid growth, and it was widely assumed Poland needed a phase of unhampered capitalism to unleash the population's acquisitive instincts. Some Poles highlight a crass materialism which swept Poland in the 1990s, as mentalities shaped by Marxism spawned a mass consumer culture, which valued individuals not for who they were but for what they had.

Others cite the importing of individualistic ideas and practices to a country with no stable infrastructure or civil society, whose institutions were weak, rulers inexperienced and citizens vulnerable and disorientated, and which sought to copy its wealthy, well-developed Western neighbours but lacked appropriate checks and balances. Talk of a 'third way' was derided by intellectuals, academic specialists and media commentators, who took the side of businesses and corporations, portraying them as heroes of freedom and enterprise against the dead weight of organised labour and the welfare state. With talk of state involvement, social justice and concern for the poor distrusted as totalitarian hangovers, the argument was framed as if there were only two choices: a vigorous, often brutal capitalism or a turning back towards communism.

The result has been a crude distortion of democratic and free market values, in which failures and setbacks have been obscured by a steady propaganda of success. Despite its Catholic traditions, Poland was rated one of the European Union's most corrupt member-countries by Transparency International following its 2004 accession, while negative phenomena from police brutality to road accidents are among the most rampant.[10] In 2006, the OECD launched an investigation into Poland's booming Western hypermarkets, after complaints that they flouted international norms for rest and maternity leave, as well as adequate pay, insurance and health assistance, and trade union rights. In a May 2006 survey by Ernst and Young, twice as many company employees as in the rest of Europe admitted to cheating, claiming others did the same, while a third of Polish firms said it was 'normal' to entertain clients with strippers and call-girls. The survey's designers said the practice had resulted from a 'culture of advancing one's interests', which would fuel the popular association of capitalism with 'moral dissoluteness'.[11]

Joanna Krupska, chairman of Poland's Union of Large Families, which has campaigned unsuccessfully for fairer policies, thinks public opinion has been kept in the dark, and encouraged to believe the poor and marginalised are to blame for their own hardships and should not be given help, according to the maxim, *biednyś boś głupi, głupiś boś biedny*. Each New Year's Day, thousands of young volunteers help in a nationwide fund-raising 'Orchestra of Holiday Help', conceived and run by lay activists to help sick children. 'But when it comes to poverty, Poles are ashamed, and most people are simply unaware of the plight of fellow-citizens', Krupska explains. 'The elites who dominate politics and the media deliberately downplay the scale of the problems and discourage any sense of empathy. Most Poles refuse to believe the facts and figures when confronted with them.'[12]

Ewa Leś, a specialist at Warsaw University's Social Policy Institute, agrees. She points to a huge asymmetry between the much-vaunted macro-economic statistics and the social situation on the ground. When organisations like the Main Statistics Office publish their data, these are routinely ignored or manipulated to disavow the real scale of the problems. 'Every official can naturally blame the current downturn and say Poland is poor compared to its Western neighbours. But none of this is true—what we are seeing is a one-sided sense of priorities, caused by a primitive application of liberal paradigms', Professor Leś argues. 'It's dangerous when a society doesn't know the scale of its own problems, and is persistently told that a neo-liberal ideology of enterprise and self-determination offers an ideal answer to every question'.[13]

Both Krupska and Leś have hoped for guidance from Poland's Catholic Church, as the only national institution which can effectively highlight the problems and apply pressure for a fairer approach. To date, their hopes have been disappointed. In 1999, on the eve of the Millennium, a national Church Synod criticised the absence of a pro-family tax policy, as well as the lack of sufficient unemployment benefit and the high salaries paid to government officials, and called for social structures which would 'more effectively protect the weak and guarantee all people equal access to the common good'. In a pastoral letter two years later, the Polish Bishops Conference criticised the 'radical ideology of capitalism' which now held sway in their country. 'After 12 years of systemic changes in Poland', the letter noted, 'we must contend that many people responsible for the shape of public life uncritically believed that the fall of Marxism would automatically lead to a just society, and in free-market mechanisms which would guarantee the wellbeing of all in every sphere of life. In the place of collectivist ideology appeared a distorted version of liberalism, which conceived the whole of reality solely in economic categories. In this way, the development desperately needed in our country was identified only with economic growth'.[14]

If such critical Catholic perspectives were evident at the time, however, they have long since faded from the public discourse. The Polish Church maintains an extensive nationwide charitable network, and an infrastructure of parish-based self-help initiatives. Yet it can be argued that these treat the symptoms, not the causes, of current injustices, and come nowhere near to 'addressing the social and political dimensions of the problem of poverty', as stipulated in Catholic social teaching.[15]

In the 1990s, Pope John Paul II repeatedly highlighted the harsh conditions facing his country. Preaching at Legnica in 1997, he deplored the plight of poor families, single mothers, abandoned old people and under-fed children, as well as the sick in under-resourced hospitals, the growing numbers of homeless, and the 'phenomenon of exploitation' manifested 'in conditions of employment in which the worker not only has no guaranteed rights but is subjected to such an atmosphere of uncertainty and fear for the loss of his job that he is in practice deprived of any freedom of decision'.[16] In 2002, during his last homecoming, he urged that the 'hearts of the prosperous' be opened to 'the needs of the poor and suffering'.[17]

Some Catholic intellectuals admitted finding the Polish Pope's appeals to social conscience hard to understand, assuming human rights problems had been resolved with the advent of 'freedom'. These have now been written out of the script in favour of more traditional interpretations of his teaching, which focus on moral and spiritual priorities rather than social and economic needs. If the Pope saw a role for the state in protecting the weakest and poorest, this aspect of his mission has been comprehensively ignored. There is, indeed, much in the Polish Church's current stance which profoundly contradicts the vision of an ethical society contained in his teaching.

Since early 2009, Bishops Conference representatives have called for a pro-family policy at occasional closed-door meetings of a joint Church-State commission, and talked of setting up a family affairs commission. Remarkably little has been said publicly, however, about the causes and consequences of poverty and exclusion. Local Catholic parishes sometimes hand out food and clothes, while some Church leaders, such as Archbishop Damian Zimon of Katowice, in Poland's depressed mining region, have spoken up for worker rights, and the Church's Catholic information agency, KAI, has given coverage to family hardships. Yet when it comes to pastoral priorities, the Church has shown little awareness and concern about the hardships facing so much of its flock.

'The state can do much less directly for the unemployed themselves—the barriers they struggle with are hidden within themselves, and related to their lack of education and appropriate virtues', explains one influential Jesuit, Fr Krzysztof Mądel. 'Our crisis also has some good sides. Work efficiency and company competitiveness are growing all the time in our country. I know this isn't good news for the unemployed, since 'increased productivity' means *de facto* more redundancies. But I wouldn't neglect this fact, since it clearly shows a change is happening for the better and everyone is feeling it'.[18]

In August 2009, when, for the first time since the fall of communism, the Bishops' Conference published a report on family hardships, it declared moral problems to be the most important, and devoted more than a hundred pages and 265 footnotes to counselling families against the evils of abortion, in-vitro fertilisation and other immoral practices. Only three paragraphs, by contrast, were concerned with their material and economic difficulties, even though the report itself acknowledged that these were in violation of Catholic social principles.[19]

In December 2009, the bishops urged couples in a pastoral letter for Holy Family Sunday to be 'witnesses of love in body and spirit' and to avoid pornography, pre-marital sex and 'improper talks and films'. Nothing was said, however, about their social and economic hardships. Nor was any mention made of them that January, when the Polish bishops' Pastoral Commission outlined its tasks for the next four years, or when Church pastors and experts on family life met that February.[20]

Defenders of the bishops insist the Church has no expertise in economic and social affairs, and no business speaking out on 'political issues' which are the responsibility of government, especially when long-term outcomes are necessarily uncertain. Yet some Poles believe the Church has sought to repudiate communism as absolutely as possible by returning to the stratified social order of rich and poor which it knew from the pre-War years, an order which combined a *laissez-faire* economy with opportunities for private charity. Others see the influence of a neo-conservative US Catholic lobby, with little real understanding of local conditions, which has used Poland as a distant battleground for its own domestic purposes by pressing the Church to reject the social market models advocated by Catholics in neighbouring Germany, and to show the possibility of combining Catholic popular devotions and moral standards with maximum individual enterprise and self-reliance.

Not everyone in the Church has been taken in by this. Fr Zbigniew Sobolewski, who heads the Church's Caritas charity, which feeds many of the 650,000 Polish children suffering from malnutrition, has condemned the 'shameful silence' towards current social problems, and warned that the growing 'dichotomous division between the very rich and those struggling to survive' could lead to a Latin American-style social rift in Poland.[21]

For now, however, the Church's leaders have taken a different view. 'The equal sharing of public riches, collected earlier by methods of force (in the form of public levies) is not only unjust, but also unfavourable to the common good', noted a report from Poland's Poznań Archdiocese, which declared itself firmly against any 'egalitarianism' which forced people 'to help others against their will'. 'A badly conceived state protectiveness, in which public structures interfere too deeply in the life of citizens, and replace them in realising many important life tasks, can weaken the Gospel commandment to multiply one's talents and take responsibility for one's own life. It also arouses a complaining attitude towards society'.[22]

There may be another reason for the failure to speak out. The Church has been a conspicuous beneficiary of post-1989 changes, and could well provoke accusations of hypocrisy if it defended the rights of the poor. Although differences have opened up between richer and poorer parishes since communism, Polish priests are perceived to be well-off, often enjoying luxurious conditions. In early 2008, the Bishops Conference cautioned clergy to see the priesthood as a 'service', rather than a 'career' offering good pay and prospects. It should not be treated, the bishops reminded them, 'as a type of job evaluated by worldly norms'.[23]

Meanwhile, in a November 2010 open letter, the Bishops Conference president urged Catholic priests to stop demanding high payments for dispensing sacraments, and to remember that 'offerings collected on these occasions must remain 'offerings', and not 'prices' for services'. The Church had always recognised the need for 'money and material offerings', Archbishop Józef Michalik told clergy, and could be thankful that it still had 'many poor priests' in Poland, 'ascetics who radiate freedom from fear about the material future'. But it should also reject the desire of some priests to obtain a 'regal living standard from material wealth and power'. Such an outlook violated Gospel principles and the specific teachings of Vatican II, which caution that 'the poor and the weaker ones have been committed to their care in a special way'. It also infringed the Canon Law injunction for priests to 'follow a simple way of life and avoid anything which smacks of worldliness'. Catholic pastors had a duty to address 'structures of injustice in a world of rich and poor', Archbishop Michalik continued. They would jeopardise their own salvation if they remained indifferent to 'poverty, hunger and loneliness'.

'Pastoral work among young people and special groups will not develop if a priest doesn't support it materially, making his own home, time and main personal wealth available', said the Bishops Conference president.

> A priest should also keep clean and clear accounts in financial matters with the people, since virtually everything is known about in our conditions. People have a duty of care for the maintenance of their priests; and clergy, for their part, have an obligation to share their acquired wealth with the poorest.[24]

For a life of simplicity and modesty, Archbishop Michalik commended the example of St Jean-Marie Vianney (1786–1859), France's celebrated Curé d'Ars. This could be considered wishful thinking. Although priestly and monastic vocations have fallen sharply since 2005 in Poland, accompanied by signs of declining Mass attendance, the Church is still investing massively in ornate new places of worship, to add to the 2000 Catholic churches dedicated in an unprecedented building boom in the 1980s and 1990s.

In June 2004, Poland's largest church, modelled on St Peter's in Rome, was dedicated at the central village of Licheń, in one of Poland's poorest regions, with room for 30,000 people in its five naves and forecourts. The Blessed Virgin basilica, the largest built in Europe for a century, boasts the world's highest columns and biggest bell, as well as a 450-foot tower and giant copula with 20,000 gold-plated tiles. The elderly Marian order priest who built it, Fr Eugeniusz Makulski, commissioned a statue of himself welcoming Pope John Paul II to the site during his 1999 Polish pilgrimage.

Work is also underway on an 81,000-square foot Basilica of Divine Providence in Warsaw, being built at a cost of

GBP 40 million in thanksgiving for the collapse of communism. In November 2000, a committee of experts warned its initiator, Cardinal Józef Glemp, that his preferred design, featuring a 160-foot glass canopy symbolising the Holy Spirit, would pose an 'excessive burden on the faithful'.[25] The cardinal modified the plans, but was still unable to raise the donations required. So the basilica was reclassified in early 2008 after a year's suspension as a cultural project, thus enabling parliamentarians to vote money for it from Poland's state budget—a move which was still being investigated by Poland's Constitutional Court three years later.

Controversy over extravagance by the Polish Church, which is estimated to have unveiled a hundred statues annually to the late John Paul II since his death in April 2005, intensified in 2009–2010, after media revelations that its religious orders had made hundreds of millions of zloties, at the cost of local councils and the State Treasury, speculating on land awarded in compensation for communist-era seizures. The shadowy Property Commission which handed out the land, composed of Bishops Conference and Interior Ministry representatives whose decisions could not be challenged or legally appealed, was closed down amid public hostility in early 2011. But huge sums of money are still being acquired by Catholic parishes and institutions. In January 2011, the District Court in Poznań awarded the single parish of St John of Jerusalem 75 million zloties (GBP 18 million) from the State Treasury in compensation for 15 hectares of land taken from it in the 1950s for use as a public water sports park.[26]

In 2002, the Church's southern Tarnów diocese distanced itself from plans by US-based Poles for a GBP 20 million statue of Christ the Saviour, which would have been taller that New York's Statue of Liberty, claiming the project 'could easily become an anti-evangelical act' at a time of 'serious social and economic crisis'. In November 2010, however, the world's largest statue of Christ the King, towering at least 40 feet above that of Rio de Janeiro in Brazil, was unveiled in a small Catholic parish at Świebodzin in western Poland. A spokesman for Poland's Zielona Góra-Gorżów diocese, Fr Andrzej Sapieha, said the statue's costs had not been disclosed by the parish, whose new twin-towered church and presbytery were consecrated only two years before.[27]

In his open letter to priests, Archbishop Michalik warned that 'only poverty, humility, purity and disinterested love' would truly satisfy the calling of Christ. 'In the process of evangelisation, what's important isn't only my personal detachment from riches, and my testimony of self-distancing from material goods and my poverty, but also the atmosphere of universal distancing and restraint, and simply a correct hierarchy of values', the Polish Bishops Conference president added. 'Creating such a collective way of thinking is an unavoidable precondition for effective evangelisation. But we must always start with ourselves, and then seek out allies in this good cause'.[28]

For now, the Polish Church's past claims to have taken a 'preferential option for the poor' may have acquired something of a hollow ring. But much can still be done to bring an end to the complacency, create a robust analysis of current injustices, and exert the kind of 'strong moral pressure' prescribed by Catholic social teaching to ensure 'structures of sin', where they exist, are 'purified and transformed into structures of solidarity'.[29]

For this to happen, the Polish Church will need to take Catholic social principles more seriously, and look again at how it formulates its values and defines its moral priorities. It will need to remember the injunction of St Matthew's Gospel that it will be judged by its concern for the poor and downtrodden (Mt 25:31–46); and it will need to ask searching questions about how exhaustively and insistently it has championed the criteria of the common good set out in the Church's Pastoral Constitution *Gaudium et Spes* —'the provision of essential services to all, some of which are at the same time human rights: food, housing, work, education and access to culture, transportation, basic healthcare, the freedom of communication and expression, and the protection of religious freedom'.[30]

Ewa Leś, the social policy specialist, thinks the Church should be doing far more to overcome the silence surrounding Poland's social problems if serious conflicts are to be avoided. Social surveys, including an annual 'Social Diagnosis' prepared by Warsaw University's Social Monitoring Council, have shown levels of personal trust are now lower in Poland than anywhere else in the world, in another striking reversal of the Solidarity legacy and the values promoted by John Paul II. They have also highlighted a depleted sense of the common good, and a sharp decline in the social capital accrued in the struggle against communist rule—all areas in which Catholic social teaching could have made a decisive contribution. 'Of course, the Church's historic role is a good one, and it does a lot to help at local level', Professor Leś says. 'But there's no question that its moral priorities since 1989 have been selective. It should have used its possibilities to highlight and counter the deep problems affecting our society. Its passivity and indifference in these areas have been a great loss'.[31]

Notes

1   Konferencja Episkopatu Polski, *Służyć prawdzie o małżeństwie i rodzinie* (Wydawnictwo Diecezji Tarnowskiej: 2009), no. 149.

2   'O pełną realizację przesłania Sierpnia 1980: Apel członków Zespołu ds. Rodziny Komisji Wspólnej Rządu i Episkopatu Polski'; Katolicka Agencja Informacyjna (KAI) report, 27 August 2010. Jonathan Luxmoore, 'Poverty, exclusion remain on Poland's Solidarity anniversary', Ecumenical News International, 10 September 2010.

3   John Paul II, Encyclical Letter *Laborem Exercens* (14 September 1981), no. 8. Pontifical Council of Justice and Peace, *Compendium of the Social Doctrine of the Church* (Libreria Editrice Vaticana: 2004), nos. 300–322.

4   Główny Urząd Statystyczny, *Zasięg ubóstwa w Polsce w roku 2009*

(Warsaw: 2009). See also *Regiony Polski 2009; Dochody i warunki życia ludności Polski (raport z badania EU–SILC 2008)*, December 2009; Rządowa Rada Ludnościowa, *Sytuacja Demograficzna Polski. Raport 2008–2009* (Warsaw: 2009); and *Informacja o sytuacji społeczno-gospodarczej kraju* (Warsaw: 2011).

5   Eurostat news release (data from EU–SILC survey), 18 January 2010. 'Thirty-two percent live in poverty in Poland', *Spiegel Online*, 20 January 2010. Poverty Dynamics in Poland—Selected Quantitative Analyses'; Report 54, Social Science Research Network, July 2009, pp. 1–121. KAI reports, 24 November 2009. European Commission, *Joint Report on Social Protection and Social Inclusion* (Brussels: EC, 2009), pp. 421–431.

6   Organisation for Economic Co-operation and Development, *Doing Better for Children* (September 2009), pp. 23, 34–6. KAI report, 29 February 2008. This was the first OECD report on child wellbeing indicators. See also UNICEF's 2007 report, *Child Poverty in Perspective: An Overview of Child Well-being in Rich Countries.* 'Pockets of Poverty in Poland', in *Spiegel Online*, 10 May 2008. Government report, 'Polska 2030'; *Gazeta Wyborcza*, 30 June 2009.

7   GUS, *Informacja o rozmiarach i kierunkach emigracji z Polski w latach 2004–2009'* (Warsaw: 2010). *Baza Eurostat-u w zakresie statystyki migracji i azylu* (Warsaw: 2011). Jonathan Luxmoore, 'The poor are not the priority'; *The Tablet*, 20 March 2010.

8   *Zasięg ubóstwa w Polsce.* 'Polityka rodzinna nie jest dziś priorytetem państwa', KAI reports, 24 November 2009.

9   Małgorzata Glabisz-Pniewska, 'Mamy najwięcej biednych dzieci' (interview with Antoni Szymański); *Idziemy*, 19 September 2010.

10 Poland is currently rated the EU's tenth most corrupt country, an improvement on previous rankings; see Transparency International's *Corruption Perceptions Index* (Berlin: 2010).

11 'Czy mamy już biznes o wzorowym morale?', *Gazeta Wyborcza*, 16 October 2007. Jonathan Luxmoore and Jolanta Babiuch, 'Poland: a nation divided'; *The Tablet*, 20 May 2006. Polska piąta na świecie: Ernst i Young o atrakcyjności krajów; *Gazeta Prawna*, 16 May 2006. OECD, *Economic Survey of Poland* (Warsaw: June 2006).

12 Personal interview, Warsaw, 10 February 2010. Jarosław Gowin, *Kościół w czasach wolności 1989–1999* (Kraków: Znák, 1999), pp. 273–4. Franciszek Kampka, *Antropologiczne i społeczne podstawy ładu gospodarczego w świetle nauczania Kościoła* (Redakcja Wydawnictw KUL, Lublin, 1995), p. 26. Stanisław Musiał,

Dwanaście koszy ułomków (Wydawnictwo Literackie, Kraków, 2002), pp. 89–95.

13 Personal interview, Warsaw, 12 February 2010. Jonathan Luxmoore, 'Polish church challenged to speak up for poor and marginalised', Ecumenical News International, 12 March 2010.

14 'W trosce o nową kulturę życia i pracy—list Episkopatu Polski na temat bezrobocia', KAI report, 30 October 2001. The synod's ethical reflections on social and economic life have generally been ignored by the Polish Bishops Conference.

15 *Compendium of the Social Doctrine of the Church*, no. 184. *Catechism of the Catholic Church* (Libreria Editrice Vaticana, Rome, 1993), nos. 2443–8. Gerald Beyer, *Recovering Solidarity: Lessons from Poland's Unfinished Revolution* (Indiana: University of Notre Dame Press, 2010), pp. 157–203.

16 Pope John Paul II, Homily at Legnica Airport (2 June 1997). Jonathan Luxmoore and Jolanta Babiuch, *The Vatican and The Red Flag* (London: Geoffrey Chapman, 1999), pp. 314–6.

17 Pope John Paul II, Homily in Blonia Park, Krakow (18 August 2002). See also *Program dla Kościoła w Polsce: Jan Paweł II do polskich biskupów* (Krakow: Znak, 1998), nos. 36–7.

18 'O. Mądel: głęboki kryzys państwa wymaga radykalnych zmian (wywiad)', KAI report, 26 June 2003. See also Aniela Dylus, *Zmienność i ciągłość: Polskie transformacje ustrojowe w horyzoncie etycznym* (Warsaw: Centrum im. Adama Smitha, 1997), pp. 27–8.

19 *Służyć prawdzie o małżeństwie i rodzinie*, 149–151.

20 'Bądźmy świadkami miłości': List Episkopatu na Niedzielę Świetej Rodziny; KAI report, 17 December 2009. 'Komisja Duszpasterstwa KEP o zadaniach Kościoła na najbliższe lata'; KAI report, 25 January 2010.

21 'Ponad jedna czwarta polskich dzieci żyje w biedzie (wywiad z sekretarzem Caritas Polska)', KAI report, 29 February 2008. Beyer, *Recovering Solidarity*, pp. 191–9

22 'Rada Społeczna przy Arcybiskupie Poznańskim krytykuje interwencjonizm państwa', KAI report, 4 December 2007. The archdiocese's social council was set up by Archbishop Stanisław Gądecki to provide an ethical evaluation of current issues.

23 'List biskupów do księży: tożsamość kapłana to służba', KAI report, 23 February 2008.

24 Archbishop Józef Michalik, letter to priests, 'Ubóstwo kapłana realizacją Ewangelii'; Przemyśl, 28 November 2010.

25 *Gazeta Wyborcza, Rzeczpospolita*, 24 November 2000. The official Basilica website makes no mention of any controversy.

26 'Poznań: sąd przyznał parafii 75 mln odszkodowania za utracone w PRL mienie', KAI report, 12 January 2011. 'Proboszcz poznańskiej parafii: odszkodowanie za utracone mienie – m.in. na działalność społeczną', 27 January 2011.

27 Jonathan Luxmoore, 'Polish parish to dedicate what it says is largest statue of Christ', *Catholic News Service*, 9 November 1010.

28 Michalik, letter to priests, supra.

29 *Compendium of the Social Doctrine of the Church*, nos. 189, 193, 201.

30 *Ibid.*, nos. 160, 165–7. Vatican II, *Gaudium et Spes* (7 December 1965), 26.

31 *Gazeta Wyborcza*, 16 July 2009; and interview with Janusz Czapinski, 29 December 2009. The latest 'Social Diagnosis' was conducted in March–April 2009 ' among 26,000 Poles, and was the fifth since 2000.

The English Bishops, *Caritas*, and Civic 'Prophecy' after the 2010 Papal Visit

FRANCIS DAVIS

In the aftermath of Pope Benedict's visit to Britain in September 2010 the English Bishops, developing themes advanced by the Holy Father himself, announced that they would be refreshing their attempts to encourage a culture of deeper 'social responsibility'. Immediately their (tiny, and multi-tasking) staff team in London announced that they would hold a 'major' consultation and conference in Liverpool. This would then be followed by a think-tank style seminar to assess modern policy thinking to be staged at Archbishop's House, Westminster and followed (again) by a 'major' conference in London to attract the interest of elected politicians . Concurrently the Bishops' secretariat and its associated *Caritas* Social Action Network sought to gather more information on the views, scope and impact of Catholic voluntary action in England and Wales. As the process developed increasingly vocal voices from among these Catholic social welfare charities called for the 'Church to speak out' , to 'be prophetic'. By the time of the final conference (Easter 2011) Archbishop Vincent Nichols was saying he was 'up' for a more publicly political role. He was echoed in this view with even more enthusiasm by Archbishop Peter Smith, the prelate charged with leading for the Bishops on public affairs. Nichols pointed to the example of *Caritas* Austria as particularly worthy of emulation because of its 'advocacy' rooted in extensive practical welfare action at the local level. Subsequently Archbishop George Stack, while being enthroned in Cardiff, also called for the Church 'to speak out against the structures of injustice' in our society. For some this was collectively perceived to be a major step-change in tone and approach.

But, for a minority English Church in a changing Europe, what exactly did such a call for 'prophecy' mean? While such language was clearly designed to appeal to biblical imagery, and to transmit a sense of being willing to 'lead' or 'act' in the public sphere it was not entirely clear what the detail of such an appeal might involve: Were the Bishops being called upon to 'speak out' to protect the budgets of Catholic charities or in 'defence' of their schools at a time of state retrenchment and reform? . Were they hoping to advocate for the poor in general? Or, *pace* the Bishops' earlier discussion document on the role of taxation in building the common good did they see themselves as having a duty to 'advocate' to 'protect' a British welfare settlement that had been in place since 1945 and which was unravelling (actually) under pressure from all major political parties?

The question then was to what extent an 'idea' of 'prophecy' was shaping Church actions and if such an aspiration was , or might be embedded, in an institution or practice? And the Bishops secretariat itself seemed unable to answer either by explaining their clear goals.

At a further 'major' conference still, in July 2011, the Church's practical response seemed to be to decide to work towards the strengthening of its domestically focused *Caritas* network with this conclusion supported by resolutions from the Bishops' Conference itself. This step both made sense of Archbishop Nichols' earlier words of approval for *Caritas* Austria's 'advocacy', and began to locate the English Bishops' 'responsibility' efforts in a classically Catholic organisational framework namely the use of a formally sanctioned charitable network as the means to establish or sustain social action.

This chapter seeks to locate an English reach for the *Caritas* model in a wider European context and ask what it may or may not be able to tell us about any expressed desire to be 'prophetic' (namely to have some kind of influence on state policy making behaviours, or on the 'civic virtues' of citizens.) It does so by drawing on a major 22 country study of the 'prophetic' advocacy' against poverty of national *Caritas* agencies. As such it assumes that an expressed desire to enhance 'social responsibility' points to a sure conviction of an intention to make such language a concrete reality.

A 'Welfare State' Among Many?

European welfare state strategies since the Second World War have often been loosely typified as owing their roots to 'socialist' (Nordic countries); Bismarckian (central Europe); liberal (Ireland and the UK) and South Mediterranean (Spain, Italy, parts of SE Europe) models.[1] While these typologies are not perfect they do serve as a useful shorthand for demonstrating the *multiplicity* of means by which governments have sought to provide protection against the traditional social risks of the post-war era. They also serve to highlight the variety of needs, family, economic structures, and social balances to which such policy actions were intended to respond: the 'Bismarckian Model' is said to rely strongly on a 'social insurance' principle for welfare provision; the Nordic model on a large state presence and income payments grounded in a high theory of 'rights' ; the Liberal model on more markets and voluntary action; and the South Mediterranean approach on a combination of strong family support with a basic social insurance. In the case of the voluntary sector the models have had profound shaping effects too as varieties in law and the forms of legal personality—including for churches—have significantly impacted third sector institutional forms and roles Along with studies in the third world, there is now an emerging view that the interaction of expressed principles, institutional form, resources and human engagement are significant for the impact and the concretisation of values.

Because such huge variation nestles under many normative terms, which in much Catholic talk are rarely distinguished, the omission of the task of discerning them gives
rise to a new danger: That in the speedy move to policy
implementation little attention will be given to the appropriate design of a balance between ideas, institutions and
strategies of governance in relation to Churches , and
especially with regard to the struggle against poverty.

A singular narrative of Catholic Social Teaching?

It is difficult for many Western policy makers to understand
the Catholic Church. Even many of its own adherents
perceive it as the most centralised of institutions. This
perception may increase after a meeting with formal Church
representatives. Civil servants and policy makers alike live
under tight deadlines, constantly sensing an accountability
to each other, to an exponentially growing range of 'per-
formance criteria', not to mention demanding electorates.
However, the Church prides itself on an ability to to call
each person back to a recollection of the ultimate purpose
of life which is to prepare for death.[2]

This formal Church also extols a corpus of publications
that together comprise the official 'Catholic social teaching
tradition'.[3] Normative in claims, these documents comment
on the nature of capitalism, the state, the need for development, purposeful work and more. In Los Angeles, Glasgow
and London to name but three, they have been the basis of
Episcopal rhetorical resistance to draconian immigration
laws.[4]

Crucially for the present study this formal body of
teaching is also deemed by the Church to be the theological
basis—the theory of organisation—upon which Catholic
social welfare, educational, health and other institutions
should be governed. In purely empirical terms, this is a
command to a huge number of institutions, representing
one quarter of the health care in Sub-Saharan Africa and,

globally, more welfare bodies (Froehele and Gautier 2003) than all Catholic parishes and Dioceses combined.

Nevertheless these institutions are all seen by the formal discourse of the Church as 'The Church's' contribution. Their relationships are more often than not defined by church law in a fashion that is not always compatible with civil law.[5] Official recognition as 'an agency of the Church' brings with it a strong discourse of participating in the single 'social teaching tradition'.[6]

The largest of these officially recognised Catholic institutions is the *Caritas International* network, which is also the second largest NGO federation in the world. In the EU, *Caritas* is the only social welfare and justice network present in every member state and likely future member states. (*Caritas* 2008)

To Caritas in Europe[7]

Caritas Europa is the umbrella body for all of the official national Catholic social welfare and development agencies in Europe. It is both like and unlike other civil society networks. It is like them in that it sees itself clearly as located in civil society — rather than confined to a 'Religious sphere' This mainstream presence makes it a service provider of domiciliary care and hospitals, community development, social enterprises and student volunteering, soup kitchens and homeless centres, refugee centres and older peoples' services, nursing homes and research institutes, to name but a few of its operations. This practical experience also causes *Caritas* to see itself as an advocate for a 'preferential option for the poor' — in secular terms it takes a strongly progressive approach to welfare rights and the responsibilities of government combined with a dim view of the marketisation of services.

The network harnesses hundreds of thousands of volunteers and paid staff. It is a major economic as well as social force. In Germany and Austria alone it employs 411,000 paid staff.[8] In Lithuania the local *Caritas* is at the forefront of work on combating human trafficking, while in Spain the agency is pioneering new models of 'personal accompaniment' to address long term and chronic poverty issues.[9] In the German case, *Caritas* agencies also raise millions of restricted and unrestricted income streams from voluntary donations and then add to these through partnerships with national, regional and local governments.[10]

Caritas takes its pan European role as a catalyst for social reform seriously For example, *Caritas Austria* and *Caritas Italy* are significant funders of new work in South East Europe while *Caritas Germany* supports social innovation in Poland and Ukraine. *Caritas Europa* as an umbrella body also makes major contributions through its capacity building programmes to new and emerging *Caritas* agencies across the former USSR. At the start of each EU presidency, *Caritas Europa* sends a delegation to meet with incoming Ministers and brief them on migration and other policy related topics. In all of these activities, *Caritas* sees itself as existing for the benefit of all and especially the most socially excluded.

However, *Caritas Europa* is unlike other networks in that it also has a complementary relationship with one of Europe's largest faith communities—the Catholic Church. While this link could be downplayed as being of little interest in secular policy debates, such a perspective would underestimate the current social contribution that arises from this interface and also the striking scale of its presence. It would underestimate the way that the social and institutional location of the Church in particular localities would influence the self understanding of the *Caritas* agency as part of 'the Church' and its strategic options.

A Caritas Europa Dimension

As I have suggested above, at the national level the member organisations of the *Caritas* federation track policy exchanges, reforms and debates related to their national social inclusion strategies; and have been matching them with advocacy and new services. However, it is only since 2006 that *Caritas Europa, Caritas International*'s European region, has begun to work in a highly structured way to seek to influence debates as they are shaped by member states at the European level, and within the European Commission itself, and to harness those insights to influence national level debates towards engaging members at the European Commission and Council level. Because there have been limitations to the political authority of the European Commission to act on issues of 'social inclusion', when such actions did commence they were particularly linked to the the so-called Lisbon agenda which aimed to accelerate the marketisation of the European arena but also out of a sense of social concern as the 'banking crisis' gave rise to other social and economic pressures (*Caritas*)

The CONCEPT Programme: A Religious Response to European Policy Making

As part of an attempt to add a social dimension to the Lisbon process from 2001, on a three yearly cycle every member state of the European Union was required to prepare a national anti-poverty or social inclusion strategy and to feed this back to the European Commission and the Council of Ministers responsible for social affairs (known as ECOSOC) . As this initiative was deemed to be a vital means by which to renew and sustain Europe's social responsibilities, governments hoped that fresh methods might be found to maximise the possibilities to improve national level policies and inter-governmental peer collaboration that might arise from this triennial planning exercise.

Because of concerns about the relative lack of social voices in policy making in the first plan, by 2006 the European Commission agreed to partner with a number of civil society networks and chose to work with *Caritas* as its only faith based partner. This partnership took two main forms. First, this entailed commencing a dialogue on improvement and innovation as part of what the Commission and member states call the 'open method of co-ordination'.[11] Second, the partnership agreement provided two year's worth of funding to enable *Caritas Europa* (along with other selected European civil society networks) to contribute to the EU social inclusion process at the European level.

Caritas' engagement in this work became known as CONCEPT. The key aim of the CONCEPT project[12] was to build a network of experts on social inclusion within the *Caritas Europa* confederation of members. Initially this network included member organisations from 12 EU Member States and Bulgaria but later it gradually expanded to cover 24 EU Member States. (Davis et al)

In the first year (1 December 2005–30 November 2006), the key goal of CONCEPT was to enable the network participants to contribute to the process of developing the design of their own national social inclusion strategies. This gave rise to the *'National Strategy Plans for 2006-08'*. In pursuit of this goal, *Caritas Europa* used twinning arrangements under which each of the 13 *Caritas* member organisations taking part in CONCEPT encouraged and facilitated active involvement by other European *Caritas* member organisations. This led the network to expand and created the development of bilateral partnerships between *Caritas* member organisations in the field of social inclusion.

To be able to engage effectively in the national strategy process, CONCEPT participants familiarised themselves with the first and second waves of their state's National Action Plans (2001-2003, 2003-2005), their country's chapter in the Joint Report on Social Inclusion and Social Protection and its assessment by the European Commission. They also contacted the ministries in charge of the national strategy design, national members of their relevant Social Protection Committee, as well as their designated lead civil servant on the process at the EU level. In most cases, this served as the beginning of more or less effective dialogue with national governments which enabled CONCEPT participants to contribute to the design and monitoring of the national strategies in their country for the period 2006-2008.

In the second year (1 December 2006 - 30 November 2007), CONCEPT participants, now representing 24 countries, aimed to monitor the initial implementation of the national strategies at national, regional and local level. To further build their capacity and facilitate mutual learning on a broader scale, *Caritas Europa* enhanced the 'twinning arrangement' idea by encouraging mutual working via geographical and thematic groups.

Geographical groups sought to bring together CONCEPT participants from countries with similarities in language, culture, state structure and social policy challenges. These groups agreed to focus on governance processes, and on experiences and challenges in relation to implementation. By contrast, thematic groups sought to network on the grounds of expertise and organisational concern. It was intended that this would enable deeper reflection around the key social policy issues. Both 'geographical' and 'thematic' groups were a useful tool for sharing national strategy-related insights, challenges and best practices between CONCEPT participants. They added to the up-scaling of EU social policy expertise.

These groups completed their work by setting out joint policy recommendations at the EU, national and *Caritas* network level with regard to civil society participation in the social inclusion process and key social policy issues. These recommendations covered topics such as the grounds for minimum income legislation, the future of the 'European Welfare Model', and the financing of home care. A consistent concern was that the position of 'migrants' had been omitted from the majority of the social inclusion plans across the European Union.

While the European level policy proposals that *Caritas Europa* evolved are of significance and interest in their own right, we will also now note the variety of contributions that the CONCEPT process gave rise to in the advocacy realm. The examples that follow are emblematic rather than comprehensive. Nevertheless they provide some insight into the complexity by which seemingly normative, transnational, religious Catholic social principles were concretised at the national level. A single idea has had many consequences.

Ireland

Ireland has a unique Social Partnership which pre-dated the national strategy process. It consists of four pillars: employers, unions, farming organisations and the community and voluntary sector. In total, 17 voluntary sector organisations were involved in the Social Partnership process leading up to the national anti-poverty plan. They represented 10 strands of social life: older people, children and youth, labour market, housing, poverty, disability and caring, local and rural, housing, gender, social analysis and the voluntary network.

The *Caritas* partner in Ireland, CORI Justice Commission,[13] was the only organisation representing the social analysis strand and has been described as 'unique in the Irish context for both its formal role and the informal high regard it is held in by those of all parties.' (CORI 2008) Both formal and informal routes to influence were used in this case and in others. One of these was brokering a resolution of a log jam in inter-party negotiations inside the coalition government.(Reynolds 2008; Jordan 2008))

Moreover, CORI Justice was a key participant and influence in the national strategy process and has been actively involved in the Social Partnership since 1996. CORI drew government attention to the fact that Ireland was following a number of meta-strategies—the Lisbon Strategy, the National Development Plan, the National Spatial Strategy, the national strategy for social inclusion—but that they are to some extent overlapping and therefore have to be properly integrated. CORI, as part of the Social Partnership Agreement, is now involved in monitoring the implementation of the national social inclusion strategy.

Sweden

Caritas Sweden has been involved in a wide variety of social policy work, despite the limited size of the Catholic community in the Nordic countries. In Sweden, a 'Network Against Exclusion' has long been established, which includes representatives from NGOs, the trade unions and faith organisations, including *Caritas*. This network is the primary dialogue partner with the government on social issues and *Caritas* sits on the 'national social partnership council' which is the official means by which government involves other sectors in policy improvement.

In 2003 the Swedish Government decided to set up a Commission for service-user influence on social development issues. It is located in the Ministry of Health and Social Affairs and is chaired by the Minister for Public Health and Social Services. The Commission includes representatives from the Network Against Exclusion, the Swedish Association of Local Authorities and the Regional and National Boards of Health and Welfare. The Commission's work is focused on particularly vulnerable service users and on monitoring the implementation of the national social inclusion strategy. It meets four times a year and between meetings acts as a network. *Caritas Sweden*, together with other stakeholders, is continuously involved in the consultation and monitoring of the implementation of the social inclusion policy.

There has been good collaboration across government departments and with civil society in the implementation of the Swedish social inclusion plan. Consequently, most of the proposals put forward by *Caritas* and other NGOs have been included in the plan. Because they were involved in the CONCEPT process, *Caritas Sweden* were able to bring an EU dimension to discussions within the NGO network that 'added to their negotiating traction'.

United Kingdom: Publications, Press and Politicians

In the UK, the local *Caritas* agency, *Caritas* Social Action, was going through a process of re-organisation at the start of the CONCEPT process. This meant that while its Scottish wing was able to feed directly into the early parts of the project, its England and Wales branch joined CONCEPT only half way into its first phase. Northern Ireland was looked after by the Irish CONCEPT partner as *Caritas* is organised as a single Island of Ireland entity.

These factors did not prove a major obstacle from a *Caritas Europa* perspective. However, in the UK the government had already established its formal group of partners as part of the highly structured—and innovative—'*Get Heard*' process.[14] Other civil society actors expressed some reservations as to the appropriateness of the local *Caritas* agency joining the formal grouping at this stage. Some Church groups were already networked into the secular European Anti-Poverty Network which is active in the UK. Consequently a plan was devised to formally involve *Caritas* at the civil service level at a subsequent stage.

In the meantime *Caritas* focused on a number of different strategies to put the national process, and the social inclusion debate, on the map in the UK.
In the UK *Caritas* Social Action:

- Circulated background briefings to faith based community groups across the country and held local discussions, and not only in Church based groups.

- Jointly with an academic research centre published a pamphlet by a member of the government which called for a new faith based coalition to 'make poverty history' on the domestic front. This led to new collaboration between the pamphlet's author and other anti-poverty groups active on the social inclusion process.

- Held meetings with the leading back bench politicians and the Prime Minister's envoy on the faith communities.

- Made over 20 speaking engagements and lectures across the country in which the national anti poverty strategies were discussed.

- Worked hard to gain a media profile. *Caritas'* critique of migration policy became the subject of a major article in the national Church press and the focus of a leader column in a major national newspaper. It was further quoted on the UK's leading TV current affairs debate programme.

France: Harnessing the Voice of the Poor

The French contribution to CONCEPT was slowed down by staff changes and issues of language but took a step forward when a former senior French civil servant agreed to act as the CONCEPT link as a volunteer. Subsequently, he was replaced by a senior member of the *Secours Catholique* management team who acted with speed to fully integrate the work located in France into the CONCEPT process.

It is of note that this fresh networking would then draw a major *Secours Catholique* programme into the CONCEPT level, both adding capacity to *Caritas Europa* and providing fresh evidence and insights at the European Commission level.

To summarise the programme briefly, it involves a nationwide action-research survey that would secure questionnaire responses from 4000 people, including children, with direct experience of poverty. The insights gained will form the basis for future mobilisation and advocacy with a particular emphasis on involving poor people themselves in speaking out. The final report would form a part of the advocacy platform for the whole of *Caritas Europa*.

Moreover, during the French presidency of the European Union (July to December 2008), *Secours Catholique* worked closely with *Caritas Europa* to put forward recommendations to tackle child and family poverty arising from its activities. The key strength of the programme is that it gives children living in poverty an opportunity to express their views on their lives, their hopes, aspirations and fears for the future.

From the *Caritas Europa* perspective *Secours Catholique's* work is now regarded as a strikingly innovative 'national pilot project' which could be replicated in other member states in due course.

Romania: Taking the First Step

This was not only the first time that *Caritas Romania* had become involved in national strategy design but also the first time that civil society had engaged in such a fashion with government policy development. This was a risk for both *Caritas* and the government but one that thus far has begun to bear fruits. Romanian *Caritas* engaged in advocacy activities which stretched its small national office. For the Romanian state the very attempt by *Caritas* to establish a framework for an external accountability was culturally significant. This is not surprising given the unique heritage of Romania even within the former Soviet bloc.

Austria: Social Innovation

In Austria *Caritas* turns over in excess of 400 million euros and works both in national social welfare and international development. During the national social inclusion process, *Caritas's* health outreach programmes for refugees and asylum seekers were specifically praised as an example of good practice. The depth of work by *Caritas* in Austria is such, however, that the agency could just as well have pointed to other social innovations taking place outside the formal strategy process. Working with the Erste Foundation, *Caritas* has founded a bank for the 'unbanked', providing a route to financial inclusion for the poorest members of Austrian society. Each year *Caritas*, with a number of corporate and NGO partners, also runs a national day on which young people give a day as volunteers, for which they are paid and their pay is then recycled to help fund social projects. This financial recycling helps with the sustainability of the projects and has been so successful that it is now being replicated in the former Yugoslavia and viewed with interest by the new National Council on Social Action in the UK. (*Erste Stiftung* 2009)

Questions of Legitimate Public Action?

According to many of its own board members, *Caritas'* actions 'in defence of the poor' provoke an immediate affirmation. *Caritas Europa*'s own interim self assessment saw its 'networked' coordination as 'the Church in action', 'an embodiment of the Catholic social teaching tradition' and as the kernel of an 'epistemic community of ideas across Europe to advance poverty reduction'.[15] Within this formal discourse the CONCEPT programme is easily presented as a resounding success. After all, it is reported, the shared aspiration to develop habits in keeping with the normative social teaching traditions has seemingly been achieved and advocacy has been delivered in the name of 'the Church' and in defence of the most excluded.(Davis et al)

However, it could also be argued that a wider set of issues are at stake. While it is true that *Caritas* has engaged in active advocacy across the EU, theoretically how do we account for the huge variety of means by which different members of the same 'Church', with the same formally expressed 'idea' of mobilisation , have engaged in what is an increasingly integrated yet diverse polity? And what light might such an account shed on the putative plans to take *Caritas* even further in England and Wales?

In almost every country this ecclesiastical institution has shaped and re-shaped its strategy while simultaneously working to discern a 'common European position'; pooling its insights and even the governance of its advocacy. At the national level *Caritas* agencies have perceived themselves as having a 'thick' conception of social justice but in developing a European position this has become 'thinner' as the objective needs of Eastern European countries have been in dialogue with more subjective definitions of 'need' found in the richer Western ones. (Interviews 2008)

Has this variety been a simple local strategic choice or the abandonment of principle? Is it likely that parts (rather than agencies) of other faith communities would experience such institutional morphing if they were to commit to an advocacy for and with the poor in a changing European environment?

In the UK, as we saw, an approach closer to a distinct discourse was adopted but this was more as a result of timing, the size of the local Catholic community and inter-religious considerations than of divergent convictions. Advocacy outside formal state governance processes was secured by enforced social irrelevance rather than the principled passion that some of the UK activists claimed for their 'social teaching' engagement (Interviews 2008). In the Swedish case authenticity came more easily because the design of the state allowed *Caritas* access on its own terms despite the marginal social position of Catholicism (Interviews 2008). In Romania there was a tentativeness on all sides and the Director of *Caritas* Romania observed that the very act of conversation was 'miraculous'.[16] Meanwhile in France a huge grassroots initiative and range of activities perhaps suggested a direction that could be both a source of learning for the Church and the state together?

Even within a strong normative discourse then, supported by rich horizontal information flows between parts of the religious third sector network, the vertical capacity, insights and impact of the religious third sector body are shown to be intensely variable. While the size of the agency matters so too does the size and form of the related extended faith community. Perhaps most crucially the quality and timeliness of policy making was crucial. What the state did or did not do had the biggest impact.

In fact *Caritas* across Europe identified a number of patterns that, when present, had a devastating effect on the role of third sector bodies in general: To name but two; state consultation that was undertaken too quickly, or which harnessed IT facilities out of kilter with third sector skills and capacity destroyed civic initiative rather than building it. Meanwhile, constructive feedback from the third sector bodies which was then fully excluded from the country's final national anti-poverty action plan, had a similar disempowering effect.

Conclusion: Putting the English Community in Perspective

In describing the work of the *Caritas* Federation over a particular two year window we have re-located the 'local' to the national level while also noting the emergence of an embryonic common European platform against poverty. This common platform is in turn the cause and consequence of new innovations at the sub-national level.

In addition, and perhaps most significantly, this dialectic between various levels within the religious voluntary organisation has been complemented by what can only be called an isomorphic response to particular state structures: Despite shared and normative claims as to what might constitute the ideal state, market and even NGO *Caritas* has morphed with great speed and detailed engagement when faced with the task of speaking for those who it considers to be 'voiceless'. As such its development of particular practices has been more vital to its work than the articulation of any motivating ideas, ideological framework or collective episcopal view of 'prophecy'.

In the English context such a realisation might conceivably provoke at least three responses: First, an attempt to make the Catholic response 'purer' by an increasingly energetic appeal to the 'distinctiveness' of Catholic social teaching. This might include a narrowing of what kinds of charities may be acceptable as members of the new '*Caritas* Network'. Second, the identification of clearly Catholic issues so as to protect the control over agendas of the Church. This might mean an increasing focus on abortion, family or authority as areas where an emerging generation of Bishops feel they have special insight. Finally, it may lead to deeper reflection on the how the links between words, institutions, and practical action might be sustained . This might include testing whether the Church's own budgetary allocations match those it is demanding of the state, whether the skills are present in the Church's staffing structures to read the detail of policy proposals and patterns and, most especially, that while the English Church uses the same 'grand' theory of Catholic Social Thought the Church's local institutional reach is relatively marginal.

In turn marginality may mean that any expressed desire for increased 'social responsibility' to be taken seriously, cannot be anything greater than a rhetorical desire presented as having real significance. Or that its concretisation requires an effort so organisationally fundamental that its likely implications have not yet been grasped by any of those involved. As Europe continues to change only time will tell.

Bibliography:

This chapter draws heavily on a series of studies funded by the European Commission and undertaken by the Von

Hugel Institute, Cambridge for *Caritas* Europa 2005-08 authored by the present author and Jolanta Stankeviciute and Jenny Rossiter and an earlier discussion of related topics: F. Davis, (2009) 'Ideas, Institutions and Poverty Reduction: Questions For A Theology of Governance', *International Journal of Public Theology*. Brill. Leiden

See also:

Buchs, M., *New Governance In European Social Policy: The Open Method Of Coordination* Palgrave Macmillan: 2007.

Froehle, B and Gautier, M., *Global Catholicism — Portrait Of A World Church* Orbis: 2003.

Campbell, H. E. F., 'The Church And Globalisation', Lecture at Las Casas Institute, Blackfriars Hall, University of Oxford: 2009.

Davis, F., The 'Big Society' — how can the Catholic voluntary sector respond? In *Pastoral Review* (2011).

McCabe, H., *God Matters* Continuum: 2005.

Taylor-Gooby, P., *New Risks, New Welfare* Oxford University Press: 2004.

Walsh M.and Davies, B. (eds), *Proclaiming Justice And Peace — Papal Documents from Rerum Novarum to Centisimus Annus* 23rd Publications :1991.

Website of the Catholic Bishops' Conference for England and Wales www.cbcew.org.

Notes

[1] P. Taylor-Gooby, *New Risks, New Welfare* (Oxford: OUP, 2004).

[2] H. McCabe, *God Matters* (London: Continuum, 2005).

[3] For example , see M. Walsh and B. Davies (eds.), *Proclaiming Justice And Peace – Papal Documents from Rerum Novarum to Centisimus Annus* (23rd Publications: 1991).

[4] I am referring here to Cardinal Mahony and Cardinal Murphy O Connor's calls for "regularisation" of illegal migrants in the

period 2006 to 2008.

5   According to leading UK charity lawyers Blake Lapthorn Tarlo Lyons, "canon law has no more status than the rules of a club". (November 2007 briefing to trustees.) The Chair of the Roman Catholic Diocesan Financial Secretaries Association, Rev Stephen Morgan, goes further to say that Episcopal governance and civil governance are "incompatible". (Correspondence with author May 2009).

6   For further discussion of this reality (and its complications) see F. Davis, 'A Political Economy of the Catholic Church', in K. Wilson and N. Timms (eds) *Authority and Governance In The Roman Catholic Church* (London: SPCK, 2001).

7   See the website: www.caritas-europa.org.

8   Figures are taken from from the global *Caritas* website which helpfully summarises local impact and staffing statistics. See www.*Caritas*.org.

9   In the UK, *Caritas* comprises 11 larger and several smaller voluntary organisations which have recently distanced themselves from aspects of Church control to allow continued work in adoption in compliance with equalities legislation.

10 K. Kramer (2009) *The Ecclesiological Concept of the Second Vatican Council and the Reality of the Church as a Worldwide Network*. Paper at St Edmund's Cambridge, September 2004.

11 See M. Buchs, *New Governance In European Social Policy: The Open Method Of Coordination* (London: Palgrave Macmillan, 2007).

12 CONCEPT stands for '*Caritas* Organisations Network To Combat Poverty and Exclusion'.

13 Conference of Religious in Ireland Justice Commission, see www.cori.ie/justice.

14 For information on 'Get Heard' see www.ukcap.org/getheard/pdf/whatisgetheard.pdf.

15 See F. Davis et al (2012) forthcoming.

16 Interview with CONCEPT representative from Romania.

Europe's Future:
The Nation-State and EU Enlargement

MICHAEL SUTTON

What should be the place of the 'Catholic social conscience' in reflections on the future of civil society and politics in Europe? Such a question is vast in scope, and a very short answer, from a Catholic standpoint, would surely be that it should be immense. However, if by 'Europe' is meant solely the international institution called the European Union (EU), there can be no very short answer, while any longer answer should be circumspect and qualified, since it is not immediately clear that the 'Catholic social conscience' has necessarily a great deal to say about the workings of the EU.

The EU is a *sui generis* political entity, perhaps best described as an exceptionally tightly integrated society of nation-states, and one of its many striking features is that social security has remained, at least until now, very largely a national responsibility. More generally, the political parameters governing the pursuit of social justice within the EU area tend still to be primarily national ones. For instance, the functioning of the EU's economic and monetary arrangements may have consequences that are judged socially unjust or regrettable, but remedial action or social protection to help the economically disadvantaged lies usually at the door of national governments, rather than at that of the European Commission in Brussels.

These cursory remarks are not to dismiss what has been achieved over the past half century in the laying down of broadly defined norms for social policy, which, in EU parlance, means essentially policy relating to labour relations. The Treaty of Rome (1957), which established the original European Economic Community in 1958, provides for a Community social policy (Part Three, Title III). These provisions have been strengthened by the Single European Act (1986), so as to include health and safety under the umbrella of social policy, and also by the Treaty of Maastricht on European Union (1992) and the Treaty of Amsterdam (1997), which, in a two-phase process, incorporated the *Community Charter of the Fundamental Social Rights of Workers* into the same EU-wide legally binding social policy provisions—this Charter had first been agreed at a European Council meeting in 1989, but at that time, because of British dissent, not unanimously so. These social rights were further developed in the *Charter of Fundamental Rights of the European Union* (Title IV, headed 'Solidarity'), which, after having been drawn up in 2000, became legally binding on the present twenty-seven EU member states—albeit with some degree of exemption for the United Kingdom and Poland—by virtue of the Treaty of Lisbon (2007; ratified in 2009).

In the light of these developments, which have established general norms for social policy, it is legitimate to speak of a widespread shared commitment to a 'European social model', and the latter may be associated not only with the post-war German concept of *Soziale Marktwirtschaft* but also, in a different vein, with the tradition of Catholic social thought flowing from Leo XIII's great encyclical *Rerum Novarum* (1891). Yet, as has been indicated, the norms represented by this 'European social model' do not translate into an EU system of social policy or protection. Social policy in any concrete, activist sense is still a national competence. More importantly, social security arrangements have remained a national preserve; this has been for a variety of reasons including nation-bound historical circumstances, the huge expense of social security funding, and the crucial role that social security has come to play in founding the very legitimacy of the contemporary European nation-state.[1]

The practicalities of the pursuit of social justice within the EU area tend therefore to be much more the concern of the EU's individual member states than directly of the EU itself. Yet this does not mean that the process of European integration, as experienced until now, should be considered of secondary significance from the standpoint of the 'Catholic social conscience'. If attention is turned to the EU's role as an international actor, the issue of social justice extends beyond the world of the EU's own citizens. Twenty-one countries or territories outside Europe, with small or tiny populations, are still formally associated with the EU in order that the latter may advance their economic and social development. More important, in terms of the scale of the ambition, are the EU's treaty provisions for development cooperation with third countries and humanitarian aid. Lastly, the EU is committed to developing a common asylum and immigration policy and is practically-speaking bound to do so, since the process initiated by the Schengen agreement of 1985 has resulted in the creation of a huge area free of internal travel controls, an area that encompasses most of the EU and some other parts of Europe also (the EU; minus opted-out Ireland and the United Kingdom; minus, for the moment, Bulgaria, Cyprus, and Romania; and plus, officially or on a de facto basis, Iceland, Monaco, Norway, San Marino, Switzerland, and the Vatican City). In this century, there have been hundreds of thousands of asylum seekers or illegal immigrants arriving in the EU each year, often in desperate conditions; how best to cope with these migratory flows poses obviously great challenges, challenges that are frequently allied to questions of ethical principle.

Furthermore, the EU's role as an international actor touches directly on matters of peace. The pursuit of justice and peace go hand in hand, the interrelationship between the two being a constant of Catholic teaching. If account is taken of the vital necessity of peace for the proper functioning of both civil society and the state, which is a precondition for the flourishing of justice, a quite different aspect of the process of European integration comes into view, namely its actual or potential contribution to peace itself. In this context, Catholics and other Christians in Europe who scrutinize their consciences, with a view to adopting an ethically informed position on international issues, may well find it pertinent to address the following twofold question: has the EU been a factor making for continental and indeed world peace and, if so, is there further potential or scope for this positive action?

In partial answer, it would appear that the record to date has broadly speaking been extremely positive. A conceptual problem should be acknowledged here, that of comparing what has been with what might have been, since all sorts of scenarios, both benign and malign, can be imagined in the realm of historical counterfactuals. However, to compare two different periods in the past, thus obviating the need to resort to counterfactuals, it may be confidently asserted that the continent that has been partly shaped over the past sixty years by the process of political and economic integration initiated by the Schuman Declaration (1950) is a Europe that stands in very favourable contrast to the wretched Europe of so much of the inter-war period, at least if the criterion is the existence, or not, of international arrangements in Europe which promote peace and security.

To summarize, the great achievements of the 'construction of Europe' since the middle of the twentieth century have been, first, the contribution made by the integration process to the securing of a durable peace for most of the continent lying to the west of Russia and Ukraine (the notable exception being the area of former Yugoslavia) and, secondly, the promotion of economic growth and prosperity. This peace and this economic growth have been related to one another. That being said, from a Christian standpoint, peace should be ranked as the higher of the two achievements. A new, utterly transformed relation between France and West Germany was the key force for good in the 1950s and 1960s, and it has been the bedrock of so much that has been realized subsequently. That the path to German unification proved so smooth and peaceful a few decades later was partly because the Federal Republic of Germany and France agreed in 1990 to link unification to a major advance in European integration, which they did by proposing to their fellow member states the ambitious architecture of what was to become the EU as a result of the Maastricht Treaty. Beyond the Franco-German core, the accession of Spain and Portugal to the European Communities in 1986—only three years before the fall of the Berlin Wall—brought these countries out of their long European political quarantine. In the 1990s and the 2000s, following the end of the Cold War, the path was progressively cleared for the accession to the EU, in 2004 and 2007, of a large number of post-communist states from central and eastern Europe, of which the biggest by far was Poland—the country at the 'heart of Europe', to borrow Norman Davies's book title, whose fate in 1939 made it the *causus belli* of the Second World War. This new phase of EU integration, conjoined with NATO's expansion of its own membership, has effectively created a vast zone of peace and security covering much of the continent, even if relations with Russia have yet to be put on a satisfactorily stable and mutually advantageous footing.

To come to the second part of the question, if the EU has been a factor making for continental peace and security along the lines summarily outlined here, Christians pondering the future, and seeking to discern the best way forward, must ask themselves whether the further expansion of the EU could improve still further the prospects for lasting peace and security on the continent. Accession negotiations are under way with Croatia, Iceland and Turkey. The former Yugoslav Republic of Macedonia awaits a green light.

Albania, Bosnia and Herzegovina, Montenegro, Serbia, and Kosovo, have all been officially identified as 'potential candidates' and indeed some of these states have already formally submitted their applications. There are many reasons to believe that the progressive enlargement of the EU to encompass the entire Balkans would generally be a positive factor for peace and security in Europe, provided each accession is carried out in strict accordance with the preconditions represented by the EU's own 'convergence criteria' (national institutions guaranteeing democracy and the establishment of the rule of law; the existence of a functioning market economy; the ability to take on all the obligations of membership) as established at the Copenhagen meeting of the European Council in 1993.

Tiny Iceland is a special case. So too is Turkey, but partly for the opposite reason, namely the huge size of its population, at least in an EU context. Already today its population is not greatly smaller than that of Germany—the most populous EU member state—and by the end of the present decade Turkey's population will no doubt be bigger than Germany's. According to OECD demographic projections, Germany's total population will decrease—yes, decrease—from 82.8m in 2008 (13.8% aged less than 15) to 81.0m in 2030 (12.7%), whereas Turkey's population will continue to rise in a pronounced fashion, from 74.8m in 2008 (27.3% aged less than 15) to 90.8m in 2030 (21.1%). These demographic projections show that the Turkish population's age structure in twenty years' time is set to be relatively less weighted towards the young, but even so, it will be an age structure still markedly younger than the age structures of those countries in the present EU that continue to have growing populations (for instance, the United Kingdom and Ireland), not to speak of the 'grey' and youth-deprived age structures of those countries, such as Germany, experiencing actual population decline. Such structural population imbalances within Europe, including Turkey, point to the likelihood of continuing large-scale migration flows through the play of push-and-pull economic factors, and this westward bound migration would no doubt be facilitated in the event of Turkey's accession to the EU. As to absolute levels of population, not only would Germany lose its position as the EU's biggest member state in the event later this century of Turkish accession—a politically symbolic change, if nothing else—but the other big member states, namely France, the United Kingdom, Italy, Spain, and Poland, would also lose something in terms of their relative rank (for instance, by having a lower country representation in the European Parliament than Turkey).

These considerations are part of the background to the present poor state of the flagging Turkish accession negotiations. They help explain, in particular, the strong hostility of France's Nicolas Sarkozy to the very idea of Turkish membership and also the more muted but still real opposition evinced by Germany's Angela Merkel. As to the opening of the negotiations, the European Council accorded Turkey the formal status of 'candidate country' in 1999, though it was not until 2005 that the actual negotiations began. That the negotiations now appear stalled owes much to the opposition mounted on the Franco-German front. It should also be stressed that if the negotiations are ever to be successfully concluded—an outcome appearing increasingly doubtful but not yet impossible—Turkey will have to make considerably more progress towards meeting the Copenhagen 'convergence criteria', especially on the political front.[2] To complicate matters further, a regional issue hampering the negotiations has been that of the future of the Turkish-controlled northern part of the partitioned island of Cyprus, with the Greek-speaking Republic of Cyprus (an EU member state since 2004) demanding immediate access to the ports in the north by virtue of Turkey's existing customs union treaty with the EU.

There is, of course, another question overshadowing the negotiations, namely the greatly controversial question of whether Turkey is part of Europe at all. The refusal of the quality of 'European' to Turkey, by politicians and opinion makers speaking from within the EU, is often expressed in crude geographical terms: Asia begins to the east of the Bosporus Strait, meaning therefore that Turkey lies largely outside Europe, and so any application for membership should be rejected out of court. Such an argument, amounting to atlas nitpicking, squares ill with the fact that Turkey joined the Council of Europe in 1949, the year of the latter's foundation, and also with the fact that Turkey's eligibility for membership of the EU (and earlier of the European Communities) has never been denied on geographical grounds by the European Commission, the gatekeeper institution for handling all membership applications.

The quite different argument, whose logic is not strictly geographical, is that Turkey does not belong spiritually or culturally to Europe. The argument may be variously expressed. One of its strongest expressions takes the form of the assertion of an incompatibility between the values represented by Islam—the religion of the vast majority of the Turkish population—and the values held to have shaped Europe and left a lasting imprint on it, particularly by virtue of the continent's Christian past. If this argument is deemed worthy of attention, it follows that it is also relevant *mutatis mutandis* for the making of judgements on the merits of the application for EU membership from Albania and any future application (at some indeterminate date) from Kosovo. In the case of Turkey, a counter-argument is that the Republic of Turkey, founded in the early 1920s under the leadership of Mustafa Kemal Atatürk, has been committed by its constitution, ever since 1928, to a sharp separation between state and religion, this divide being remindful of the legal separation between church and state introduced in France in the early years of the twentieth century; in short, Turkey is a secular republic, which means that religious considerations should not be allowed to stand in the way of its EU candidacy. A second counter-argument, bearing directly on the issue of values, denies any exclusive spiritual or cultural identity to modern-day Europe. A start to this counter-argument might draw on the history of ideas, stressing that it was only between roughly the fifteenth and seventeenth centuries that the words 'European' and 'Christian' became interchangeable with one another, before the idea of Europe (in more than just a geographical sense) separated itself from the dying idea of Christendom.[3] And the same counter-argument might conclude by looking at the present state of European society, one of whose distinguishing features is wholesale religious indifference, with the marginalization of Christian thought amongst the intelligentsia being one of its sad reflections.

Discerning the right path through the complexities of this type of debate can be difficult. In seeking to find such a path, the question of peace and security may be addressed anew. For the sake of economy of argument, let us retain our focus on Turkey. If from a consciously Catholic standpoint, there are good reasons for Turkey's eventual accession to the EU, there are likely to be even more good reasons for the enlargement of the EU, to the west of the Bosporus, to include the entire Balkans.

In the case of Turkey, it is noteworthy that strong support for its accession to the EU has come from both the United States and the United Kingdom. Thus, during the past twenty years or so, following Turkey's first (unsuccessful) bid in 1987 for membership of what was then the European Communities, these two powers—irrespective of the changes of government in Washington and London—have shared the position that Turkey's accession would be a positive development for Europe, the Mediterranean area and the Middle East. On the American side, three successive presidents, Bill Clinton, George W. Bush, and Barack Obama, have been strongly of this view. On the British side, there has been a similar consistency, with Tony Blair, as prime minister, having been its most eloquent advocate.[4] In some continental European capitals, however, there has been a tendency to suspect a new mischief on the part of perfidious Albion: the suspicion that London wishes to put a spoke in the wheels of European integration by having the EU widened inordinately, and thereby enfeebled, through Turkey's accession. But the views of the United States and the United Kingdom—two of the five permanent members of the UN Security Council—cannot be dismissed simply on the grounds of ulterior motive. Within the EU, the United Kingdom has not stood alone. During the course of the present troubled negotiations, Sweden, in very outspoken fashion, as well as Finland, Italy, Poland, and Spain, have all shown themselves in favour of the Turkish bid and have joined the United Kingdom in forming an informal caucus to support it. Not the least of their considerations has been the geopolitical one of widening the area of peace and security outwards from core Europe, especially in the aim of bringing a greater degree of stability to the Middle East.

The potential for progress of this kind may well have been compromised, at least temporarily, by the deterioration that occurred in 2010 in relations between Turkey and Israel. Nonetheless, it would still seem that if the EU enlargement question in respect of Turkey is being assessed solely from the standpoint of the EU's contribution to international peace and security, the prospect of the country's accession should in all conscience be judged positively. But a proviso should be attached to this judgement. This proviso has nothing to do directly with economics—Turkey has a successful, fast growing market economy. It concerns rather the ethical underpinnings of both public and private life. We have described the EU as an exceptionally tightly integrated society of states. The concept of a 'society of states' has been borrowed here from the school of academic thought that goes under the name of the English School of International Relations and, in particular, from the writings of Martin Wight (1913-1972), an Anglican by Christian belief and devotion, who taught after the Second World War at the LSE before moving on to the newly founded University of Sussex. According to Wight, essential to any international society of states is a sense of solidarity and commonality of purpose, and the tighter that international society, the stronger must be its sense of solidarity and commonality of purpose. Wight identified the idea of an international society of states, be it global or more narrowly limited to Europe, with what he termed the 'Grotian tradition' of international thought. Yet it is in the writings of the Spanish Jesuit philosopher and theologian, Francisco Suárez, rather than in those of his near contemporary, the Dutch Protestant, Hugo Grotius, that he found his best definition of the tradition at the outset of the modern period. 'The human race', Suárez wrote, 'though divided into no matter how many different peoples and nations has for all that a certain unity, a unity not merely physical, but also in a sense political and moral bound by charity and compassion; wherefore though every republic or monarchy seems to be autonomous and self-sufficing, yet none of them is, but each of them needs the support and brotherhood of others, both in a material and a moral sense. (Therefore they also need some common law organizing their conduct in this kind of society.)' (*De legibus, ac Deo legislatore*, Book II, chapter XIX, 9—translation taken by Wight from *The Catholic Tradition of the Law of Nations*).[5] In other words, an integrated international society of states requires the glue of shared ethical values, whether derived from natural law type reasoning or from religious belief.

To return to the issue of EU enlargement and, in particular, Turkey's desired accession, how should Catholics judge in good conscience whether there is enough of the ethical glue in question? The Magisterium provides some guidance for this sort of appraisal. However, the extent of this guidance is perforce limited, since what is entailed in the appraisal is not only recourse to general principle but also to historically-informed practical judgement. Pope John XXIII's encyclical *Pacem in Terris* (1963) lauds the principle of active solidarity between nations in the pursuit of the universal common good. Yet it includes no consideration of regional political and economic integration as one of the possible paths towards peace. Somewhat more detailed considerations about peace are to be found in the Second Vatican Council's Pastoral Constitution on the Church in the Modern World, *Gaudium et Spes* (1965), whose second part ('Some Problems of Special Urgency') contains a last chapter headed 'The Fostering of Peace and the Promotion of a Community of Nations'. Put to the fore is 'the permanent binding force of universal natural law and its all-embracing principles'.[6] But the dominant perspective is a global one, with attention paid, for instance, to the arms race and to relations between 'developing nations' and 'advanced nations'. For our purposes, perhaps a more instructive document is the Second Vatican Council's Declaration on the Relations of the Church to Non-Christian Religions, *Nostra Aetate* (1965). Its exhortation 'Christians and Muslims [...] let them together preserve and promote peace, liberty, social justice and moral values' certainly bears on the question of whether Christians and Muslims should be associated together in further developing the EU as an international entity.[7]

While the Magisterium is an essential reference for all Catholics engaged in deliberation of conscience over appropriate responses to practical ethical questions — including ethical questions with a strong political dimension — help may also be had from other quarters in the shape of works of philosophy or theology that have the power to improve our conceptual framework for handling these same questions. Here mention may be made of the French philosopher and theologian, Gaston Fessard (1897-1978), who was closely associated with his fellow Jesuit, Henri de Lubac, and was also a friend of Raymond Aron and Gabriel Marcel.[8] In *'Pax Nostra': Examen de conscience international* (1936), a book whose starting point was Nazi Germany's growing threat to peace, Fessard elaborated an original conceptual approach for the exercise of moral discernment in international affairs. In particular, drawing on a theology of Pauline inspiration and on a dialectical method of philosophising, he explored the rightful roles of modern nations, or nation-states, in their diversity. They are each to steer between the dangers represented by both pacifism and nationalism and look to the 'common good'. Their plenitude, according to Fessard, is to be realized through the building of a 'community of nations' founded on justice and charity. Justice (expressed through nations rendering to one another their due, not only in accordance with the letter of international law but also with its spirit) and charity (expressed by acting with benevolence) are the concepts that should govern one's discernment of what is appropriate or acceptable in international affairs, with charity enriching justice, yet not overriding it. The relevance of the analysis in *'Pax Nostra'* to the question today of EU enlargement resides especially in Fessard's effective claim that the very diversity of nations, each with its own 'moral personality', is an essential rather than contingent feature of the properly founded community of nations. In other words, if availing of his analysis, we look at the international community of nations formed in Europe by the EU in the early twenty-first century, might it not be the case that an inner diversity is to be welcomed rather than feared?

Pope John Paul II, for one, was very conscious of the rich and legitimate diversity of Europe's national cultures. In speaking of his own country, he could implicitly ascribe a moral personality to the Polish nation by linking its vocation down to the present day with the proud and tolerant spirit of the old Polish-Lithuanian Commonwealth as represented by the nineteenth-century poet, Adam Mickiewicz. The Polish pope's great religious ambition for Europe as a continent was that of realizing substantial progress towards the eventual unity of the Catholic and Eastern Orthodox Churches, bringing together the Christian traditions flowing from Rome and Constantinople respectively.

Yet, to come back to our reflections on the subject of EU enlargement, it may be noted that John Paul never made any pretence that Europe had been exclusively Christian during most of the Christian era, now termed the Common Era. He was, moreover, keenly aware of the complex ways in which diverse religious beliefs and practices—Christian, Jewish and Muslim—had contributed to the shaping of the continent, particularly in east-central Europe and in the Balkans. In 1994 the pope was forced to abandon a visit to Sarajevo, where he was to have addressed the theme of religious tolerance, regretting that Muslim, Jew, Orthodox, and Catholic, had all been victims, in Bosnia, of violent acts of nationalism. In his New Year address in 1995 to the diplomatic corps accredited to the Holy See, he said starkly that the tragedy of Bosnia seemed like 'the shipwreck of the whole of Europe'.[9]

In debates about European identity, these considerations are pertinent for the tackling of the question of the degree of Turkey's supposed otherness. But they do not resolve the more precise issue of whether the EU could cope successfully with Turkish accession. Mind frames are of crucial importance. Pope Benedict XVI rightly stated in his intellectually rich (and controversial) address to the University of Regensburg in September 2006 that the 'inner rapprochement between Biblical faith and Greek philosophical inquiry was an event of decisive importance not only from the standpoint of the history of religions, but also from that of world history', and that 'this convergence, with the subsequent addition of the Roman heritage, created Europe and remains the foundation of what can rightly be called Europe'.[10] It can scarcely be denied that Turkey's educated classes, to the extent that they espouse Enlightenment values, belong to this Europe. Benedict himself, in the 'critique of modern reason from within' that formed the substance of his Regensburg address, said explicitly that his critique had 'nothing to do with putting the clock back to the time before the Enlightenment and rejecting the insights of the modern age'.[11] In the case of Turkey, as regards modern values, it is clear that the country's Westernization under Atatürk and later, after his death in 1938, was far-reaching and profound.[12]

Problems remain, nevertheless. Human rights issues continue to bedevil the EU accession negotiations. In particular, freedom of religion as defined by the *Charter of Fundamental Rights of the European Union* (art. 10) is not yet fully guaranteed in Turkey. The European Commission drew attention to this failure in the conclusions it drew from its latest annual report, in November 2010, on Turkey's progress towards meeting the Copenhagen 'convergence criteria'.[13] The way forward should be that indicated by Benedict XVI in his New Year address in 2010 to the diplomatic corps accredited to the Holy See. With particular reference to Europe, only a month after the Treaty of Lisbon had come into force, he called for a spirit of *laïcité positive* — in the face of the widespread hostility shown in certain Western countries to religion, especially Christianity — this being an open-minded spirit founded on the 'just autonomy of the temporal order and the spiritual order'.[14]

To conclude, for reasons relating to peace and security in Europe, the Mediterranean area, and the Middle East — reasons which should indeed count from the standpoint of the Catholic conscience — there is much to be said in favour of Turkey's application for EU membership. The (uncertain) prospect of Turkey's accession does raise difficulties from a Christian perspective. But they should not be deemed insuperable. The restoration of a European Christendom is an anachronistic pipedream. Greater confidence on the part of Catholics in drawing on the riches of the natural law tradition would allow for more optimism in the forging of a wider Europe. But, for any country, a precondition today for EU membership is full respect of the *Charter of Fundamental Rights of the European Union*. On this point, in the case of Turkey, the jury is still out.

Notes

1   What was formally called the European Community, and prior to 1993 the European Economic Community, remains very much an economic construction centred on the founding concept of a common market. In the present consolidated version of the *Treaty on the Functioning of the European Union* (essentially the updated Treaty of Rome), the place accorded to social policy is a secondary one, particularly when compared with the far-reaching and concrete nature of the consolidated treaty's economic and monetary provisions. In Part Three, which is headed 'Union Policies and Internal Actions', Title X covers 'Social Policy', but it is relatively short on content, despite the additions and changes wrought by the Single European Act and the Treaties of Maastricht and Amsterdam; and its provisions are pitched at the level of general principle. The main substance of Part Three resides in the matters covered by Titles I through to VIII. Crucial herein, without any social considerations attached, are the provisions relating to the following: freedom of movement of goods; freedom of movement of persons, services and capital; and economic and monetary union. Matters such as the scope of collectively financed healthcare, or the actual level of social protection afforded by old-age pension entitlements and unemployment benefits, lie outside the purview of the consolidated treaty and hence outside the EU's remit.

2   See the European Commission's latest annual progress report, in November 2010, on Turkey in respect of meeting the 'convergence criteria'.

3   See Denys Hay, *Europe: The Emergence of an Idea* (Edinburgh: The Edinburgh University Press, 1957).

4   A subject touched upon in his memoirs. See Tony Blair, *A Journey* (London: Hutchinson, 2010), p. 540: 'I was and am in favour of Turkey's accession. I want Turkey looking west and Europe looking east, and, handled correctly, Turkey's membership would do us all good. It is very dangerous—for us and for them—to push Turkey away, because it would appear to underscore the fact that Judaeo-Christian and Muslim civilisations cannot coexist. The implications of estrangement are very large. After I left office, Turkey was politely but firmly pushed back in the direction of something less than full membership. It is a perilous mistake for both parties.'

5   Martin Wight in Gabriele Wight and Brian Porter (eds.), *Interna-*

tional Theory: The Three Traditions, (London: Leicester University Press for The Royal Institute of International Affairs, 1991), p. 22.

6 Vatican II, *Gaudium et Spes*, 79.

7 Vatican II, *Nostra Aetate*, 3.

8 On Fessard's thought, see Michel Sales, 'Gaston Fessard (1897–1978)—Genèse d'une pensée', in Michel Sales (ed.), *Le Mystère de la Société: Recherches sur le sens de l'histoire*, (Bruxelles: Culture et Vérité, 1997), pp. 5–133; Frédéric Louzeau, *L'anthropologie sociale du Père Fessard* (Paris: Presses Universitaires de France, 2009).

9 See Michael Sutton, 'John Paul II's Idea of Europe', *Religion, State & Society*, vol. 25/1 (1997), pp. 17-29.

10 Pope Benedict XVI, *Address at the University of Regensburg* (12 September 2006).

11 *Ibid.* Cf. Joseph Cardinal Ratzinger and Jürgen Habermas, *Dialectics of Secularization: On Reason and Religion*, (ed.) Florian Schuller (San Francisco: Ignatius Press, 2006); Joseph Ratzinger, *Europe Today and Tomorrow: Addressing the Fundamental Issues*, (San Francisco: Ignatius Press, 2007).

12 Noteworthy on this subject: Andrew Mango, *Atatürk* (London: John Murray, 1999); Norman Stone, *Turkey: A Short History* (London: Thames & Hudson, 2011).

13 Extract from the Communication from the Commission to the Council and the European Parliament *Enlargement Strategy and Main Challenges 2010-2011* in respect of Turkey: 'As regards *freedom of religion*, freedom of worship continues to be generally respected. The implementation of the law on foundations has been continuing, albeit with some delays and procedural problems. The dialogue with the Alevis and non-Muslims continued but has not yet produced results. Members of minority religions continue to be subject to threats by extremists. A legal framework in line with the ECHR [European Convention on Human Rights] has yet to be established, so that all non-Muslim religious communities and [the] Alevi community can function without undue constraints, including the training of clergy.'

14 Pope Benedict XVI, *New Year Address to the Diplomatic Corps accredited to the Holy See for the traditional exchange of New Year greetings* (11 January 2010). The New Year address was given in French in accordance with diplomatic usage. The word *laïcité* in French is perhaps impossible to translate into English; in any case the expression 'secularity' is inadequate.

Part 3:
Broadening the English Perspective

Roman Catholicism and the Welfare Society: Catholic Ideas and Welfare Institutions after Labour[1]

FRANCIS DAVIS

The 2010 Papal Visit to England and Scotland has been described as 'the highlight' of some Catholics' lives. In addition to pastoral events, state dinners and private meetings it comprised a number of addresses in which the Holy Father exhorted those present to pay particular attention to the twin demands of 'reason' and 'faith'. A year later, in September 2011, Archbishop Vincent Nichols returned to these themes again claiming 'reason' and 'faith' as the ground of a common good. Speaking at Birmingham University on the occasion of the tenth anniversary of the city's faith leaders group he went further still citing these two complementary themes as essential to the very heart of a shared commitment to social action. But how might 'ideas' gain 'traction' in a rapidly changing environment? And how fit is the Catholic community for such a purpose?

This chapter explores aspects of the thorny question of the embodiment, the practice, of Episcopal calls to civic virtue. It draws on new research. First, I describe some of the sensitive issues that researching the Catholic community throws up not least for researchers who come from that community. Second, I summarise the findings of three recent inter-related studies. Finally I draw out some questions that this exploratory research may suggest for the case of the English Roman Catholic Church[2] in particular as it seeks to discern its relations with the 'welfare state' and 'the big' or 'welfare society ' in the Cameron/Clegg years and beyond.[3]

English Roman Catholicism: A Note of Caution

The public history, role and civic contribution of the Roman Catholic community in England and Wales is highly contested academic territory. [4]That contestation is not reduced by reference to the still relatively tiny body of empirical work carried out on the community's habits, policies and attitudes since the 'restoration' of the English Episcopal hierarchy in 1850.[5]

Consequently, while rhetorical appeals may be made by some Catholic community leaders to the 'recusant', 'Brideshead convert', 'Irish' and new 'East European migrant' strands in English Catholic life the huge variations in physical resources, geographical location, political access, social class , educational attainment and numbers that these represent(ed) may be more empirically opaque notwithstanding their metaphorical significance to some. Indeed I have argued elsewhere that the instinctive Catholic reach for 'metaphor', untested by evidence, can enhance this opacity and may even cause a profound confusion between the 'is' and the 'ought' in the assessment of the community's position and its social context.[6]

Even when the effort is made to gather an evidence base to inform Catholic reflection the task may not be as simple as at first it may seem. Fr Andrew Greeley, for example,[7] has reported criticism of his studies from Church leaders when the findings have uncovered personal convictions among lay Catholics which do not conform to formal Church teaching. It would be better, his critics have suggested, to repeat the studies until the 'right' answer has been found (despite rigorous sampling techniques) than to publish findings that may cause scandal, or that come from those who have an 'axe to grind' (no matter their academic standing). Similarly, even in Britain and Ireland, the decades since the Second Vatican Council have seen a study of the needs of Irish migrants suppressed,[8] a study of the 'Renew' process in the Diocese of Arundel and Brighton met with 'concern',[9] and reported laments of the ethnic chaplains about their position in London treated with resistance [10]

English Roman Catholicism: A Context

An awareness of episcopal caution in this regard is important for in the three years up to the appointment of Vincent Nichols as Archbishop of Westminster, and President of the Catholic Bishops' Conference of England and Wales, British Catholic advocacy took on a new urgency in its form and tone.[11] Opposing the proposed quotas for non-religious pupils in religious schools, the extension of legal rights to members of the gay community regarding adoption, the liberalisation of embryology and a possible change of law on abortion, key Bishops attempted with force to secure 'opt outs' from political discipline and public policy proposals arguing that they represented a threat to the moral life of their community, the health of the Catholic voluntary sector and an articulation of the virtues of 'the common good'. Proposing 'regularisation' for (im)migrants without legal papers to be resident in the UK, they named the plight of refugees, asylum seekers and migrants as a political and pastoral priority for the Church, and the nation too. [12]

Throughout this period a striking feature of the Catholic Church's manifestation of its civic presence were the very public voices of its senior Bishops. They claimed to speak 'on behalf' and 'in the name' of the Catholic community. While this may not surprise those familiar with Roman Catholic theology such a position takes on political overtones by providing a clear and central network of authority and representation for the Church in relation to the state's governance in these key areas. Such a node point of representation is largely absent in other faith communities[13] and thus, in an era of exhortation to 'social cohesion',[14] is doubly notable.

But whereas the Bishops may ground such public authority in a theological reasoning their public utterances also give rise to a form of civil accountability whether it is sought or not. Political conversation is at least a two way process and the Bishops were engaged in making specific proposals. Consequently, in a liberal democracy the ability of the Bishops to evidence some of their principles and positions becomes a matter of legitimate public interest.; indeed even a matter of the authenticity of 'reason' and what is judged to be 'reasonable'. These in turn can have a public impact on the credibility of ecclesial voices notwith-standing theological claims to legitimation. How significant then is the Catholic civic contribution? How 'cohesive' are it schools? Are its resources being redistributed from the top to the bottom of society rather as it suggests the state should do?

Later, in 2010 the Bishops themselves seemed to take aspects of this conundrum on board. The English Bishops Department for Christian Responsibility and its Caritas Social Action Network published a 'snapshot of the Church's social welfare contribution. However, the presen-tation of the figures—which were intended to clarify credibility—raised fresh questions again suggesting as they did that Catholic prison chaplains visited more prisoners every year than were found in the entire prison system; and that some Catholic charities had client loads in proportion to other resources that were up to 300% more effective than even award-winning secular counterparts. The need for extended research to underpin Catholic reflection could not have been clearer.

Three Studies of Exploration

During 2008 and 2009 we undertook three inter-related but separately commissioned studies. In the first, we surveyed one thousand five hundred Church going Catholics as to their attitudes to relationships, and their knowledge and understanding of key aspects of Catholic teaching. In the second study we sought to map the contribution to care and advocacy of Catholic institutions in the field of migration, refugees and asylum seekers. This was deemed especially important given the major public stand that the Catholic Bishops had taken in this area. This study included a phone interview with three quarters of the area Deans nation-wide[15], communications with every Bishop, and approaches to regional agencies and local projects. Lastly, we carried out an in - depth research enquiry into the work and current profile of one of the very largest Catholic voluntary organ-isations. The Bishops' advocacy had, after all, been at least partly an attempt to protect the 'unique' factors that such bodies were said to bring to society.[16] While it is not possible, in a single chapter, to describe the findings fully the overarching patterns that began to emerge were signif-icant.

First, in our survey of Mass going Catholics, we discov-ered that while 84% of those who replied said that they would attend Mass weekly,[17] their offspring had much less regular patterns of attendance. Of those who had at least one child under 18, 55 per cent indicated that their children attended Mass once a week, another 23 per cent attended almost every week, 7 per cent once a month, and another 7 per cent on major feast days and/or several times a year. Confession, now often called the Sacrament of Reconcilia-tion, and a cornerstone of traditional Catholic observance, had little place in many people's lives.

Despite these quite high levels of Eucharistic practise the knowledge of formal Church teaching — or a willingness to conform to its precepts — was low. Only 26% said that they were 'fully aware' of the Second Vatican Council. Nearly half of those who responded were unaware of *Humane Vitae* [18]while half had no awareness of the English Catholic Bishops' previous major advocacy initiative entitled *'The*

Common Good And The Catholic Church's Social Teachings'.
[19]Given the formal public opposition to all abortion by the Bishops it was perhaps most notable that 15% of this Catholic sample 'wouldn't mind' using the morning after pill, and 10% already had done so, despite the fact that in formal Catholic eyes this acts as a concrete action of termination. A full 68.8% were using condoms in direct contravention of formal Catholic policy.

Turning from individual responses to the formal institutions of the Church our findings with regard to the Church's actual engagement in the field of migration, refugees and asylum were equally notable.

For example, it became clear that new patterns of demographic change effect all Dioceses nationally. Table 1 shows this clearly. This table reports the number of Deans who said, across England and Wales, that these topics were now impacting upon their work and life. For ease of reference the Deaneries are tabulated alongside the Diocese in which they are located.

However, the local expression of need did not tally with local responses: In the parishes 10% of Deans expressed 'no interest' in the topic while at least a third reported themselves as thinking negatively, or having had negative experiences, with regard to the new arrival communities. In some areas, for example Wales, objective need was very high but the practical response of the Church had been very low. While in some Dioceses, such as Westminster, meaningful action was taking place, it was still outstripped by need and comprised a very small proportion of ecclesiastical resources and assets invested in all activities despite the public assertion that this was a 'priority' area on the part of the Bishops. In a nation where migration is set to rise despite Prime Minister Cameron's attempt to impose a 'cap' on numbers, this makes notable reading.

Table 1

Diocese	Deaneries with significant presence of migrant groups †
Arundel & Brighton	4 out of 9
Birmingham	14 out of 17
Brentwood	10 out of 12*
Cardiff	5 out of 7
Clifton	11 out of 13
East Anglia	5 out of 8
Hallam	4 out of 5
Hexham & Newcastle	11 out of 16
Lancaster	5 out of 9
Leeds	14 out of 42**
Liverpool	13 out of 17
Menevia	3 out of 6
Middlesbrough	5 out of 9
Northampton	6 out of 8
Nottingham	8 out of 10
Plymouth	3 out of 4
Portsmouth	15 out of 24
Salford	8 out of 12
Shrewsbury	2 out of 4
Southwark	16 out of 20*
Westminster	15 out of 19
Wrexham	4 out of 6

† = Based on the number of deaneries from which we were able to get a response.
* = Based on interviews with diocesan representatives.
** = Based on interviews with parishes.

Seeking further data we turned to the Catholic Church's flagship voluntary agencies but here too the response was no more extensive: Two agencies—both small, and both in central London, had had to restructure their services to meet overwhelming demand from new arrivals. Nevertheless, only two other agencies nationally reported that half or more of their work was alongside migrants, refugees and asylum seekers. The largest agencies in the country use only 25% of their revenues in this client group area with only the St Vincent De Paul Society (SVP) reporting an active 'increase' in the range of services provided to migrants, refugees and asylum seekers. Even so, this still only represented 1% of the SVPs total expenditure.

A factor in this limited response to new needs was the high dependency of the Catholic bodies surveyed on statutory income streams. In some cases they were as high as 70%. Given that statutory funds in the migration, asylum, and refugee field are scarce this suggested limitations on the potential to innovate and a structural constraint too (not of the government's making) on any likely attempt by agencies, currently undertaking high levels of other work, to broaden their service provision. Overall then action, advocacy and provision was, at the least, patchy and would be sorely tested if the Catholic voluntary sector entered a period of public sector retrenchment.

Our third study sought to tease out how challenges may be constrained or affirmed by the issues faced by particular organisational factors. To achieve this we agreed to undertake an in-depth study of a charity that in this chapter I shall call *Angel*.[20]

Angel's self-description of its role and purpose is to be a 'Catholic organisation which is at the service of the whole community', and which seeks to relieve poverty. In pursuit of this aim it recruits 'thousands' of volunteers though local parishes. *Angel* has also established a number of special and professionalised social welfare projects across the country which employ paid staff, and are funded by a mixture of statutory, foundation and national lottery funds to 'provide services to users of all backgrounds.' They include community enterprises, recycling projects, and residential provision for those who have found themselves homeless.

Over the last three years *Angel* has stepped up its own public role, enhanced its claims to be available to all, begun new work to establish branches in Catholic schools, and this process culminated in parliamentary receptions to promote its work to which MPs and Peers of all backgrounds were invited. Indeed, among *Angel's* patrons was one of the Archbishops most publicly associated with national media advocacy against the Labour reforms that had so upset senior Bishops. As such *Angel* is a useful exemplar when it comes to assessing Catholic-welfare state interfaces and the health of the community's civic action. This is especially the case when we turn to the evidence gathered within the organisation.

First, we discovered that the bulk of *Angel's* clients are aged in the 60 to 75 age group. Figure 1 shows the relative distribution of clients across age bands.

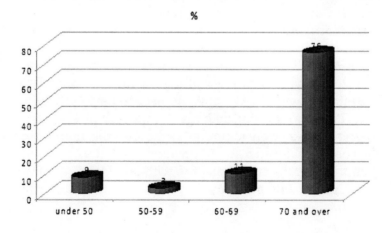

Figure 1: Age of the Angel beneficiaries (%)

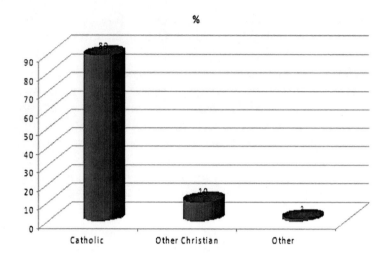

Figure 2: Religion of clients

Figure 2 gives us further information by adding to an understanding of the age profile of *Angel's* clients and a knowledge of their religious affiliation. The chart reveals a clear client concentration among Roman Catholics with only 1% of all clients coming from beyond the Christian community as a whole despite *Angel's* diverse—and diversity encouraging—funding base.

However, this is not an un-needy group of people. More than half reported physical illness with just under 50% saying they were 'lonely' and had needed help with 'basic jobs'. Perhaps reflecting their age profile a full 94% said that *Angel's* workers were important to them for the 'friendship' they offer, followed by their 'practical help'. It would seem then that *Angel's* engagement is with an elderly and frail client group but a highly Catholic and almost wholly Christian one.

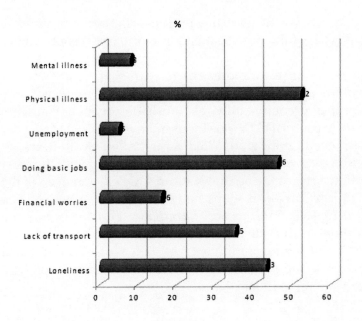

Figure 3: Responses to the question: Which of the following do you experience?

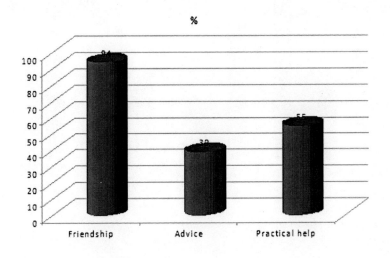

Figure 4: Does Angel provide you with help on the following?

When we turn to the profiles of *Angel's* volunteers themselves the organisation's rhetoric of diversity comes under further pressure. 63% of all volunteers have been active in *Angel* for more than 10 years with a quarter of all volunteers active for more than 25. What is more, not only are they predominantly religiously observant as Catholics but, in contrast to the one thousand five hundred Mass goes surveyed for the study cited earlier, *Angel's* volunteers are strongly aware of spiritual figures associated with the relief of poverty, of the Second Vatican Council, and even of the English Catholic Bishops statement *The Common Good And The Catholic Church's Social Teachings*. Perhaps even more striking is the extent that they stay involved as a manifestation of their commitment ' to their parish', to 'spiritual reading' and their own search for friendship. 65% of them are in long term marriages.

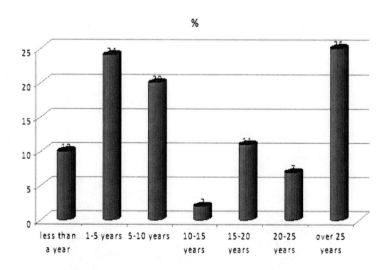

Figure 5: How long have you volunteered for Angel?

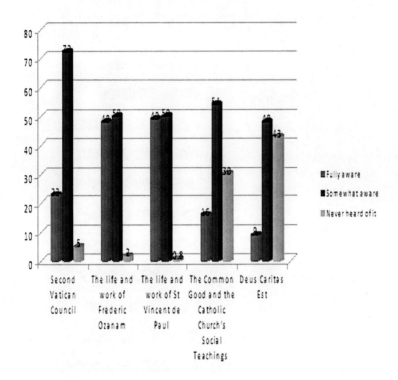

Figure 6: How aware are you of the following?

Of the organisation's paid staff 47 out of the 55 who replied said they would recommend working for the organisation while there was an almost uniform clarity of purpose to 'alleviate poverty' for all those in need. As with respondents to other surveys of Christian charities half consider their project 'unique' with a quarter suggesting they are 'better' than 'similar' voluntary sector bodies.[21]

In (Catholic) schools, despite rhetoric of modernisation on the part of the organisation, those who have not signed up to its groups said that they thought *Angel* 'a bit old fashioned', 'not really seen in the best light', or as 'admirable but basically the God squad'.

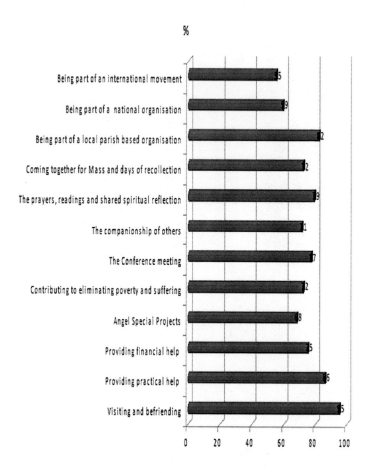

%

Being part of an international movement
Being part of a national organisation
Being part of a local parish based organisation
Coming together for Mass and days of recollection
The prayers, readings and shared spiritual reflection
The companionship of others
The Conference meeting
Contributing to eliminating poverty and suffering
Angel Special Projects
Providing financial help
Providing practical help
Visiting and befriending

0   20   40   60   80   100

Figure 7: Reasons for being part of Angel

Meanwhile, all the Bishops we surveyed expressed 'strong approval', an affirmation of the agency's work with 'the youth, the migrant and the elderly' and thought that there was much hope for the future.

Notwithstanding such affirmation Catholic parliamentarians were less enthusiastic with regard to *Angel*'s work. Surveying all Catholic MP's our response rate was high and so it was notable that all were aware of its activities, but not a single parliamentarian thought it 'an effective agent for social change.'

Conclusion

Taken together the three studies that I have described in summary here form one of the largest exploratory empirical research enquiries ever undertaken within the English Roman Catholic community.[22] Drawing as they do on findings at the end of the Labour era, and in a period of increased public stridency on the part of the Bishops that I referred to earlier, they also set the backdrop for the renewed English episcopal call to social responsibility following the Papal Visit and not least the context for the ears, hearts and institutions to which part of the exhortation to 'reason' and 'faith' with which I started are addressed.

A number of vital questions seem to emerge from the research. These are of significance for the English Roman Catholic Community in particular but may also suggest avenues for further enquiry for other denominations as ageing (and immigration) change the shape of British Christianity more generally.

First, a disjunct has emerged between the Church leadership's view of itself, its understanding of its public legitimacy, and the convictions of those ('the members')who may be said to give their words democratic weight or legitimation in a liberal democracy. While for Bishops this divergence between those people surveyed in parishes, and their own 'formal' positions, may suggest the need for renewed catechesis, harsher Church discipline, or simply be a matter of theological interest its demonstration effect to wider civil society and decision makers could risk undermining all Episcopal utterances.

Second, this mismatch of words and convictions between the Episcopal and the parochial level is matched by a further disjunct between an expressed priority of 'The Church' nationally and the actual number of people hours and proportion of financial resources being allocated to that priority. As we have seen when it comes to the pastoral and social needs of migrants, refugees and asylum seekers the Catholic Church in England and Wales could be responding more consistently than thus far it has found itself able to. Again, public legitimacy and institutional authenticity is at stake in the context of public deliberation in a liberal democracy.

Last, the case of *Angel* points to the possibility of underlying demographic trends that could compound the first two patterns: *Angel* represents a large and loved Catholic voluntary agency which exists for the whole community. Based on our research though it has become neither and thus finds its members diverging from the new outlooks of parishioners in the parish life that its members hold dear and the needs of the wider neighbourhoods for whom its receives statutory, foundation and lottery funding. Indeed, *Angel's* elderly, and intensely devout Catholic volunteers, may receive so much episcopal approval because they are more akin in social and ideological profile to the kind of Catholics that Bishops globally might wish for in their parishes as opposed to those that we found in the parish study. Such a 'purer' Church—larger and elderly or, later, young and small may have theological attractions but will likely have reducing institutional capacity to concretise principles in action for a good wider than the Church's own.

This exploratory group of studies of the English Roman Catholic case may suggest contrasting patterns: Indeed, it may just be that at the very moment that the English Roman Catholic Bishops have found their public voice to engage in debates about 'civic virtue', 'social responsibility' and even very specific proposals on migration, abortion, embryology and equalities legislation, and are calling upon 'reason and 'faith' to shape the mission of their people and institutions, that the chairs are falling out from underneath them in terms of parish solidarity, the profile of their activists and the ability to match any public exhortation and words to practical actions and habits.

For a theological call to the 'common good' this may have no impact on the authenticity of such an exhortation, nor its significance. However, if such research findings were repeated in wider and deeper studies they would in due course likely raise significant questions as to the fitness for purpose of Catholic institutions to respond in deed as well as word, and to act as a means by which ideas of 'reason' and 'faith' can be sustained. Ideas, as George Weigel often says, 'must have consequences'. In turn such a discovery may require a fresh approach on the part of both the Church and government as the former loses some weight/legitimation in the public square while the latter moves on to seek out civic allies embodying the social capital and habits that European societies in an era of austerity will so desperately need. To say so may be perceived as risky in some quarters but without risk mission, it could be argued, rarely endures.

Notes

[1] For other studies of the Christian interface with New Labour see, for example, P. Manley Scott et al (2009) *Remoralizing Britain?: Social, Ethical and Theological Perspectives on New Labour* (Continuum) by Peter Manley Scott (Author, Editor), Christopher Baker (Editor), Elaine L. Graham (Editor) and and M. Chapman (2008) *Doing God Religion And Public Policy in Brown's Britain* (DLT).

[2] England and Wales is used deliberately representing as it does a single Catholic administrative unit known as a Bishops' Conference, in this case comprising 22 Dioceses. Scotland and Ireland have their own Episcopal Conferences.

[3] The full versions of these studies are available from the author on lascasas@bfriars.ox.ac.uk. They comprise *The Tablet Survey* published in part over two weeks in June 2009, see http://www.thetablet.co.uk/article/11769; J. Stankeviciute, F. Davis and J. Rossiter (2009) *A National Mapping Of the Roman Catholic Church's Work in England and Wales with Migrants, Refugees And Asylum Seekers* Caritas/Von Hugel Institute; J. Rossiter, J. Stankeviciute and F. Davis (2008), 'A Study of *Angel*' Von Hugel Institute.

4   For example, V. Alan McClelland and Michael Hodgetts (1999) *From Without the Flaminian Gate: 150 Years of Roman Catholicism in England and Wales 1850–2000* (London: Darton, Longman and Todd Ltd.) and M. Hornsby-Smith 2000 *Catholics In England 1850-2000- Historical and Sociological Perspectives* (London: Cassells).

5   See, for example, the work of Kieran Flanagan http://www.bristol.ac.uk /sociology/staff/kieranflanagan.html; Michael Hornsby-Smith (Surrey), http://www.soc.surrey.ac.uk/staff/mhornsby-smith/index.html, and A. Archer (1985) *The Two Catholic Churches: A Study In Oppression* SCM.

6   F. Davis (2001) *A Political Economy Of The Catholic Church* in N. Tiims and K. Wilson (eds.) *Authority and Governance in the Catholic Church* (SPCK).

7   See A. Greeley (2001) The Catholic Imagination Univ Of California Press and http://www.agreeley.com/booklist.html, but also F. Davis (2009) *Editorial : Religion Third Sector, Policy And Public Management* in Public Money And Management Vol 29,6 Routledge.

8   This occurred in the early seventies and was Reported by the Pastoral Research Centre to the Newman Association Conference 2009.

9   The 'concern' came from the then local Ordinary and his Vicar General in conversations with the present author. See M. Hornsby-Smith (1995), *The Politics of Spirituality: A Study of a Renewal Process in an English Diocese* (Oxford: Clarendon Press).

10 This was a part of the 2008 report *The Ground Of Justice: A pastoral research enquiry into the needs of migrants,* Von Hugel Institute (www.rcdow.org) that caused some ire. A subsequent study by the University of Middlesex, funded by the Catholic Bishops Conference Secretariat, that identified similar concerns among the chaplains is still to be widely circulated.

11 Archbishop Nichols was appointed Archbishop of Westminster on 3 April 2009, and subsequently, President of the Bishops' Conference.

12 For example, Catholic Bishops of England And Wales (2008) *Mission of The Church To Migrants In England and Wales* (CTS) and, earlier, calls from Cardinal Murphy-O'Connor for regularisation. See A. Ivereigh (2009/Oct to Dec) *Into The Light: The Strangers Into Citizens Story* in *Crucible* (SCM).

13 See F. Davis et al, *Moral, But No Compass: Government, Church and the Future of Welfare* (Chelmsford: Matthew James, 2008).

14 See Rt Hon John Denham MP *Faith And Government* http:// www.iengage.org.uk/component/content/article/1-news/592-government-and-faith-communities-speech-by-john-denham-mp.

[15] A Dean is the lead Priest for an area normally including around six local parishes.

[16] See, for example, the commentary of James Hanvey SJ, a key advisor to the Bishops: J. Hanvey, 'Charity which makes the Difference' in *Charity which makes the Difference* (London: Heythrop Institute for Religion, Ethics & Public Life, 2008), pp. 7–26.

[17] Weekly Mass attendance is the formal minimum observance.

[18] The official Papal Encyclical whereby the traditional Roman Catholic prohibition of artificial contraception was reaffirmed. For more detail (and the fall out) see P. Kearney (2009) *Guardian Of The Light: Denis Hurley—Renewing The Church And Opposing Apartheid* (Edinburgh/London: T and T Clark /Continuum).

[19] Catholic Bishops of England and Wales (1997) *The Common Good And The Catholic Church's Social Teachings* (London: CBCEW).

[20] *Angel* is a *nom de plume* given to the organisation in order to make it anonymous, in so far as is possible.

[21] Again this was regularly stated by those we interviewed for *Moral, But No Compass*.

[22] Although an even larger one will be completed for CAFOD's market research programme in late 2009. See www.cafod.org.uk.

The State and the Christian Voluntary Sector: The Challenge of Totalitarianism

Stephen Morgan

Praised be Jesus Christ, now and forever. Amen.

I was, some months ago, talking to a friend of mine about the nature and extent of the modern British state: about its involvement, I might even say interference, in the entirety of the lives of its citizens. When I had finished, she said to me that she thought that I was a pretty unreconstructed eighteenth century Tory, who felt that as long as the British Government stopped the French invading, they had done all that could be reasonably asked of them. It was, of course, a caricature of my views but, as with all the best caricatures, it had more than a grain of truth to it and it takes me to what I want to argue in this chapter. Because I am becoming ever more convinced that for the Christian Voluntary Sector, in fact for the Christian, the reach of the modern state in Britain, and in much of the developed world, has become so extensive as to be a serious danger to religious freedom and specifically to religious freedom of action. This thesis is by no means novel and I am unlikely to be able to give it anything more than a very sketchy treatment in this short paper. Nevertheless, I want to suggest that the combination of technology, a dogmatic secularist view of morality and a conception of the state as all encompassing has created what is, in fact, tantamount to a totalitarian view of the state. It may be a liberal, capitalist, democratically legitimated totalitarian state but it is one whose tentacles reach into virtual all aspects of life and which has an appetite for control that is ever the equal of those totalitarian regimes whose activities so blighted the twentieth century. I want further to argue that this should be of particular concern to the Christian Voluntary Sector because of the very nature of Christian Charity and its Christological foundations. Finally, I want to ask some questions about how the Christian Voluntary Sector should respond to the challenges this position poses. But I should warn you that in this matter, at least, I am an unrelieved pessimist.

First, however, a word about the charity with which I am primarily involved. The Portsmouth Diocesan Trust is the charitable trust through which the Catholic Church in the Diocese of Portsmouth operates. The diocese covers the Channel Islands, the counties of Hampshire, the Isle of Wight, Berkshire, and those parts of Berkshire which Ted Heath gave to Oxfordshire. From Oxford south of the River in the North to Jersey in the South: from Windsor to Portsmouth, from Bournemouth to Faringdon, we have 158 churches, 171 other properties—both residential and functional, 56 schools, 328 full-time and part-time employees and just over 150 priests and deacons, serving a Catholic population of approximately 130,000, of whom we see just over 38,000 each week and about 55,000 at least once a month. We have a total annual income of about £14million. I am the Secretary to the Diocesan Trustees and the Bishop's Financial Secretary. In this role, I am close to what the Charity Commission would see as the charities' Chief Executive but because of the enormous authority vested in a Catholic Bishop by the Church's teaching and canon law, quite properly the real authority rests very largely with him. Some of you may know of Talleyrand's dictum that 'to have all of the power and none of the responsibility is the morality of the whore'. In my role, I have, at least it regularly seems so, all of the responsibility and none of the power: what that makes me—or for that matter my Bishop—is something that bears further careful thought. Well enough of that—on with the argument.

It is fairly well established that the size and reach of the modern state is quite unlike anything ever seen in human society previously. From consuming about 15% of national income at the beginning of the twentieth century, by the close of that century, the British state consumed something in the order of 45% of GDP. Nearly one in four of the working population were employed by the state in its national or local manifestations and fully one in five of all households were dependent to a greater or lesser extent upon it for some portion of their income. The state controls 75% of all schools—and funds in whole or in part virtually all of them, it controls 80% of all medical expenditure,and it funds 85% of all academic research in the humanities and over 50% in science and technology. Its reach and influence are immense. I don't for one minute want to suggest that this is, in itself, necessarily a bad thing, but I do want to suggest that there are, in such a situation, inherent dangers and that, because of the sheer weight of this economic muscle and the ubiquity of the State's reach, the tendency towards absolutism and totalitarianism is almost irresistible. I also want to suggest two factors that exacerbate the problem. The first is that of the almost exclusive state control of education, health and social services in Britain—in contradistinction to most of our European neighbours, where the voluntary sector and specifically the Christian voluntary sector is a much more significant service provider. The second a constitutional settlement that has, for nigh on five hundred years, recognised for all practical purposes, no higher moral authority than that of the state—whether it be an absolute monarchy of a modern so-called liberal democracy. I believe that because of these two things, we are now facing a profound and acute crisis.

I want to suggest that none of this would be a problem for the Christian Voluntary Sector or for the Christian, if it weren't for two things: first, an aggressive secular liberalism which drives a 'rights' based agenda that I believe is grounded in what is at best a desire, through ignorance or antipathy to privatise religious belief and action, and is at worst a profoundly illiberal anti-religious sentiment; and, second, because for the Christian, and therefore *a fortiori* for the Christian Voluntary Sector, because of who Christ is, religious belief and practice are so inherently linked with action, that to talk of one necessarily implies the other. Indeed, Sacred Scripture says as much in the Epistle of St James: 'For as the body apart from the spirit is dead, so faith apart from works is dead' (Jm 2:26).

To hold the government of the United Kingdom, or of any western liberal democracy, to the charge of totalitarianism is a serious business. The experience of the twentieth century tells us that totalitarianism, whether of the left or the right, has been responsible for an almost unspeakable catalogue of human misery, whether it be the racist lunacy of the Holocaust or the sheer indifference to human life that lay at the heart of 50 million dead during Mao's 'Great Leap Forward'. To accuse Britain of anything remotely similar seems, at face value, to be to devalue the currency of the word 'Totalitarianism' itself. But I think not. Leaving aside, for the moment, the seven and a half million abortions in Britain since 1967 — evidence enough of what happens when the state presumes to define or redefine what it is to be a human, to set aside, by an act of legal positivism, the most fundamental of human rights — what characterises the Totalitarian state is the presumption of the absolute authority of the state to supremacy in all things. Recent developments in the UK seem to provide evidence of a creeping extension of the state into areas where previously individual freedom of conscience and action were presumed.

In the field of education this has been particularly evident. *Pace* Bishop Malcolm McMahon and the Catholic Education Service, but I simply don't buy the assurances that the Sex and Relationships Education provisions Parliament considered in early 2010 are no threat to Catholic Schools. They are, in fact, an unpardonable arrogation by the state of the rights of parents to be the primary educators of their children. The regulations, we were assured, would allow Sex and Relationships Education to be taught in Catholic schools in accordance with the 'Catholic Ethos' of the school but, says Mr Balls, that will not allow Catholic schools to opt out of advising children how to access contraceptive or abortion 'services'—a curious use of the word 'services' it seems to me, but there we are. Nor, for that matter, will Catholic schools be allowed to teach only the Catholic moral perspective, but must put before children the alternative view. Whilst that might be a worthwhile exercise in a course of apologetic, the moral confusion that it is likely to engender when attempting to teach sex and relationships education seems to me entirely regrettable, quite apart from the fact that a corresponding duty to put the Catholic perspective in State schools is entirely absent. This leaves a situation where, for example, my fifteen year old daughter can be excluded by her state school, as indeed she has been, from classes in Sex and Relationships Education when she expressed the view that the question of the morality of abortion doesn't only turn on the principle of a woman's right to choose but also on the question of at what point the child in the womb acquires the status of 'human life'. Or again, when she said that she thought that human sexual activity belongs only within marriage and that all other forms, heterosexual or homosexual are wrong. Whereas my thirteen year old son in a Catholic school will soon have to be taught that homosexual activity is, in Mr Balls' own words, 'normal and harmless' and that, should he wish to do so, he can access contraception by speaking to the staff of Connexions in the room at the end of the main corridor, where he will be given confidential advice that will enable him to commit what is a criminal offence and to behave in manner that my wife and I, those who will have to pick up the pieces, find entirely morally repugnant. Since the Coalition came to power in the 2010 General Election, despite a better climate of engagement, there appears as yet no indication that the assumptions underlying this kind of legislative intervention have disappeared from the scene.

The problems created by the legislation to outlaw discrimination on grounds of sexual orientation for the various Catholic adoption agencies are well known. It represents yet one more example of the creeping arrogation by the state of a right to direct morality and action which belongs not to that state but to the individual conscience. It isn't my purpose to examine the question of what constitutes discrimination, which if unfair is, of course, to be deplored, and what constitutes a properly responsible act grounded in conscience, but merely to ask this question: to what extent does the state have the right to compel me to act in manner that I find unconscionable or otherwise to constrain me from acting at all?

It is perhaps a relief that the Catholic Church in the UK has never been a major supplier of healthcare, but we see, in the controversies surrounding John and Lizzies and in the end of life issues surrounding both the withdrawal of nutrition and hydration and the use of, for example, the Liverpool Care Pathway, how the state has trespassed into the proper province of conscience, so that many Catholic medical professionals find themselves deeply challenged and living daily with the threat of compliance, compromise or conflict.

I do sometimes wish that the hot-button issues that so well illustrate my argument, at least so far as the UK is concerned, did not so revolve around personal moral, and often sexual, questions rather than, for example, the issues of development, justice, racism and labour rights that lie at the heart of the question of the status of illegal migrants in the US or of freedom to practice religion that is being seriously threatened in South Asia and parts of the Asia-Pacific. Nevertheless, they do go to the self-same question: that of the fundamental dignity of the human person and the rights of the state in respect to that individual. God in his infinite providence and mercy has put you and I here and now and it is the challenges of here and now that you and I have to face. We might thank God for a brief moment if we stop to consider what a gentle loving he has given us who, for the present, don't face quite the serious threats to life and liberty that our brothers and sisters in many parts of the world live with daily.

The genius of the modern secular democracy which lies at the heart of its success in extending its reach is in how it has subverted the very democracy it proclaims and in the use of language to reconfigure the moral landscape. I have to say that I am increasingly persuaded by the analysis of Professor John Keane at Westminster. In his latest book, *The Life and Death of Democracy*[1], he argues that we are witnessing the death of representative democracy and its replacement by what he calls 'monitory democracy', where scrutiny of both public and private actions lies not in open debate but in a vast collection of elected and unelected bodies, which have both the power and the appetite to recast society's moral norms. For those in the Christian Voluntary Sector, the most obvious manifestation of this is in the removal of the four hundred year old presumption of public benefit for religious charitable purposes in the 2006 Charities Act and the attendant requirement to demonstrate that they provide a public benefit in terms that can be 'justiciable', that is that can be assessed by the Charity Commission and the Courts. And here we come to the use of language.

'Public benefit' is an expression capable of wide interpretation and that interpretation falls to be provided by the Courts. So far, so good. But we live, within a judicial climate where a judge—and a practicing Catholic judge at that—in what was then the House of Lords could describe the argument put forward by the Church of Scotland to explain the relationship between the Church and a minister of religion as one which, in using language based on the concept of vocation, 'relied on redundant religious metaphor'. In such a climate, I would contend, expressions such as public benefit are nothing other than dangerous. Tolerance, diversity and community cohesion are similarly ill-defined words which really belong in linguistic realm of Humpty Dumpty, who, you will remember, told Alice that a word might mean whatever he wanted it to. Or perhaps to strike a more learned note: if Wittgenstein's 43rd aphorism in *Philosophical Investigations*[2] was right and 'the meaning of a word is its use in the language' then precisely these words can be used by those in positions of power to mean just whatever they want them to mean and can be used to whatever purpose those in power wish to turn them. In a representative democracy this is dangerous enough: in a 'monitory democracy' it is a time-bomb.

Euphemism is also used quite insidiously to advance this linguistic positivism. I have begun to notice how acts that might once have been described as 'wrong' are now routinely described as 'unacceptable', even 'totally unacceptable'. I even heard the murder of James Bulger described on the wireless as 'totally unacceptable'. What is 'acceptable' and what 'unacceptable' immediately begs the question 'acceptable to whom; unacceptable to whom?' In truth the use of these terms to replace 'right' and 'wrong' is a linguistic marker not of a moral compass that indicates a moral pole but of a moral thermometer that shows the moral temperature. It is the morality described with characteristic pithiness over sixty years ago by Mgr Ronald Knox as 'the morality of what will Jones stand'.

I have, I know, painted a bleak picture with colours perhaps too exaggerated and hinting at the sinister. Nevertheless, I am convinced that the picture bears a likeness to its subject and is, I believe a depressing one for the Christian Voluntary Sector. If the figure of Jesus Christ is but a comforting story, the implications of which can be relegated to the private sphere, then a pietistic approach might make this all just about bearable. If, however, Jesus Christ is alive and is the animating principle of love—now there's a word—of love, of caritas, of charity in which faith implies action and action faith, then we should ask ourselves how the creeping absolutism of the modern state leaves room for that love, that action, that 'faithed action' which is, for the Christian, the meaning of Charity.

What we are dealing with here is a challenge to the place of faith in the public square. I would argue that this amounts to the privatisation of belief and it is usually defended, as George Cardinal Pell writes: 'by referring to the importance of maintaining the public domain and public policy as *neutral* areas.' But as he goes on to say, 'this privatization does not favour neutrality. It is a way of silencing opponents and as such favours the dominant secular cultural identity.'[3] Indeed, far from being neutral, I would suggest that it is based on a doctrinaire secularism that is based on a denial of the existence or relevance of God that certainly no less a 'faith' statement, or, perhaps, as Lord Justice Scott might say 'redundant religious metaphor' than when you and I proclaim 'Jesus is Lord'.

I want to end with a voice from the 19th century and another from the 21st. Alexis de Tocqueville was the 19th century writer who commented on the French Revolution and on the young democracy of the United States. He foresaw very clearly the link between secular humanism and totalitarianism, even if he could hardly have foreseen the methods that would be used. He believed that the premises of secularism do not sustain democracy and liberty, but undermine it by advancing a moral relativism of belief and causing the inevitable decline in public and private morality that come close on its heels. The result, he said, would be 'a new, soft despotism, an imprisonment by a thousand silken threads.'[4] Such a despotism finds scant use and provides little space for the 'faithed action' of Christian Charity unless it is prepared to be imprisoned by those self-same silken threads, silken threads that increasingly permit the Christian Voluntary Sector to engage with the state or even to operate only on the state's terms, terms which are cast, ever more strongly, in the alloy of the state's secular, absolutist, totalitarian self-conception. The final word might reasonably be given to Pope Benedict XVI. In his address to Parliament, given in Westminster Hall, he reminded the British nation, with the first-hand insight of one who had lived under a genuinely totalitarian regime that there are proper limits to the activity of the state and that for the state's action to be moral, even in its proper sphere the voice of faith and the place of 'faithed action' must be respected:

> Religion... is not a problem for legislators to solve, but a vital contributor to the national conversation. In this light, I cannot but voice my concern at the increasing marginalization of religion, particularly of Christianity, that is taking place in some quarters, even in nations which place a great emphasis on tolerance. There are those who would advocate that the voice of religion be silenced, or at least relegated to the purely private sphere...there are those who argue—paradoxically with the intention of eliminating discrimination—that Christians in public roles should be required at times to act against their conscience. These are worrying signs of a failure to appreciate not only the rights of believers to freedom of conscience and freedom of religion, but also the legitimate role of religion in the public square.[5]

Notes

[1] John Keane, *The Life and Death of Democracy* (London: Simon and Schuster, 2009).

[2] Ludwig Wittgenstein, *Philosophical Investigations* (trans. G. Elizabeth Anscombe) (New York: 1953).

[3] George Cardinal Pell, *God and Caesar:: Selected Essays on Religion, Politics and Society* (Sydney: Connor Court Publishing, 2007), p. 55

[4] Alexis de Tocqueville, *Democracy in America*, (Chicago: Chicago University Press, 2000), p. 424

[5] Pope Benedict XVI, *Address to Politicians, Diplomats, Academics and Business Leaders, given at Westminster Hall* (17 September 2010).

Spiritual advocacy in England?
The overlapping roles of chaplains and advocates

GEOFF MORGAN

Introduction

In this chapter I aim to present an integrated model of advocacy practice based on spiritual and cultural aspects of the qualitative study on which it is based. A comparison between groups (between advocates and service users, and especially between chaplains and advocates) could highlight aspects of the broad advocacy role and how attitudes to the practice complement each other. Although the article in principle covers qualitative research, contrasts between spiritual care coordinators or chaplains and advocates may be enhanced by some relevant figures. In relation to numbers of full-time equivalent (FTE) chaplains, recent figures showed that at the beginning of 2010 there were around 425 full time, and approximately 3000 part time chaplains employed by the National Health Service. In addition there were 'numerous volunteer chaplains of all denominations and faiths' (Hospital-Chaplaincies-Council 2010, p. 5).

Against this, it was more difficult to discover numbers of FTE advocates because it is not known exactly how many services there are nationally. This, according to Martin Coyle, Head of Quality and Development at Action for Advocacy, is because there is 'no obligation for groups to record or report this data', which would include the number of volunteer and of part-time advocates. Also, there are a number of organisations who say their work includes advocacy where the services listed do not appear to reflect this appropriately, and vice versa, a few who may be providing advocacy without describing it as such. However, on the basis that every local authority in England (and Wales) must provide the statutory services of Independent Mental Capacity Advocates (IMCAs) and Independent Mental Health Advocates (IMHAs) and an aggregation of numbers of advocates depending on known provider organisations, the following figures emerge.

With approximately 600–800 advocacy organisations in the country, an educated estimate would suggest an average of 8 advocates per group, and this would indicate a total number in the range of 4800–6400. It was also unclear what effect the variable of volunteer advocates would have on this number, in the same way as it was for chaplains.

There is not a definitive list of trained IMHAs or IMCAs — which must be provided in every Local Authority, but estimates of the number of trained IMCAs tend to be around 500. It would be reasonable to assume a similar number for IMHAs, according to Coyle (2010) although commissioning patterns across the country makes this assumption unclear (Coyle 2010).

Therefore it is possible to view the number of 425 full-time and 3000 part-time paid chaplains alongside at least 4800 full-time paid advocates, with the further possibility that there may be up to 1000 more, when IMCA and IMHA numbers are taken into account. On this basis, paid advocacy activity could outweigh paid spiritual care practice in certain areas, and it is at least interesting — and with funding and commissioning pressures bearing down on chaplaincy and advocacy — to note the minimal spiritual or possibly 'pastoral' functions ('beliefs and values') which the Department of Health has now ascribed to the role of the IMCA, as we shall see below.

In the light of this arguable limited reconfiguration in pastoral practice within health and social care, the theme of a renewed social conscience and a Catholic reshaping of the social sciences will also frame the fruits of the research I want to share. I will seek to set 'independent advocacy' and 'spiritual care' alongside one another, conceding that this is not an obvious pairing. But I want to argue—alongside the possible rising numbers of advocates compared with chaplaincy provision—that the interface with spiritual carers could be enriching for both disciplines, and that it could provide a framework for the mutual recognition of secular and religious parties, whether volunteers or professionals, in a common response to the needs of the most socially vulnerable.

But let me now turn to advocacy. Amongst the diversity of roles which it embraces, the requirement for IMCAs and IMHAs, which passed into English and Welsh law in 2007 and 2009, underlined the growing significance of advocacy in health and social care and the emergence of these particular roles as occupations undergoing professionalisation. Growing out of the 'Patients' Rights' advocates' and the consumer and civil rights movements in the US of the 1970s (Mallik and Rafferty 2000), advocacy in health and social care sparked a debate about whether nurses could effectively advocate for their patients, or whether greater independence from the employing health provider was desirable (Ravich and Schmolka 1996; Bateman 2000; Llewellyn and Northway 2007). There was evidence that social workers and other practitioners were in a good position to 'advocate' for their clients (Mallik 1998); however advocacy was seen as a 'risky role to adopt' for nurses and not one which their career should embrace (Mallik 1997 pp. 130, 135). And if the 'central tenet of independence is missing from an advocacy relationship in which the advocate is also acting as a professional...' (Forbat and Atkinson 2005, p. 331), for a social worker it could also be problematic or bring them into conflict with their employers (Faust 2008, pp. 295–6; Gilbert 2010). Atkinson stated that the rejection of the professionalisation of the role of nurse-advocate by the nursing élite left a gap needing to be filled (Atkinson 1999). This was the gap which voluntary sector organisations, funded increasingly by central government, were to fill. Thus independent advocacy came to be separated from 'the system' in order to be better able to support and represent clients, patients or service users. The Department of Health described IMCA — a service for the 'un-befriended' — as the creation of 'a new form of advocacy, a new profession and a new safeguard'. (Dept.-of-Health 2008). Specifically in respect of safeguarding adults, there was a wider role for IMCAs since 'those who lack capacity who have family and friends can still have an IMCA… in… adult protection procedures' (Dept.-for-Constitutional-Affairs 2006, p. 198; see also Redley, Platten et al 2008). So far, so independent. But how should advocacy be defined?

Advocacy: voices to raise, rights to know, choices to face

Clearly much could be said in terms of legal and theological definitions of advocacy, e.g. 'one who pleads or speaks for another': the Shorter Oxford Dictionary, while it describes the legal process, also actually refers to the person of Christ in this context (Little, Fowler et al 1983). Rather, a pragmatic approach is taken below. The wide range of advocacy roles- from mental health to children's advocacy and other varied forms, which I cannot develop in detail here, whether citizen advocacy which is mostly performed by volunteers, or professional advocacy carried out by paid staff — this range calls for some kind of comprehensive definition, bearing in mind that nuances depend on the field and style of the expression. Atkinson (1999) as described it as 'speaking up', and writes that 'everyone, sooner or later, needs help in making their voice heard — and advocates are people who can provide the time and support to enable this to happen.' (Atkinson 1999, pp. 5–9; Henderson 2005, p. 206).

This help is provided in different modes: either as instructed or non-instructed advocacy. 'Instructed advocacy' describes activities which support those who can request or direct that support, or exercise choices in order to be able to 'speak up' for themselves. By contrast, 'non-instructed advocacy' focuses on individuals with disabilities or mental health issues, who are vulnerable or have been deemed to lack specific capacity and who therefore need specialist support (such as IMCA) in decision-making in their 'best interests.' In summary, independent advocacy happens when practitioners or volunteers are commissioned to support individuals to make choices, take decisions and secure rights and safeguards in relation to health, social care and housing, either on an instructed or non-instructed basis, as previously stated.

Advocacy as cultural and spiritual support

The Department of Health's asserted 'new profession' of IMCA advocates (Dept.-of-Health 2008) included the statutory responsibility to take into account 'any beliefs and values (e.g. religious, cultural, moral or political) that would be likely to influence the decision in question' (Dept.-for-Constitutional-Affairs 2006, pp. 20, 65), in accordance with the 'best interests' of a client. The Human Rights Act framework (specifically, Article Nine: Freedom of Conscience [Thought and Religion]) and the fact that public authorities uphold rights to 'manifest one's religion and beliefs'(Dept.-for-Constitutional-Affairs 2006) both locate a conduit for these principles to apply to independent advocacy.

This article is part of a larger study in which advocacy and spirituality are analysed, including a spiritual history of advocacy. Indeed there are distinctive views about the inception of advocacy: on the one hand it can be seen as arising in the 1970s, and in the post-modern context of de-institutionalisation, social rights and political activism

(Traustadóttir 2006; Thompson 2008). A longer view, as argued elsewhere (Morgan 2010), could take in the spiritual concerns of early mental health reformers such as Pinel and Perceval and apply these to a history of independent advocacy in terms—to use a theological model—of a 'preferential option' for the oppressed, if not for the poor (Pattison 1994).

Mental health, spirituality and advocacy — gaps in the literature

Increasing material has related religion and spirituality to health care and mental health, and to learning disabilities, (Fulford, Ersser et al 1996; Swinton 2001; Cornah 2006; Cox, Campbell et al 2007; Coyte, Gilbert et al 2008; Gilbert 2008). The growth of the special interest group in spirituality of the Royal School of Psychiatrists, which had a membership of 1900 in 2008 (RCPsych 2008), the appearance of new journals, such as *Anthropology and Medicine* and *Mental Health Religion and Culture*, in which authors discuss culture and healthcare and issues such as prayer and well-being, are indicative of a renewal of research interest (Foskett 2004; Maltby, Lewis et al 2008). My research sought to correlate advances in the rapport between mental healthcare and religion and spirituality with the increasing influence of independent advocacy.

Mapping projects have also begun to delineate the extent of the influence of advocacy initiatives (Carver and Morrison 2005; Forbat and Atkinson 2005; Foley and Platzer 2007; Coyle 2008). Tew (2003) wrote that a different value base will include people as active participants or partners in their own recovery (Tew, 2003, p. 24); in her account of user involvement, Wallcraft (2003) found that black people were marginalised and needed their own networks (Tew 2003; Wallcraft 2003, p. 29). Given a lack of an integrative, comprehensive study of advocacy practice, and in particular one which sought to illuminate and complete gaps with spiritual, cultural or theological dimensions in that practice,

I want to show that the longstanding work of generic mental health advocacy, as well as other statutory forms of advocacy, are improved through awareness and training in culture, spirituality and theology.

Methods

With the complete study in view, I produced, by means of interviews and questionnaires, a selection of informal views and opinions on advocacy practice from 4 data sources and 3 groups, namely advocates, spiritual care coordinators/chaplains and advocacy clients. The 41 respondents to interviews and questionnaires gave written permission before taking part; names and some details were changed to protect confidentiality. Initially I sought to use a grounded theory approach to write up the data and set out *in vivo* or 'live' phrases from interview participants coded, for example, by references to 'power' or 'equality'; I also explored a possible and partial 'ethnography' of advocacy although my methodology remained flexible to the purpose.

Qualitative data

Comparing the practices of advocates and spiritual care coordinators/chaplains:

The voice of the advocate

1.*'a bit of a mouthpiece'*

> In many cases communication may be a problem if (a client) comes from a different cultural background—an advocate who has more understanding of the language may talk on behalf of the person. (Zablon 2008, September 19)

Earlier we visited the definition of advocacy as 'providing time and support to enable voices to be heard.' In describing BME-specific advocacy services, Zablon, a spiritual care coordinator drew attention to the uses of cultural background and interpreting skills in the craft. There is a difference of opinion as to whether advocacy and interpretation can be a dual function, however (El Ansari, Newbigging et al 2009).

Questioned about the role and tasks of the advocate, the participant Janine elaborated further on the need for authenticity in communication:

> I see advocacy as trying to smooth the … communication process between service users and professionals … they feel they are just not listened to… even though as I say I'm the 'mouthpiece', … and I tell them it's their experience, not mine… and (they say), 'Ah, you will know how to put it better,' and (I say) 'No, it's not about me, it's about you…' (Janine 2007, October 1)

The term 'mouthpiece', which emerged in this interaction was counted as a 'live category' to be applied to many of the responses, such as 'advocating for people, supporting people, speaking on their behalf', which Fauzia drew out (Fauzia 2007, October 1). It is worth noting the different nuances of meaning I reported in comparing advocates whose role is to speak up for clients who cannot do so, with those who support clients to speak up for themselves. This is illustrative of the different styles—instructed and non-instructed advocacy—to which I alluded above.

2. Action based on Equality (ABE): *'like an equaliser'*

> You are a partner, an equal relationship… (Nebi 2007, October 22)

> I suppose the overall idea of an advocate is to be like an equaliser, is to try, with the people you are working with,… that they have an equal say, … and have access to their rights as though they didn't have

a disability or whatever it is that defines the client
group. (Sam 2008, February 13)

Another category which emerged as relevant to advocacy
roles and tasks was the term 'equaliser'. The notion that the
advocacy role consisted in ensuring equality was raised by
participants, Nebi and Sam, from different data sources.
The principle point of partnership and the need to conduct
a levelling exercise, as Sam described, were sharply
expressed by both participants. In terms of his advocating
for individuals from a religious and pastoral perspective,
Norman's views resonated with the above:

> I don't know how secular advocates would define
> their role but I would define it as one of solidarity,
> one of empowerment, one of levelling out the
> imbalances of power... (Norman and Colin 2008,
> September 11)

Earlier in the interview, Norman spoke of his role as picking
up advocacy functions, where no such service exists, 'in my
intuitive sort of way' (Norman and Colin 2008, September
11). This statement indicated the way in which the role of
an independent 'witness' (an expression with legal and
religious overtones, also used by this participant) is
employed in mental health, for example: while chaplaincy
services were viewed as independent by patients or clients,
advocacy services may have a more distinctive claim to be
so. In a comprehensive model of independent advocacy
practice, which arose in my broader study, I used the term
'action based on equality' (ABE) to summarise the rebalancing practice delineated above. In the quotation above, Sam
stressed the 'equal say' which she wanted clients to have,
who are often preferably designated 'partners'; she wanted
them 'to have access to their rights as though they didn't
have a disability'. The description and the actions, which
assert the rights of the 'partner' and address inequalities

both under the law and in terms of individual treatment, belong to the concept of ABE.

Voices of the advocate and client/ self-advocate

3. Reconstructed Empowerment (RE): 'it's so good, I'm powerful… I'm taking over your job'

> it's satisfaction when you get results and see someone quite happy. And, kind of, we don't have any power but we can empower them and I think, you know, that is why I continue doing my job. (Jana 2007, October 22)

> (Co-f = Co-facilitator)

> Co-f: How do you feel when you're in the group together? How does that make you feel?

> M: Good, good

> P: Talk to people, talk to them, have a good experience, make a good idea so people with learning disability can say things, people need friends, people need colleagues, people like us, it's so good, I'm powerful… I'm taking over your job (Laughter…) (Louise, Michael et al 2007, November 23)

It was revealing to note the positive connotations in the use of 'power-based' words by participants to explain their feelings when advocating from, or being supported in a position of powerlessness. In this second example, the speaker was acting as a spokesperson for 4 other self-advocacy group members. It demonstrated how the self-advocacy group had provided the opportunity for one of its members to express publicly (to me as a researcher and a complete stranger) how she was strengthened by the support from the group. These examples, amongst others, provided evidence for a 'spiritual' if not a theological approach to advocacy in which ego is subjected to client needs. Putting the client or self-advocate at the centre of decisions is a process I described as 'reconstructed empowerment' (RE). Jana's statement (above) that her motivation related to the 'satisfaction when you get results and see someone quite happy', followed by the problematic claim: 'we don't have any power but we can empower them', are relevant. While independent advocacy has progressed in occupying a clear space whereby decision makers have legally to take account of statutory advocates and there is some kind of power (e.g. with the IMCA role), in many areas (generic mental health advocacy) the actual power which advocates had was related to the potential in the relationship between the client (or 'partner') in the area they were being supported to negotiate, as well as to the validation of the advocacy function by professionals in the social work context. The way unpaid advocates used their space for their clients' advantage was striking:

> N: That's the reason the whole movement came about, that we're independent of it, we're not paid
>
> B: Yeah
>
> N... so we won't lose our job whatever we do...
>
> B: I've got to be honest if the choice came between following [name of organisation] party line and doing the best I could for the person, I'm going to go for the person. (Norah and Bella 2009, December 14)

In citizen advocacy, where the advocate may be a volunteer, there was a strong link with the partner which was divorced from the advocacy provider as some participants said they would put the relationship with the partner before loyalty to the organisation, as was the case with Bella (above). It was in these variations that the empowerment process was seen to be 'reconstructed' and constituted the description, RE.

Advocating behaviours and moral or religious motivation

Advocates interviewed only made an explicit connection on two occasions between their own practice and spirituality or religion, but as the researcher I noted implicit comparisons and contrasts between the two areas in the combination of interviews with advocates and spiritual care coordinators. These are made explicit in the narrative and link to principles of charitable behaviour in Judaeo-Christian and in Islamic theology. For example, the foundational injunction of the Torah, the Shema, to love God and one's neighbour as oneself (Bible: Deuteronomy 6:4–9; Mark 12:29–30), the practice of alms-giving (Zakat) in Islam, and the practical action of compassion exemplified in Christ's teaching in the parable of the Good Samaritan (Bible: Luke 10:25–37) were related in my study to the practice of advocacy. Although such a comparison may be anathema to some advocates and secularists, it may be acceptable when framed in terms of 'well-being', which was reflected in my wider study. Layard (2009), who does not hold theological views, noted the need for altruistic direction:

> We desperately need a social norm in which the good of others figures more prominently in our personal goals. (Layard 2009, September 14)

These factors contributed both humanistic and religious colouring to a picture of advocacy practice, including, for example, the statutory role of the IMCA acting for the 'unbefriended' — for those with no family or friends to support or represent them. In Christian theology and ethics, this sat with the pastoral and social activity described as 'pure religion' in supporting 'widows' and 'orphans' (James 1:27).

Advocates meeting 'cultural needs'; 'social needs'; and 'spiritual needs.'

Although they are technically independent, advocates could find themselves meeting broad social needs bordering on the spiritual; this would be included in the role which signposted clients on to other services, or which offered limited emotional support without setting out to do so. (see Janine 2007, October 1, ll.172–177). The assumption of the overall study is that there is a partial deficit in terms of the capacity of the current practice of independent advocates to reflect upon their role, to be totally clear in their approach, to gather usefully from existing theory and history in order to assemble a structural base for future development. I argue that principles of 'action based on equality' and 'reconstructed empowerment' induced from the qualitative study, would assist with this. Willingness by the devout participants and spiritual care coordinators I interviewed is contrasted with the National Secular Society which questioned whether the NHS should fund chaplaincy (see also the medical ethicist, Sokol 2009, who argued for the value of chaplaincy; BBC–News 2009, April 8; Gammell 2009, Feb 7). This stance can be viewed as a specific northern or western global cultural problem when large parts of the (sub-Saharan and Islamic) world (and parts of UK inner cities) depend culturally on spirituality or religion as part of a way of life (Gilbert and Nicholls 2003; Foskett, Marriott et al 2004). Does the fact, as we have seen above, that advocates may now be more widely deployed numerically than chaplains, mean that they will need to have broader cultural and spiritual understanding in order to support individuals to have their needs met holistically?

As a further example therefore, we consider an advocate who worked with refugees who had fled across the South China Sea, and had learnt their spiritual language. She noted that when they talked of ghosts and conversations with the dead, some were misdiagnosed as having schizophrenia. In fact, some professionals had been unaware of a tradition that a Chinese household (from Vietnam) appoints a separate room for the 'ghosts' of the families ancestors to inhabit and in which 'communion' can take place (Sam 2008, February 13).

Specific cultural knowledge and behaviour can improve understanding amongst clients and be spread by advocates: a Muslim, who wore a traditional beard and clothing, explained his method. When he and a colleague 'go to the wards together, some people approach her and others approach me; if they have religious beliefs, Muslim people might just approach me...' (Habib 2007, October 1). In other ways cultural religious symbols may make communication more difficult: another advocate who wore a 'headscarf', in her words, recounted being called a 'terrorist' by a patient/bystander on a ward; in yet another example, a Christian chaplain was told how he had not prayed hard enough and felt that this was because Pentecostal spirituality was seen by the patient to require a loud praying voice; the chaplain was more interested to talk with the client and felt slightly uncomfortable to pray on a ward rather than in a church or chapel (Fauzia 2007, October 1; Zablon 2008, September 19).

Advocacy clients themselves reported about a training session they had led to raise awareness of discrimination with the police (Louise, Michael et al 2007, November 23); another group related how they had spoken about religion in a 'culture group' as part of their self-advocacy. (Micky, Einstein et al 2008, May 14)

The intriguing advocacy role of religious professionals in providing a 'check on individuals' beliefs' was made clear by 3 examples from spiritual care coordinators. In one case a chaplain had to write in a patient's notes that his beliefs 'were consistent with his faith group'. In another hospital, a chaplain was asked if an individual had 'genuine religious ideas'. Not that such an interrogation was unknown in the Church herself, as the late Dominican Fr Edward Schillebeeckx could have testified (Stanford 2010).It may be that chaplaincy roles can be related to those of IMCAs in what they need to do in establishing the views, including the religious views, of clients whom they are supporting in their non-instructed roles. In another example, an advocacy client needed reassurance he was not 'psychotic' on account of the fact he had been praying to African gods. (Ruth 2007, November 21; Zablon 2008, September 19).

Examples of the social and spiritual support given by local churches to individuals recovering in the community were produced. In relation to a refugee, a consultant told a chaplain:

> what you've done is give this woman a family... people in the parish... have supported her incredibly well, and that's made a great deal of difference to her. (Bernard 2008, August 19)

With regard to spiritual needs, it was not straightforward to separate what were clearly spiritual or theological as opposed to cultural needs. One issue which was common in discussion with both Muslim and Christian participants was the phenomenon of 'possession' in relation to mental health.

> people got better... It was because they were being told that it was not them who were going mad, they got better, it was amazing, they made speeches saying, 'We are better...' (Fauzia 2007, October 1).

Another patient had told a chaplain that he felt he was 'possessed' and the chaplain had preferred to speak with him rather than pray with him. (Zablon 2008, September 19). More research is needed in this area, and is being undertaken in the field of spirituality and mental health. (Coyte, Gilbert et al 2008; Gilbert 2008)

Conclusion

In this article, following the background of a possible increase in advocacy provision compared with chaplains/spiritual care coordinators, I have set out definitions of independent advocacy, and suggested that the coverage of the population in some areas by advocates may be more extensive than that reached by chaplains. I then focused on the synergy between the practices of advocates and chaplains and included the views of clients. There were implications that both disciplines may have practices and training which they could beneficially share. The proposal of twin best practice principles, Action Based Equality and Reconstructed Empowerment may assist with such a project.

Finally, in relation to whether independent advocacy or spiritual care initiatives could in themselves meet the needs of those who are 'un-befriended', or desperately need support in a period of economic austerity, it is doubtful. But a society, which upholds tangible safeguards, including expressions of independent advocacy flowing from the Mental Health and Mental Capacity Acts, redounds to the public good and is more socially integrated, I argue. And alongside similar services, such as funded chaplaincy, which view the individual not only holistically, but also in spiritual terms, together all must find new, efficient and practical ways to keep faith with the most vulnerable individuals and groups in that society.

Acknowledgments

The author acknowledges with gratitude the support given by all participants in the study and thanks Dr Peter Duncan and Dr David Thompson for their comments during drafting of the article.

References

Atkinson, D. (1999). *Advocacy—a Review*. London, Pavilion/Joseph Rowntree.

Bateman, N. (2000). *Advocacy Skills for Health and Social Care Professionals*. London; Philadelphia, Jessica Kingsley Publishers.

BBC–News. (2009, April 8). 'Church should fund NHS chaplains' Retrieved 23rd April 2009, from http://news.bbc.co.uk/1/hi/health/7988476.stm.

Bernard, A. (2008, August 19). Interviewer: G. Morgan, Advocacy interviews, Ivs–BA London.

Carver, N. and J. Morrison (2005). 'Advocacy in practice: the experiences of independent advocates on UK mental health wards.' *Journal of Psychiatric & Mental Health Nursing* **12**(1): 75–84.

Cornah, D. (2006). *The Impact of Spirituality on Mental Health*. A Literature Review. London, Mental Health Foundation.

Cox, J., A. V. Campbell, et al, Eds. (2007). *Medicine of the Person : Faith, Science and Values in health care provision*. London, Jessica Kingsley Publishers.

Coyle, M. (2008). *Here for good? A snapshot of the advocacy workforce*. London, Action-for-Advocacy.

Coyle, M. (2010). Email. G. Morgan. Leeds.

Coyte, M. E., P. Gilbert, et al, Eds. (2008). *Spirituality, Values, and Mental Health :Jewels for the Journey* London; Philadelphia, Jessica Kingsley Publishers.

Dept.-for-Constitutional-Affairs (2006). *Human rights : human lives : a handbook for public authorities*. [London], Department for Constitutional Affairs.

Dept.-for-Constitutional-Affairs (2006). *Mental Capacity Act code of practice*. London, Department for Constitutional Affairs.

Dept.-of-Health (2008). *The first annual report of the Independent Mental Capacity Advocacy Service*. Year 1, April 2007–March 2008. *Annual Report*. London, Crown.

El Ansari, W., K. A. Newbigging, et al (2009). 'The role of advocacy and interpretation services in the delivery of quality healthcare to diverse minority communities in London, United Kingdom.' *Health & Social Care in the Community* **17**(6): 636–646.

Faust, J. (2008). 'Clinical Social Worker as Patient Advocate in a Community Mental Health Center.' *Clinical Social Work Journal* **36**(3): 293–300.

Fauzia, B. (2007, October 1). Interviewer: G. Morgan, Advocacy interviews, Ivs–FB London.

Foley, R. and H. Platzer (2007). 'Place and provision: Mapping mental health advocacy services in London.' *Social Science & Medicine* **64**(3): 617–632.

Forbat, L. and D. Atkinson (2005). 'Advocacy in Practice: The Troubled Position of Advocates in Adult Services.' *Br J Soc Work* **35**(3): 321–335.

Foskett, J. (2004). 'Editorial.' *Mental Health, Religion & Culture* **7**(1): 1–3.

Foskett, J., J. Marriott, et al (2004). 'Mental health, religion and spirituality: Attitudes, experience and expertise among mental health professionals and religious leaders in Somerset.' *Mental Health, Religion & Culture* **7**(1): 5–22.

Fulford, K., S. Ersser, et al, eds. (1996). *Essential Practice in Patient-Centred Care*. Oxford, Blackwell Science.

Gammell, C. (2009, Feb 7). 'Nurse Caroline Petrie: I will continue praying for patients.' *The Daily Telegraph* Retrieved 23 April 2009, from http://www.telegraph.co.uk/news/newstopics/religion/4537452/Nurse-Caroline-Petrie-I-will-continue-praying-for-patients.html.

Gilbert, P. (2008). 'Nurturing a new discourse: mental health and spirituality.' *Spirituality and Health International*: 9, 285–295.

Gilbert, P. (2010). 'Seeking inspiration: the rediscovery of the spiritual dimension in health and social care in England.' *Mental Health, Religion & Culture* **13**(1): 1–14.

Gilbert, P. and V. Nicholls (2003). *Inspiring Hope: Recognising the Importance of Spirituality in a Whole Person Approach to Mental Health*. Leeds, NIMHE.

Habib, C. (2007, October 1). Interviewer: G. Morgan, Advocacy interviews, Ivs–HC. London.

Henderson, R. (2005). Mental Health Advocacy and Empowerment in Focus. *Good Practice in Adult Mental Health*. T. Ryan, J. Pritchard, et al London; Philadelphia, Jessica Kingsley Publishers: 202–215.

Hospital-Chaplaincies-Council (2010). *Health Care Chaplaincy and The Church of England, A Review of the work of the Hospital Chaplaincies Council*. London, Church of England.

Jana, D. (2007, October 22). Interviewer: G.Morgan, Advocacy interviews, Ivs–JD. London.

Janine, E. (2007, October 1). Interviewer: G.Morgan, Advocacy interviews, Ivs–JE. London.

Layard, R. (2009, September 14). 'This is the greatest good. We have only one true yardstick with which to measure society's progress: happiness.' *The Guardian*: 32.

Little, W., H. W. Fowler, et al (1983). *The shorter Oxford English dictionary on historical principles.* London, Book Club Associates.

Llewellyn, P. and R. Northway (2007). 'The views and experiences of learning disability nurses concerning their advocacy education.' *Nurse Education Today* **27**(8): 955–963.

Louise, F., G. Michael, et al (2007, November 23). Interviewer: G.Morgan, Advocacy interviews, Ivs–LF et al London.

Mallik, M. (1997). 'Advocacy in nursing—a review of the literature.' *Journal of Advanced Nursing* **25**(1): 130–138.

Mallik, M. (1998). 'Advocacy in nursing: perceptions and attitudes of the nursing elite in the United Kingdom.' *Journal of Advanced Nursing* **28**(5): 1001–1011.

Mallik, M. and A. M. Rafferty (2000). 'Diffusion of the Concept of Patient Advocacy.' *Journal of Nursing Scholarship* **32**(4): 399–404.

Maltby, J., C. A. Lewis, et al (2008). 'Prayer and subjective well-being: The application of a cognitive-behavioural framework.' *Mental Health, Religion & Culture* **11**(1): 119–129.

Micky, K., L. Einstein, et al (2008, May 14). Interviewer: G. Morgan, Advocacy interviews, Ivs–MK et al London.

Morgan, G. (2010). 'Independent advocacy and the 'rise of spirituality': Views from advocates, service users and chaplains.' *Mental Health, Religion & Culture* **13**(6): 623–636.

Nebi, S. (2007, October 22). Interviewer: G. Morgan, Advocacy interviews, Ivs–NS. London.

Norah, A. and B. Bella (2009, December 14). Interviewer: G. Morgan, Advocacy interviews Ivs–NA & BB. London.

Norman, A. and B. Colin (2008, September 11). Interviewer: G.Morgan, Advocacy interviews, Ivs–NA/CB. London.

Pattison, S., Ed. (1994). *Pastoral Care and Liberation Theology*. Cambridge, Cambridge University Press.

Ravich, R. and L. Schmolka (1996). Patient Representation: A Patient-centred approach to the provision of health services. *Essential Practice in Patient-Centred Care*. K. Fulford, S. Ersser and T. Hope. Oxford, Blackwell: 68–85.

RCPsych (2008).
http://www.rcpsych.ac.uk/college/specialinterestgroups/spirituality.aspx, Royal College of Psychiatrists.

Redley, M., M. Platten, et al (2008). The Involvement of Independent Mental Capacity Advocates (IMCAs) in Adult Protection Procedures in England:1st April 2007–31st March 2008. Cambridge Department of Psychiatry (Section of Developmental Psychiatry) University of Cambridge.

Ruth, T. (2007, November 21). Interviewer: G. Morgan, Advocacy interviews, Ivs–RT. London.

Sam, U. (2008, February 13). Interviewer: G. Morgan, Advocacy interviews, Ivs–SU. London.

Sokol, D. (2009). 'The value of hospital chaplains.' Retrieved 23rd April 2009, from http://news.bbc.co.uk/1/hi/health/7990099.stm.

Stanford, P. (2010). Edward Schillebeeckx obituary. *Guardian*.

Swinton, J. (2001). 'Spirituality and the lives of people with Learning Disabilities.' *Updates: Spirituality and Learning Disabilities* 3(6).

Tew, J. (2003). Emancipatory Research in mental health. *SPN Paper 4: Where you stand affects your point of view. Emancipatory approaches to mental health research Notes from SPN Study Day: 12 June 2003*. S. Cochrane. London, Social Perspectives Network: 24–27.

Thompson, D. (2008). 'Advocating beyond the institution.' *Learning Disability Today* 8(1): 16–21.

Traustadóttir, R. (2006). 'Learning about self-advocacy from life history: a case study from the United States.' *British Journal of Learning Disabilities* 34(3): 175–180.

Wallcraft, J. (2003). User Focused Research. *SPN Paper 4: Where you stand affects your point of view. Emancipatory approaches to mental health research Notes from SPN Study Day: 12 June 2003.* S. Cochrane. London, Social Perspectives Network.

Zablon, V. (2008, September 19). Interviewer: G.Morgan, Advocacy interviews, Ivs–ZV. London.

Renewing the Catholic Social Conscience Means Renewing the Catholic School Curriculum: Taking *Caritas in Veritate* Seriously in Education

GERALD GRACE

Introduction

In 1988 the Catholic Fund for Overseas Development (CAFOD) in London published a booklet by Michael Schultheis SJ, Edmund De Berri SJ, and Peter Henriot SJ. (formerly staff of the Center of Concern in Washington, DC) under the title, *Our Best Kept Secret: The Rich Heritage of Catholic Social Teaching*. The intention of this work was to disseminate knowledge about Catholic social teaching more widely in the community because, they argued, such teaching 'seems to have been forgotten, or never known, by a majority of the Roman Catholic community'.[1] Given that the Church has a 'rich heritage' of such teaching in the Papal encyclicals of Leo XIII (1891), Pius XI (1931), Paul VI (1967) and John Paul II (1981, 1988) and in major scholarly texts such as Donal Dorr's, *Option for the Poor* (1983) and Walsh and Davies' collection of Papal documents, *Proclaiming Justice and Peace* (1984), how was such ignorance to be explained?

Michael Schultheis and his co-authors saw the major problem to be the lack of access, by the majority of the Catholic population, to the formal discourse of Papal encyclicals or to the academic discourse of the major interpretive texts. What was lacking was the provision of mediating texts which could convey the essentials of Catholic social teaching through parish discussion groups. The relative success of the booklet, *Our Best Kept Secret* (1988) demonstrated that it was effective as a mediating text and that it answered a real need in the Catholic world.

The argument of this paper is that Pope Benedict XVI's (2009) Encyclical: *'Caritas in Veritate*: on integral human development in charity and truth', provides a great opportunity for further renewal and dissemination of Catholic social teaching. This renewal could be realised not only through the agency of parish discussion groups but also through the agency of Catholic secondary schools and colleges across the world. It is universally recognised[2] that the curricula of Catholic schools internationally are in danger of losing their distinctive identity and contents in the face of contemporary pressures for conformity to 'national needs' (as expressed in national curriculum requirements), academic productivity (as expressed in national testing regimes) and a global culture where, 'many young people find themselves in a condition of radical instability... They live in a one-dimensional universe in which the only criterion is practical utility and the only value is economic and technological progress.'[3]

A strong emphasis upon Catholic social teaching, and, in particular, *Caritas in Veritate* in the curricula of Catholic secondary schools and colleges could assist significantly in resisting these processes of cultural incorporation and ensuring that a Catholic school curriculum is, in practice, and not just in rhetoric, distinctive and counter-cultural.

How can the teachings of Caritas in Veritate permeate the curricula of Catholic schools and colleges?

From a close reading of *Caritas in Veritate* (CV), at least three major themes can be discerned:

1. Religious, moral and cultural issues.

2. Economic, business and enterprise issues and
3. Social, environmental and political issues.

Insofar as Catholic schools and colleges, internationally have curricula constituted by Theology and Religious Education, Philosophy and Ethics, Personal and Moral education, Mathematics, Business and Enterprise studies, Economic and Social Sciences, Politics, Environmental and Physical Sciences and Humane subjects (Literature, History, Languages, Geography etc.) the potential for permeation of Catholic social teaching is considerable across many subjects.

Religious, moral and cultural issues

In this sector of the school curriculum, study sessions for senior students could be constructed as discussion topics related to specific CV extracts, with assignment questions designed to elicit personal, critical responses from the students. Some examples would be:

- 'Charity demands justice: recognition and respect for the legitimate rights of individuals and peoples. It strives to build the earthly city according to law and justice. On the other hand, charity transcends justice and completes it in the logic of giving and forgiving.' (para 6, p. 7)[4]
  In what ways does charity 'transcend' justice?

- Underdevelopment is the lack of brotherhood among individuals and peoples. As society becomes ever more globalised it makes us neighbours but does not make us brothers. Reason can establish civic equalities but it cannot establish fraternity. (para 19, p. 20)
  Outline your understanding of the Christian doctrine of fraternity and indicate how it could be applied to international development.

- 'Today, people frequently kill in the holy name of God… This applies especially to terrorism motivated by fundamentalism which generates grief, destruction and death and obstructs dialogue between nations.' (para 29, p. 33)
  How would you answer the arguments of Professor Richard Dawkins that this is the inevitable outcome of religious belief?

- 'When he is far away from God, man is unsettled and ill at ease. Social and psychological alienation and the many neuroses that afflict affluent societies are attributable, in part, to spiritual factors.' (para 76, p. 88)
  To what extent do you agree with this statement?

- 'The greatest service to development then, is a Christian humanism… Openness to God makes us open towards our brothers and sisters and towards an understanding of life as a joyful task to be accomplished in a spirit of solidarity.' (para 78, p. 91)
  Does the record of Christian social action in the world support, in your view, this assertion?

A study programme based upon this section of *Caritas in Veritate* must clearly be based upon a resource book of readings covering issues such as conceptual distinctions of forms of charity, developing ideas of social justice, interpretations of fraternity, study of the various types of religious fundamentalism, engagement with the work of the 'new atheists' e.g. Dawkins (2006) and historical study of Christian social action. While this will be demanding for both teachers and students it can be suggested that senior students in Catholic schools are likely to engage with these issues with interest and vigour. In other words it should contribute powerfully to a renewed and better informed Catholic social conscience among the young.[5]

Economic, business and enterprise issues

The development of curriculum subjects and curriculum materials related to the study of Economics, Finance, Business administration and Enterprise is a growing feature of Catholic schools and colleges internationally. This reflects, in part, the expectations of government, parents and senior students that these subjects are a necessary preparation for an increasingly competitive, mobile and globalised world of international corporate business, finance and trade. The utilitarian appeal of these subjects is high.

A challenge for Catholic schools and colleges is that the addition of these subjects to the curriculum may represent an entirely secular and utilitarian cultural implant in their programmes unless these subjects are brought into an organic relation with the religious, moral and social teachings of the Church. But, is this happening? There is little evidence that this organic relation is being developed in the schools. The cultural problem here is that many writers on Economics and related subjects have kept religious and moral issues outside the boundaries of their subject content and analysis.

In a recent publication, *The Credit Crunch: making moral sense of the financial crisis* (2009), Edward Hadas has argued: 'In addition to greed itself and bad ideas about human nature, one other factor may have played a role in the pre-crisis abdication of responsibility in finance. This is the refusal to take morality seriously in any economic discussions' (p. 42)[6]. It must also be admitted that the 'rich heritage' of Catholic social and moral teaching relevant to these subjects has, in general,[7] been ignored in many Catholic schools internationally. That is why this present situation, marked by a global economic and financial crisis (salient in the thoughts of contemporary students) and the publication of *Caritas in Veritate* which addresses these issues from a Catholic perspective, provides an opportunity for all Catholic schools and colleges to focus upon the relevance of Catholic social teaching to contemporary conditions.

Caritas in Veritate presents an agenda of issues for discussion and reflection which all senior students in Catholic education should encounter in their studies. The following are some examples of what Pope Benedict offers for their consideration:

- 'The world's wealth is growing in absolute terms but inequalities are on the increase. The scandal of glaring inequalities continues.' (para. 22, p. 25)

- 'The conviction that the economy must be autonomous, that it must be shielded from the influences of a moral character, has led man to abuse the economic process in a thoroughly destructive way.' (para. 34, p. 39)

- 'The market can be a negative force, not because it is so by nature, but because a certain ideology can make it so.' (para. 36, p. 42)

- 'John Paul II taught that investment always has moral as well as economic significance.' (para. 40, p. 47)

- 'Financiers must rediscover the ethical foundations of their activity so as not to abuse the sophisticated instruments what can serve to betray the interests of savers.' (para. 65, p. 77)

Catholic schools and college teachers have the potential to be significant innovators in bringing together the study of Economics, Finance, Business administration and Enterprise with an in-depth understanding of Catholic religious, moral and social teaching, so that a higher order level of knowledge and understanding can be achieved in these crucial contemporary subjects. *Caritas in Veritate* could be the catalyst for this necessary cultural transformation.[8]

Social, environmental and political issues

The intrinsic appeal of social, environmental and political issues to senior students in Catholic schools and colleges is considerable.[9] They are, after all, the inheritors of a world which many of them believe is in a dysfunctional state on all three dimensions. As a generation they are probably possessed of more information and consciousness of the nature and extent of social, environmental and political dysfunctions in the world than any previous generation. It is entirely likely that they expect their school and college programmes to engage seriously with these issues, not only in knowledge terms but also in suggesting what Catholic social action is needed to help a process of change and development.

In meeting these expectations, *Caritas in Veritate* has much to offer because Pope Benedict XVI shares their concerns and provides profound guidance for action and transformation: 'The crisis thus becomes an opportunity for discernment in which to shape a new vision for the future' (p. 24). The Pope's discernment and vision is developed in a number of strong statements which have the potential to animate the consciousness and action of Catholic youth in their subsequent vocations and roles in adult life.

Such statements include:

- 'The processes of globalisation... open up the unprecedented possibility of large-scale redistribution of wealth on a world-wide scale; if badly directed however, they can lead to an increase in poverty and inequality.' (para. 42)

- 'Today the material resources available for rescuing peoples from poverty are potentially greater than ever before, but they have ended up largely in the hands of people from developed countries who have benefited more from the liberalisation that has occurred in the mobility of capital and labour.' (para. 42)

- 'The way humanity treats the environment influences the way it treats itself... This invites contemporary society to a serious review of its life-style, which, in many parts of the world is prone to hedonism and consumerism, regardless of their harmful consequences.' (para 51)

- 'Every migrant is a human person who, as such, possesses fundamental inalienable rights that must be respected by everyone and in every circumstance.' (para 62)

- 'There is urgent need of a true world political authority... vested with the effective power to ensure security for all, regard for justice, and respect for rights.' (para 67)[10]

It is sometimes the case that senior students in Catholic schools and colleges begin to distance themselves from the practice and discourse of the Faith because they perceive it to be disconnected from the many challenges of the 'real world' in which they live.[11]

Detailed study of *Caritas in Veritate* has the potential to show that, on the contrary, the Christian religion in the Catholic tradition is integral to an understanding of these challenges and a valuable source of guidance in ways of responding to them. There is a Heavenly City to which all believers aspire but there is also an Earthly City which believers are called upon to perfect by social action. As Pope Benedict expresses it:

> Development requires attention to the spiritual life... trust in God, spiritual fellowship in Christ, reliance upon God's providence and mercy, love and forgiveness, self-denial, acceptance of others, justice and peace. All this is essential if 'hearts of stone' are to be transformed into 'hearts of flesh' (Ez 36:26), rendering life on earth 'divine' and thus more worthy of humanity.[12]

In other words, what is projected to contemporary youth as the 'real world' is in fact a construct of globalized materialism from which religious faith is either marginalised or represented by the media in its distorted and fundamentalist extremes. Catholic social teaching, and in particular the teachings of *Caritas in Veritate* show to the young the authentic face of religion and show a 'real world' that can be attained by social action inspired by faith.

Catholic social teaching and the Catholic school curriculum

In 1999, Dr Robert Davis wrote a ground-breaking chapter with the title, 'Can there be a Catholic curriculum?' His purpose was to generate a debate among Catholic educators about this crucial issue at a time when both government and economic agencies internationally appeared to be dominating the content, assessment and purposes of curricula.[13] Davis' argument was that discussion of this issue had virtually disappeared from the considerations of Catholic educators.

His thesis was that

> the price Catholic schools have had to pay for their accreditation as appropriate centres for the 'delivery' of the modern curriculum is a restriction of their Catholicity to those features of school life where secular society is prepared to permit the manifestation of Catholic ideas—mainly worship, ethos and Religious education.[14]

While worship, ethos and Religious Education are clearly central to the maintenance of a distinctive Catholic educational mission, Davis was raising the question, was this sufficient in itself if the major part of the curriculum and discourse in the school was, in essence, secular, utilitarian and shaped by government and economic requirements?

In as far as Davis's analysis is correct, in many societies, it points to an urgent need to strengthen the Catholic cultural content of the curriculum in general to prevent a process of incorporation into a secularised and technicist educational culture.

It has been the argument of this chapter, that the rich heritage of Catholic social teaching, with its implications for the teaching of many subjects in the curriculum could provide such distinctive and counter-cultural material. While *Caritas in Veritate* provides the immediate stimulus to do this, the Encyclical itself is built upon the insights of earlier work especially from Pope Paul VI and Pope John Paul II. Taken together this is a rich resource which innovative teachers can use to illuminate a range of subjects in ways which are distinctively different to those used in state secular schools. In this way the Catholicity of the school will be strengthened not only by its worship, ethos and formal religious Education but by a total curriculum experience which integrates faith and learning through the agency of Catholic social teaching.

To bring about such a transformation will require school authorities to struggle for more relative autonomy in curriculum provision; it will require changes in professional preparation and continuing professional development programmes for Catholic teachers and it will require school leaders to be innovative agents of change. However, if the *mission integrity* of Catholic schools and colleges in an increasingly secular, globalised and technicist world is to be maintained, such cultural action is essential.[15]

Education and the Formation of the Catholic Social Conscience

Speaking of education in *Caritas in Veritate*, Benedict XVI reminds his readers that, 'the term 'education' refers not only to classroom teaching and vocational training ... but to the complete formation of the person'.[16]

As educational discourse in contemporary society becomes increasingly dominated by the language of 'training', a Catholic educational discourse which emphasises 'formation of the person' is not only counter-cultural but more humane. It insists that the ultimate goal of the educational process is the formation of good persons equipped with knowledge and skills to serve the common good motivated by faith and a Catholic social conscience. But what is this conscience and how is it formed? In his essays *On Conscience*, Cardinal Joseph Ratzinger argued that:

> conscience signifies the perceptible and demanding presence of the voice of truth in the subject himself. It is the overcoming of mere subjectivity in the encounter... with the truth from God.[17]

At the same time:

> included in the concept of conscience is an obligation, namely the obligation to care for it, to form it and educate it.[18]

In addition to the direct teaching received by the young from their parents and attendance at Mass, Catholic schools and colleges clearly represent a crucial arena for the forming and informing of conscience. The Catholic social conscience of the young will not simply result from the acquisition of knowledge about Catholic social teaching, although that is the necessary foundation. It will require the nurture of their spirituality and Christian faith by a constant interaction between such social teaching and the teaching, practice and mission of Jesus Christ and the saints. To be truly animated, such students need opportunities to be involved in Catholic social action projects in their communities and beyond. The *International Handbook of Catholic Education* (2007) records examples of such formative and practical action by Catholic schools and colleges in different parts of the world.[19] The challenge is not that such formation and expression of the Catholic social conscience is absent in Catholic education but rather that it is in danger of being marginalised in the contemporary pursuit of better academic and test results.

The history of Catholicism is rich in the heritage of the martyrs of conscience who have shown 'obedience to the truth which must stand higher than any human tribunal'.[20] Catholic schools and colleges are not lacking in role models with which to inspire contemporary students to think and act beyond a culture of acquisitive and competitive individualism. In writing *Caritas in Veritate*, Pope Benedict XVI has given them a better vision for the future and has emphasised that love of God must always be shown in love of neighbour.

Conclusion: Catholic Social teaching: a major theological and cultural resource for Catholic education

This chapter has argued that Catholic education internationally could be renewed and reanimated by a systematic permeation of Catholic social teaching across all subjects of the curriculum. This strategy would have many advantages. It would, first and foremost, have the potential to engage the interest and involvement of senior students at a time when many of them begin to question the relevance of their faith to contemporary challenges. It would help to inform and strengthen their Catholic social conscience as they came to understand that the teachings of Jesus Christ and the saints as mediated by the Catholic tradition of social analysis makes an organic relation between faith and action in the world. At the same time, it would help to prevent both students and schools from becoming incorporated into a global culture in which 'the only criterion is practical utility and the only value is economic and technological progress'.[21]

While *Caritas in Veritate* provides the immediate stimulus for making such a cultural transformation in Catholic education, and is strongly founded upon earlier Papal encyclicals which need to be re-discovered, the corpus of Catholic social teaching is more extensive than that provided by the Magisterium. An appendix to this chapter suggests a supplementary range of other sources which can be used by Catholic educators. However, it has to be recognised that serious cultural transformations in educational practice are not easy, especially in contemporary conditions where academic 'productivity', public accountability, market competition and value for money calculations are dominating educational institutions. As many hard-pressed school leaders and teachers will observe, measurements of Catholic social conscience are not included in school accountability processes by public agencies. So, while Catholic social teaching may be a valuable resource for Catholic school curricula, it may not 'count' in the public mechanisms for school evaluations and judgements of 'success'.

It is in situations such as this, that a distinctive quality of Catholic school and college leadership must assert itself. Catholic school leaders have to 'render to Caesar' but they also have to 'render to God'. They are the guardian of the mission integrity of the schools. But public accountability requirements are not the only impediments, there are workload and time pressures which block the path to religious, cultural and curriculum change. It is one thing to list the sources for the serious study of Catholic social teaching; it is another thing for already pressurised educators to find easy access to such sources for classroom stimulus material. A survey of the available literature, prior to the publication of *Caritas in Veritate* suggests that the most useful mediating text for school leaders and teachers is the Fourth Edition of *Catholic Social Teaching*, published by the Center of Concern in Washington in 2003. Here is, in effect, a valuable teacher's handbook which gives access to Catholic social teaching in classroom-related format.

To supplement and to background the profound insights of *Caritas in Veritate*, teachers and students can construct a term's programme focused on seven core principles of Catholic social teaching:

1. The Dignity of the human Person

2. The Dignity of Work

3. The Person in Community

4. Rights and Responsibilities

5. Option for those in Poverty

6. Solidarity

7. Care for Creation

Contained within these principles are discussion and analysis topics of great potential interest like the common good, structures of sin, liberation theology, human rights, resisting market idolatry, subsidiarity, peace making, the just war.[22]

In 1996 the Catholic Bishops' Conference of England and Wales published a ground-breaking document, *The Common Good and the Catholic Church's Social Teaching* in which they called for 'more participation in the future development of Catholic Social Teaching so that it is properly owned by all Catholics'.[23]

The way to ensure this ownership and the formation of a maturely developed Catholic social conscience in all members of the Church is to permeate the curriculum and the pedagogy of Catholic schools and colleges, with the rich heritage of Catholic social teaching.

References

Alford, H. (OP) and Naughton, M (2001)*Managing as if Faith Mattered: Christian Social Principles in the Modern Organisation*. Notre Dame, University of Notre Dame Press.

Arthur, J., Boylan, P., Grace, G. and Walsh, P. (2007) *Can There be a Catholic School Curriculum? Renewing the debate*. London, CRDCE.

Benedict XVI (2009) *Caritas in Veritate: encyclical letter on integral human development in charity and truth*. London, Catholic Truth Society.

Congregation for Catholic Education (1988)*The Religious Dimension of Education in a Catholic School*. London, Catholic Truth Society.

Davies, J. (1993) (d.), *God and the Marketplace: essays on the morality of wealth creation*. London, Institute of Economic Affairs.

Davis, R. (1999) 'Can There be a Catholic Curriculum?' chapter 9 in J. Conroy (ed) *Catholic Education: Inside Out/ Outside In*. Dublin, Lindisfarne Books.

Dawkins, R. (2006) *The God Delusion*. London, Bantam Books.

De Berri, E. (SJ) Hug, J. (SJ) Henriot, P. (SJ) and Schultheis, M. (SJ), (2003) *Catholic Social Teaching: our best kept secret* (4th Edition). New York, Orbis Books.

Dorr, D. (1983/2003) *Option for the Poor: a hundred years of Catholic social teaching* (2003 revised edition). New York, Orbis Books.

Grace, G. (2002) 'Mission Integrity': Contemporary Challenges for Catholic School Leaders' in K. Leithwood and P. Hallinger (Eds) *Second International Handbook of Educational Leadership and Administration*. Dordrecht/Boston Kluwer Academic Press.

Grace, G. and O'Keefe, J. (SJ) (Eds) (2007)*International Handbook of Catholic Education*, 2 volumes. Dordrecht, Springer.

Griffiths, B. (1982) *Morality and the Market Place: Christian Alternatives to Capitalism and Socialism*. London, Hodder and Stoughton.

Hadas, E. (2009)*The Credit Crunch: Making Moral Sense of the Financial Crisis*. London, Catholic Truth Society.

Hoge, D., Dinges, W., Johnson, M and Gonzales, J. (2001) *Young Adult Catholics: Religion in the Culture of Choice*. Notre Dame, University of Notre Dame Press.

John Paul II (1981) *Laborem Exercens* (On Human Work) Encyclical Letter. Vatican City, Rome.

John Paul II (1988) *Sollicitudo Rei Socialis* (The Social Concern of the Church). Encyclical Letter. Vatican City, Rome.

John Paul II (1991) *Centesimus Annus* (One Hundred Years) Encyclical Letter. Vatican City, Rome.

Leo XIII (1891) *Rerum Novarum* (On the Condition of Labour) Encyclical Letter. Vatican City, Rome.

Mofid, K. (2002) *Globalisation for the Common Good*. London, Shepheard-Walwyn.

Paul VI (1967) *Populorum Progressio* (The Development of Peoples). Encyclical Letter. Vatican City, Rome.

Pius XI (1931) *Quadragesimo Anno* (The Reconstruction of the Social Order). Encyclical Letter. Vatican City, Rome.

Ratzinger, J. (2006) *On Conscience*. San Francisco, Ignatius Press.

Schultheis, M., (SJ) De Berri, E. (SJ) and Henriot, P. (SJ) (1988) *Our Best Kept Secret: The Rich Heritage of Catholic Social Teaching*. London, Catholic Fund for Overseas Development.

Vorgrimler, H. (ed) (1967) *Commentary on the Documents of Vatican II*, Vol V. New York, Herder and Herder.

Walsh, M. and Davies, B. (1991) *Proclaiming Justice and Peace: Papal Documents from Rerum Novarum through Centesimus Annus*. North American Edition, Mystic, CT, Twenty-Third Publications.

Further Sources for the Study of Catholic Social Teaching

Booth, P. (Ed) (2007) *Catholic Social Teaching and the Market Economy*. London, Institute of Economic Affairs.

Caldecott, S. (2009) *Catholic Social Teaching: A Way In*. London, Catholic Truth Society

Catholic Bishops' Conference of England and Wales (1996). *The Common Good and the Catholic Church's Social Teaching* London, CBC.

Charles, R. (SJ) (1998) *Christian Social Witness and Teaching* (2 Volumes). Leominster, Gracewing.

Clark, C. and Alford, H. (OP) (2009) *Rich and Poor: Rebalancing the Economy*. London, Catholic Truth Society.

Coleman, J. and Ryan, W. (2005) *Globalization and Catholic Social Thought*. Ottawa, Novalis

Cullen, P., Hoose, B. and Mannion, G. (eds) (2007) *Catholic Social Justice: Theological and Practical Explorations*. London, Continuum.

Gutierrez, G. (1983) *A Theology of Liberation: history, politics and salvation*. London, SCM Press.

Hollenbach, D. (2003) *The Common Good and Christian Ethics*. Cambridge, Cambridge University Press.

Hornsby-Smith, M. (2006) *An Introduction to Catholic Social Thought*. Cambridge, Cambridge University Press.

McDonough, S. (SSC) (1990)*The Greening of the Church*. London, SCM Press.

Pontifical Council for Justice and Peace (2004) *Compendium of the Social Doctrine of the Church*. Vatican City, Rome. Libreria Editrice Vaticana.

Rowland, C. (ed) (1999)*The Cambridge Companion to Liberation Theology*. Cambridge, Cambridge University Press.

Notes

[1] Michael Schultheis, SJ, Edmund De Berri, SJ, and Peter Henriot, SJ, *Our Best Kept Secret: The Rich Heritage of Catholic Social Teaching* (London: Cafod, 1988), p. 3.

[2] See, *International Handbook of Catholic Education* (2007) chapters 7, 9, 13, 14, 16, 28, 31, and 43.

[3] Congregation for Catholic Education, *The Religious Dimension of Education in a Catholic School*, pp. 8–10.

[4] All quotations are taken from the 2009 edition of *Caritas in Veritate* published by The Catholic Truth Society. London and reproduced with permission.

[5] It also has to be accepted that some young people will disagree with the stance taken by the Pope and the Catholic church on these issues as part of their own individual critical development.

[6] There have been some attempts to bring the Christian religion and the world of economic enterprise into dialogue, eg, *Morality and the Market Place: Christian Alternatives to Capitalism and Socialism*(1982); *God and the marketplace: essays on the morality of wealth creation* (1993); *Managing as if Faith Mattered* (2001); *Globalisation for the Common Good* (2002).But this literature does not seem

to have affected school curricula in general.

7   This situation varies internationally. Catholic schools and colleges in the USA, especially Jesuit schools, have engaged seriously with Catholic social teaching in their curricula and in social action.

8   *Caritas in Veritate* could be the catalyst for this but it could also help in the re-discovery of other Papal encyclicals of Catholic social teaching. It is clear that Pope Benedict XVI was deeply influenced by Pope Paul VI's encyclical, *Populorum Progressio* (1967). See pp. 11–21 of *Caritas in Veritate*.

9   See *Young Adult Catholics*(2001).

10 This is a clear criticism of the present effectiveness of the United Nations Organisation.

11 'Real world' is a contemporary ideological device used to suggest that proposed alternatives to the status quo are impractical theory or naive utopias.

12 Pope Benedict XVI, *Caritas in Veritate*, 79.

13 For one response to this debate, see, *Can There be a Catholic School Curriculum*? published by the Centre for Research and Development in Catholic Education in 2007.

14 R. Davis, 'Can There be a Catholic Curriculum?' chapter 9 in J. Conroy (ed), *Catholic Education: Inside Out/ Outside in* (Dublin: Lindisfarne Books, 1999), pp. 221–222.

15 In first using the concept of mission integrity in 2002, I stressed the importance of the mission to the poor. However, mission integrity involves not only service to a particular category of students but also a distinctive Catholic curriculum content.

16 Pope Benedict XVI, *Caritas in Veritate*, 61.

17 Pope Benedict XVI/Cardinal Joseph Ratzinger, *On Conscience* (San Francisco: Ignatius Press, 2006), p. 25.

18 *Ibid.*, p. 63.

19 See *International Handbook of Catholic Education* (2007) chapters 6, 10, 22, 24, 33, 37 and 39.

20 Pope Benedict XVI/Cardinal Joseph Ratzinger, *On Conscience*, p. 26. See also the earlier statement of Father Joseph Ratzinger, when acting as theological adviser to the Second Vatican Council: 'Over the Pope as expression of the binding claim of ecclesiastical authority, there stands one's own conscience, which must be obeyed before all else, even if necessary against the requirements of ecclesiastical authority. This emphasis on the individual whose

conscience confronts him with a supreme and ultimate tribunal, and one which in the last resort is beyond the claim of external social groups, even the official church, also establishes a principle in opposition to increasing totalitarianism.' (Vorgrimler, 1967, p. 134).

[21] Congregation for Catholic Education, *The Religious Dimension of Education in a Catholic School*.

[22] *Catholic Social Teaching: Our Best Kept Secret* (2003), pp. 18–34.

[23] Catholic Bishops' Conference of England and Wales, *The Common Good and the Catholic Church's Social Teaching*, 31.

Regaining a Voice

TERRY PRENDERGAST

If I were to stand in front of you opening and closing my mouth for any time it would become rather tedious fairly quickly, and whilst you might pick up one or two words or meanings from me, you would be hard pressed to get the main messages that I was trying to get across to you. It seems that this is the experience today for many in our society when they are spoken to by either Church or State. The image I want to project is of someone visible, someone obviously speaking, but also someone who cannot be heard, or whose words have become difficult to hear. But let me try to put a context into this so-called *laryngitis* which seems to be a common malady. Let me try to paint a picture of what our society is like today and why I think many of our words go unheard or are not listened to.

We have lived through unprecedented levels of change during the past twenty to thirty years in many different ways. One of the biggest changes for many of us has been the rise of multi-culturalism, and the multi-faith experiences that have sprung from this, that has led many to conclude that our identity has been lost, or blurred. You may remember a song by a pop group in the 1970s where the lines suggested that we should all be in a 'great big melting pot' and end up 'chocolate coloured people by the score'. The song, I think, was a hopeful anthem of a return to the pre-Tower of Babel days where humanity was secure, where the other was understood, and there was generally peace. But, I think that this 'melting pot' has caused a lot of worry for people shaken by an erosion of identity, where many are left not knowing what is constant anymore. This assumes that anything was ever constant which, of course, it never has been. I can sit on a tube train in London and look down the carriage and see lots of different ethnicities represented and even those who look like the original white indiginous population are probably Polish, Lithuanian, or some other European domicile. So, population, certainly in terms of ethnicity, has changed hugely, and this has changed how we view our world, either for better or worse.

The digital age that really has taken off in the last twenty years has also had a huge impact on our lives. There is no doubt that the increases in communication possibilities have made life an awful lot better for many, but there are also negative aspects that we need to keep in mind. I don't just mean that annoying experience of listening to lots of different conversations on the phone whilst you are on a train or a bus. I mean the advances in the information highway that have subliminally impacted on our consciousness, that have affected how we see the world, and what we believe about it.

Finally, the impact of an increasing consumerism now practically drives everything so that the material has taken over from the spiritual in its importance and presence. What I call the 'Me! Me! Me!' culture is all-pervasive and so I have every kind of product pushed into my face, telling me that I need this, that or the other in order to have the best life, the best relationship and best well-being. Everybody seems to be so concerned about my health!

So, let me place all of the above within the context of marriage and family life and try to draw out some of the consequences for us today because of these and other changes.

Multiculturalism has meant that the established family structures have been challenged. Our many cultures have some similar expectations of family but there are some marked differences also that either challenge directly the status quo, or do so indirectly by posing questions about different life-styles and ways of living. The increase of inter-faith marriages, and some where there is faith on one side only, have increased exponentially. Certainly, in my own organisation Marriage Care, we find it unusual when two Catholics come to us for marriage preparation, for example. And, I would stress that I find nothing wrong with this situation we find ourselves in today other than it has shaken belief and structure for some, and left others worried and concerned.

The *information super-highway* has been a very positive revolution for us, bringing many of us closer in ways we would not have thought possible twenty years ago. Again, in Marriage Care, we have developed a partnership with One Plus One, the relationship research agency, to provide a web-based service for couples focused on their parenting. This is a service that people can access when and where they want, and it is free, if they have a computer. This is just one example of many where increases in this kind of communication have proved beneficial. But the increases have also posed problems or questions. There are now serious concerns about Internet pornography and it is very clear that paedophiles, who have always been amongst us do have more opportunities to prey on children and young people. And the Internet itself is so open to possible abuse, or is abusive, that there is always a need for parents to regulate what their children work on. So, it's not just unsafe for some to go outside—it's not safe to stay in either!

There are more opportunities also for our views to be shaped by the general advertising processes that hit us in the face in public places and especially on TV. We are told how we ought to look; how to be sexy; what kind of image or body shape we should have. What is important and influential in how your life should be. You can see the scale of the problem when that young Jewish girl, who answered the Angel Gabriel, and who has been offered as a role model for us all, and especially as a mother, is pitted against another kind of Madonna—nowadays I think there is probably very little contest who appears to be the more popular!

And, it is also clear that a wedding (the actual day or event) is becoming both expensive and thereby prohibitive. This is another major shift in our value base, and what we have allowed to happen. My son, who is a set builder in theatre and exhibitions, told me that he had a two-day job building a scenario for a wedding in central London that cost more than £250, 000, at a venue that cost £6000 a night to stay in. Whilst this is doubtless an extreme of what is happening, it provides the backdrop to what is confronting more ordinary members of the public. So, whilst the public commitment is very important for our society, many couples find it is costing them so much that they avoid it. The wedding industry is huge but, ironically, it seems to be working against itself.

I am not against these modern developments *per se*, but I think we need to understand them within the context of my main premise that the 'voice of authority' has been diminished or has disappeared. There seems to be so much 'noise' these days, a kind of white noise, that it's hardly surprising that we cannot hear or be heard.

In my work, I try to hold onto the early Christian concept of *diaconos* where the leader in the early Christian communities had power and influence in direct proportion to their level of service to that same community. And, I have also learned, sometimes painfully over the years in my authority roles in various organisations, the difference between power and influence—that is, I may have legitimate power over people but when I use it, that power is somehow diminished. Influence is much more potent, but also is much more difficult to maintain. Influence means getting alongside people, being credible, being congruent, and nudging change, where change is needed, and being truthful and trustworthy.

So, if we look first at Church, and it could be any Church for that matter, but focusing on the Catholic Church, power certainly seems to be wielded at times, and influence appears to have lost ground. But, I would stress it is not just our own Church that is facing these problems. At present, only 12% of people *feel* that they belong to a Church in this country. I lived during the 1990s in a smallish Yorkshire town with a high proportion of Muslims in the community — perhaps near to half the local population, but where it was clear that many young Muslims had lost the faith and views of their parents, and were alienated in an alien, Yorkshire landscape and western culture, were adrift between communities. So, it's not just a Catholic thing, but I guess we have to start somewhere and we might as well start with our own.

When my wife and I married in 1970, there was no thought of living together. Even if this had entered our consciousness, and there was a lot of flower-power around, we would not have considered it. Our families and our Church would have found it hard to accept, and this lack of acceptance certainly had an impact and moved us towards marriage rather than cohabitation. The moral authority that the Church had was, to some extent, reflected in the environment and in the State, and it had an impact on how we behaved. Whilst this was not all good, there was some comfort in hearing a voice and seeing the line that was being drawn. The erosion of Church authority is an interesting phenomenon and might merit a book or two in itself, but it is clear that for many years now, tens of thousands of Catholics have voted with their feet. The consequences of *Humanae Vitae*, for example, are well documented and debated on what is right, just and reasonable. More recently we have seen the consequences of abuse by clergy — we have probably all watched with a kind of fascination events in Ireland, perhaps hoping that it doesn't come over the water. The problem with it is that the good voices of the clergy are clearly eroded by the few, and credibility has been lost. So, we can see and probably have reflected on the diminishing guidance systems of the

Catholic Church, alongside, as I have said, the same reductions in other religious communities.

An important sub-topic here is language. One senior member of the clergy recently wondered with me about the lack of *traction* in some of our language, so that even if the throat and vocal chords had recovered from the 'laryngitis' , the language that then emerged would be lacking in some way. We are charged by the secularists for being irrelevant, out of touch, and empty moralisers. And, I have felt at times as if the more irrelevant we have appeared, the more strident we have become—a self-defeating and vicious cycle.

However, it is not just Churches that have become diminished in their voices, but it is the State also. This is why our problem today is even more complex and difficult to solve. For me, a lot of this started in the 1980's, with the rise of market liberalism, the rise of the importance of the individual, the support for the individual, as opposed to the group, in that perennial *Agency versus Structure* debate[1]. Margaret Thatcher claims she had never said *there is no such thing as society* but her voice carried that message even so and her Government led us away from a collective sense of community and thought for the other, towards an individually driven agenda, towards a lack of thought for my brother and sister, towards a consumerism and greed that I feel we have never recovered from.

The credibility of the State has been challenged over these years and with it the opportunity for politicians to take liberties with our trust. There were no weapons of mass destruction—we all knew that but it was said enough to make us believe that there might be something. What do we think about MPs and their claims for expenses, duck houses, second homes and the like? Leaving aside the morality of what appears to be dishonesty and fraud, and I am less concerned with this here, the net result is that their voices on a range of important issues have also become diminished because trust has gone. Indeed, low turn outs at recent elections appear to confirm this lack of trust[2].

And, as in the Church, the good voices are tarred with the brush of mistrust to the extent that those who do speak out on issues that are important and deserve our attention are lost in a wilderness of seeming intrigue, dissembling and opportunism. The compact between us and individuals, families, communities with our Churches and State have been reduced to zero in some places.

I want now to speak briefly of the *domestic church*, since this concept probably has some resonance for all of us. I have mentioned already about the changes in values and standards in our families, as a result of many different influences. The *domestic church* offered us an opportunity for growth and structure, but this also seems to have either come under attack or been diminished. You will note today the concern expressed by many about the apparent re-engineering of Vatican II, where the concept of the domestic church first came to our attention, and was given prominence. During the last few decades, when family has been challenged in the secular world, our concept of the domestic church offered us an opportunity to provide a different model, a new paradigm based on spirituality, love and commitment. But, I fear that we have not been able to fully develop this model and now it seems that this concept is also even under review within the Catholic Church. And, as I have said, thousands are no longer around to hear the *voice* anyway.

What appears ironic is that whilst the firm view that family and marriage is at the base of stable and good society, the very systems and structures, and values and beliefs, that support this appear to have been undermined, and steadily eroded by actions and behaviour. In early 2010, Baronnes Deech, The Chair of the Bar Standards Board in England and Wales, announced that English law no longer had a clear concept of marriage, noting that if the legal definition was the 'voluntary union between man and woman, to the exclusion of all others' then 'such is the transformation of family law and family life that not one word of this is remains true'.[3]

We also need to have a concern about marriage and family. For example, most murders and abuse happen in families—most people are murdered by someone who knows them well; most children are abused by a close relative. The pervasive image of the lone paedophile preying on unsuspecting children, whilst having some reality is not where most of our concern should be focused. We also need to remember that marriage has residues of paternalism and the denigration of women, or at least a denigration of their power, and their voice. We further need to remember that what many hold up as the paradigm of health and growth, the nuclear family of the '50s and '60s, had a very short life span and was based on many complex hopes and false premises.[4]

However, the statistics and research are consistent. Adults and children do best in marriages and families, where the adult relationship is stable, loving and committed. By the same token, the research insists that other family forms also provide this goodness where the adult relationship is strong and stable, yet there is concern about other family structures, not least cohabitation, as it appears to be flawed. It is odd that people choose such a flawed model when the evidence or experience suggests something else is better. What this shows is that it is not enough just to say how good marriage is, because it doesn't work like that. If it did, we would not be exploring what can be done, sometimes helplessly and hopelessly lost for answers.

The main competition to marriage, if it can be described as that, is cohabitation which is on the increase though it is a difficult demographic phenomenon to pin down, largely because this lobby is not organised in any way. It is an amorphous mass of people who interestingly are still following a pattern of marriage—two people coming together in love and wanting to build a life together. What they are not doing is making a public commitment to each other and they are *buying* a product that is inherently flawed and prone to breakdown. In saying this, I don't mean to criticise those individuals who cohabit. Other people's life-styles frankly are none of my business but it is fascinating, nevertheless, that increasing numbers are choosing a relationship that seems not to work for long for those who adopt it.

But, the statistics also tell us a story that is worrying. The UK Office for National Statistics figures that were published in 2010, a week after figures indicating fewer divorces, provide us with problematic evidence. Some of those involved in supporting marriage were pleased that divorces appeared to have slowed down, though with fewer marriages, there are bound to be statistically fewer divorces. The real story is in the continuing decline in the number of marriages across the country with 156,290 civil weddings in 2008 of which 105,570 were in approved premises (hotels, stately homes, etc). What we should have a concern about is the drop in religious weddings (only 76,700 and this is fewer than half the 1991 total). And religious marriages are declining at a faster rate than marriages *per se*. In the Catholic Church there were 9,932 marriages in England and Wales (according to the figures in the Catholic Directory) and these statistics have shown a steady decline of about 1000 weddings per year during this decade, whereas in 1981 the figure was 26,097.

There are broader and more covert issues in play here also and one cannot discount the rise in individualism, as I have noted above, as another factor in why people choose not to 'tie the knot' publicly. There is a fear of commitment, linked to the rise of individualism, which means that some people translate till 'death us do part' as an infringement of personal liberty.

But enough doom and gloom, and Old Testament prophesying! Let me offer some thoughts about what can be done. We in the faith communities need to take the lead in providing the solution. We need to promote marriage much more. We need to witness, as married couples, to this important and sacramental union. We need to endorse it and make that endorsement personal. For despite advertising, it is clear that most products or services tend to be bought or taken up because someone close to you has said it was a good restaurant, a good film, a good book.

I think that we have been shy about such promotion in our Church. And, perhaps, with falling Church attendances, there are fewer married couples attending who are able thereby to advertise their union. We also need to promote marriage in other ways. We need to take seriously the need for preparation. There is too much lip-service paid to preparation both by the couples preparing for marriage, and by the laity and clergy. It is right and proper that priests and religious spend so much time preparing for their lives, and take time to consider the direction they have chosen. However, why is there a discrepancy of principle when we compare what we expect of couples preparing for their lives together with that of priests or Religious, particularly when we know that the *domestic church*, or family, is the base for all of the other sacraments? This discrepancy contributes to the problem and it is pervasive and possibly subliminally destructive when people consider marrying. Despite what we say verbally, our actions perhaps suggest that we do not believe in it's worth very much. Marriage as a vocation is talked about but not developed consistently so that the spiritual aspect is often left untended. And how do we reconcile the 'fairy-tale' image built up by the wedding industry of the wedding day, when those of us who are married and have lived out the life know that it is an imperfect, troubling, dynamic yet fundamentally wholesome experience? How do you package and market that? How do you maintain and promote the 'magic' of deep and intimate love against the Disneyesque wedding industry?

I have learned both in my therapeutic and managerial practice, and in my personal life, that I can do little about other people. I can do nothing outside of my skin. And this is the real challenge for all of us. Because we are all in the same position regardless of who you are and what power you think you have. I have to behave differently myself as this is the only way that things will change. Witnessing does not mean speaking and expecting everyone to listen and follow. Witnessing means doing, leading by example with congruence and truth.

The ideas that I want to share with you are taken from Margaret Farley's work and thinking about relationships, *Just Love: a new framework for Christian Sexual Ethics*.[5] I have amended them somewhat. She suggests a number of concepts, or ways of behaving, in our relationships that will make a difference. In bringing these to your attention, with the hope that we might take on these norms or principles, I think that we need to consider the language we use in sharing these ideas so that our language has a connection with the common mass of people, it has resonance, and offers a way forward for the many who are clearly bereft. And, it has to be the language of Church, clergy and laity together in action.

Firstly, we should *do no unjust harm*. This is not just an obvious assumption, or a desired state, but a fundamental position on which all the other norms stand since we are setting the basic ground rules for how we should view and treat each other, how we should meet each other in our daily lives. And since justice is one of the foundations of the Gospels, this should not really present a problem for us in how we witness to this in our daily lives.

All relationships should be founded on *free consent*. The concept suggests to me that we as family and Church members need to want to belong and make an active choice about this and be present in our dealings all of the time. Farley suggests a much more active quality than that offered by the mere words. We know that, for example, long-term relationships are essentially dynamic and chang-ing over time, requiring mutual development for those involved, and also for the relationship and can only survive if there is a measure of consent present.

Thirdly, there is the concept of *Mutuality*. In Marriage Care we have worked with this norm which we see at the summit of relationship building, through a process of Romance, to Reality, to Power Struggles, to Finding Oneself, to Working Through and finally Mutuality. This is a structuring that can be applied to all relationships, intimate or not. We would normally apply this to the couple in our work in Marriage Care, but the graceful and grace-giving nature of a good family, for example, surely implies again a mutuality in all the relationships present in the family — again, this process of engagement suggests activity and complication, but worth also!

A fourth norm is *Equality*. We can argue that all good and sound relationships need to be founded on equality where we are aware of the uniqueness of the other and find joy in that difference, actively seeking it out and developing it for the self and other. This concept within Church might be particularly challenging for us in our different roles. But equality is not about everyone starting on the same line — none of us do — but about each appreciating the unique value and worth of the other and their contribution to the whole. For example, I have found how, in my more available phases that my children have taught me a lot, where I have accorded them equality of thought or observation, and I am now finding that my grandchildren are providing the same opportunities, if I am willing to watch for it!

The fifth and really important principle is *Commitment*. I would consider this to be one of the fundamental principles on which we base our togetherness. Indeed, the lack of commitment or a willingness to give up too easily seems to be a modern malaise, seen in marriages, family and Church relationships. Commitment has been one of the major cornerstones of thinking in the relationship support agencies for many years in relation to long-term relationships, but not a *commitment* that is associated with *contract*.

Commitments are basically decisions, or the making of choices, even making a choice to give up other choices.

The emergence of the pure relationship, an intimate partnership entered into for its own sake, which lasts only as long as both partners are satisfied with the rewards that they get from it is another challenge in relation to commitment these days. It is seen as the logical extension of the increase of individualism and the de-institutionalisation of long-term relationships such as marriage, and perhaps offers an answer to why so many relationships either in marriage or Church disintegrate.[6]

The nature and quality of relationships wax and wane as the years pass and we all have to navigate this. Robin Morgan, quoted by Margaret Farley says 'Commitment gives you the leverage to bring about change—and the time in which to do it.'[7] I also like the suggestion from the Irish Redemptorist, Johnny Doherty, about the importance and difficulty of commitment over time. He says: 'on a good day I am committed to you; on a not so good day I am committed to the relationship (or family); and on a really bad day I am committed to the commitment that I made.'[8]

Commitment is not just saying 'I do or I will'—it is making that choice actively and then working with it, staying with it, and believing in it over time. So, whilst people can be born into a family, or adopted or fostered, they have to actively make that commitment for it all to work.

A final norm offered by Farley is that of *Social Justice*. It is fundamental to the Gospels. It is very challenging to consider that all so-called good relationships are in fact diminished if there is no focus on the outside, if we only look inwards. In fact, it is possible, perhaps, within our Christian tradition to understand this as the call to be 'holy'. And, having built a set of relationships that are equal and committed, then the final challenge is to take that beyond our immediate boundary to others. Having found a language internally that makes sense and offers hope, then we have to take this beyond our own immediate families and Church. Otherwise, we are merely burying the talents, and such a situation will do nothing to help us regain a voice.

Further, this concept connects us with the importance of the faith community—such a community provides the context for the development of grace and communion, and an opportunity for going beyond and sharing in social justice. We perhaps as children repeated the rote lines of 'sacrament being an outward sign of inward grace' without any conception of what this might mean. I certainly didn't at the time but do understand it now finding meaning for it in the every day activities of care and love between people, and especially in committed, consensual and convenanted relationships that fundamentally project *sacrament*, that is, God's presence through grace.

But, it finds its fuller meaning when these relationships go beyond themselves, that is, outwards to others. Relationships that are inward and insular do not obviously display grace, and they are diminished in some way. It is only in building on and developing our strengths, by sharing, that a vital fruitfulness is passed on. I was struck by the comments on this topic by Timothy Radcliffe, in his book *Why go to Church? The drama of the Eucharist*[9], where he says that we are gathered as a people of hope and not because we like each other—we may not like each other that much. But, the important matter is that 'we gather in hope, as people of love, to be slowly *infected* by God's grace working in us.' Being part of the community is not the end rather it is the beginning. This is Social Justice, and it is our challenge to be the source of infection thereby.

I hope that I have provoked thought about relationships in a different way, with the hope that this will offer us back a voice. And I suggest that we as Church regain a voice to others by living within and by these principles and witnessing by our actions to each other, and then to those beyond our normal boundaries. We also need to work hard to find a language that makes sense for today, so that it not obscure or inaccessible. The early Christian community were noticed by the way they behaved, the way they did not conform to usual ways of being—'see these Christians, how they love one another'. This marked them out and this gave them influence, where others then sought them out. It is very clear that just telling people how to behave will have little or no impact. The recent publication by the Bishops in England and Wales, *Choosing the Common Good*, is another good example of how we can set out our programme, but then we have to live it because just putting in down on paper will have no impact if the messenger, and message thereby, is already deemed to be flawed.

The way we live our lives today and the 'traditions' we establish will, if we adhere to the norms I have suggested, provide a better world and environment for those who come 'downstream of us'. The real challenge is, however, a deeply personal one that we need to commit to individually. The challenge is clear and simple, though difficult. Taking that famous title from Primo Levi's novel: *If not now, when?*[10]and adding the American Senator, Jesse Jackson's additional phrase *if not me, who?* we have the means and method clearly set out for us.

Notes

[1] Z. Bauman, *Thinking Sociologically. An introduction for Everyone.* (Cambridge, MA: Basil Blackwell. 1990).

[2] UK election turnouts have dropped significantly since 1992. They reached their lowest point in 2001 at 59% and recovered slightly in 2010 to 65%. This is set against a post war average of approximately 75%. House of Commons Research Papers 01/54, 05/33 & 10/36.

[3] A. Thompson, 'We mustn't divorce ourselves from marriage' in *The Times* (March 2010).

[4] S. Coontz, 'In search of a Golden Age' in *Caring for Families* (1989).

[5] M. Farley, *Just Love: a framework for Christian Sexual Ethics* (London: Continuum International Publishing Group Ltd, 2006).

[6] A. Giddens, *The Transformation of Intimacy* (Stanford University

Press: 1992).

7   Farely, *Just Love.*

8   J. Doherty CSSR., *Commitment in relationships.* Unpublished presentation to Marriage Care's Marriage Preparation Conference (Manchester: 2005).

9   T. Radcliffe, *Why go to Church: the drama of the Eucharist.* (London: Continuum International Publishing Group Ltd, 2008).

10 P. Levi, *If not now, when?* (translated by W. Weaver) (London: Abacus, 1994).

From Best Kept Secret to Social Norm? The Catholic Social Conscience

Keith Chappell and Francis Davis

We opened by suggesting that the Church's social tradition was a constant resource. However, in English speaking Roman Catholic circles there is an often repeated mantra that 'the Church's social teaching' is also 'it's best kept secret'. Seized on equally by those who would do a little social action and those that might reach for theologies of liberation alike this mantra has come to reflect both a mechanism of defence of those accused of 'not doing enough' and a strategy for exhortation for those who would have us all 'do more'. As such the secretive element finds itself both a vice and a virtue depending on the perspective of the moral judge. In this process it is conceivable that a series of categories of intellectual and practical endeavour have been buried or at least inadequately excavated. In the essays that have preceded this concluding chapter we have sought to begin this task of excavation but also to establish navigation points for discerning the present, initial foundation stones for a future journey of conversation, and new studies to undergird exploration and fresh practice. We believe that each of the chapters sheds light on Christian challenges in general.

That said, as will be clear, we have not set out to destroy or criticise what has come to be the 'formal' or clerical tradition of Catholic social encyclicals. Quite the opposite. Neither have we promoted revolutionary strategies that by-pass, or seek to undermine, institutions in a quantum leap of historical change. But neither are we content with the simple categorisation by some, for example, Francis McHugh which give the formal tradition an automatic primacy. Consequently, in seeking to reflect on European experience widely put we have perhaps created a space where the question can be asked as to whether the traditional clerical or Episcopal outpouring of publications and words is adequate as a method of communication, a means by which to stimulate formation, and as a basis for renewed social action for and with the most frail.

Does the phrase 'social teaching' then only encompass the Roman clerical tradition of encyclicals and Vatican documents? Does its history begin in 1891 with *Rerum novarum*?[1] Or might it incorporate teaching letters issued by Bishops' Conferences?[2] Or embrace the 'distinctive' contributions of particular religious orders to theory and practice whether that be, for example, the social venturing, especially in education, of Breton Religious Women and Men, the internal democracy of the Dominicans or the far-reaching educational contributions, and intense identification with the needy, by many rooted in Ignatian spirituality?

More contentious in some Roman curial theological circles still, might be the suggestion that the biographies, judgments, ideas, and institution founding of lay Catholics tells us more about the essence of concrete social thought in history than any number of other utterances. To what extent do lay thinkers and organisations drive the agenda? In this scenario the social innovations of a (vaguely religiously observant) Paul Farmer[3] or ('frustrated with the Church') Barbara Ward[4] become foundational and as worthy of 'reception' as curial publications. Meanwhile at the elite level the contributions of, for example, a Ruth Kelly[5] in the UK Blair government, Michael Tate in Bob Hawke's cabinet[6], Mary Jo Bane[7] in the Clinton Administration, and those closely advising Ministerial 'cabinets' become key sources even before the rich history of Christian Democracy and the rise of Catholic neo-conservatism.

Perhaps even more difficult to assess might be the sense that those in other Christian traditions, or indeed other faith communities, are leading the way and that Catholic teaching might now be playing a mere catch-up or reduced to the accommodation of other's thought and pioneering action into the body of Church doctrine and practice. From the nineteenth century protestant social reformers, to the astounding generosity of the Jewish diaspora, to the social action of Muslim communities,[8] to Anglican social enterprise in Australia in the twenty-first century the context of Catholic social teaching cannot sit in splendid isolation and is challenged to assess where it stands, and whether it has analytical traction, despite the attempts by some to secure or claim a foundational 'distinctiveness'.

At stake of course are some fundamental theological questions, not least the authority of the Church in provinces not only occupied by, but also aggressively defended by, other disciplines; or, conversely, Catholic social teaching's openness to challenging findings from other academic and practical fields. The empirical research we have shown here shows observant Catholics with behaviours well outside the formal norm of the Church's expressed expectations; and the Church leadership's sweeping words sitting in tension with the actual (in) coherence, impact, demographic profile and reach of its charity and other institutional work. While theology inspires, mobilises, explains, challenges and cajoles, such complementary findings run the risk of being treated as heterodoxy even before their implications are thought through. Likewise debates about 'spirituality' when Cardinals may praise a 'thirst for spirituality' among the young that closer research is revealing to be a reflexivity bound up in the role and meaning of 'brand values'.[9]

One response of course is to discount a rich and varied approach.[10] While even a supposedly 'liberal' interlocutor such as the former Master of the Dominican order Timothy Radcliffe OP would assert the primacy of the 'Queen of Sciences' of 'theology' and 'imagination' over 'facts' and 'evidence'[11]; at what point of empirical push back does an imaginative articulation of ideas of the Church and a putative 'common good' become accountable to an avalanche of findings in social research, not to mention the rejection of even neo-Thomism by philosophers?

Following from this what weight is given to the natural and social sciences in testing theological arguments more broadly? This applies both when long-held theological positions are challenged by new empirical finding, the Galileo moment, and also when the weight of scientific and social information demands a response hitherto ignored by theology or where 'theological' claims are put under such pressure that it becomes clear that self-declared 'Catholic social thought' is actually a distraction from meaningful social reality and action. And this is not just a problem for the Roman Curia: Early liberation theologies, for example, made much use of dependency theory whose analytical veracity was already under intense challenge in mainstream development studies and which has subsequently been largely discredited[12]. Meanwhile, reflecting concerns that we have noted from sociologists, in both the UK and the US Bishops have lamented that high quality empirical studies of the civic and sexual habits of Catholics so clearly reflect the failure of formal Catholic teaching to take root in their congregations that ' the sample' or 'the researcher' must be at fault. In such situations even social researchers profoundly loyal to the formal Magisterium can find themselves accused of theological convictions that they have never held

Less controversially from a Roman point of view the recent sudden rush of theological reflection and Church teaching at varied magisterial levels on environmental questions would seem to suggest that a critical pressure can be reached at which a minor matter, worthy perhaps of some spiritual consideration, becomes one central to social justice and the mission of the Church and so a tipping point is reached and the dam bursts. This same subject again provides challenges relating to all the questions raised above about what might be considered part of Church social teaching—St Francis, Bonaventure, Boff, Benedict XVI? And in turn this may raise the question of the contingency of any Church teaching.

Even for Bishops the defining and description of principles and reasons is all well and good but we must also recognise the pragmatic dimension, or indeed the realpolitik, of the ideation and implementation of social teaching. A Cardinal, for example, might choose to resist abortion laws in a specific historical moment out of peer pressure from other Cardinals globally as much as in response to any local need or in response to any classically articulated 'theology of life' while another might 'go big' on migration for the lack of any wider vision for his Diocese or, by contrast, because of a lifelong exposure to immigrant parishes Likewise 'orthodox' Catholic legislators may choose to support the death penalty despite its prohibition by the Catechism while their campaign literature includes images of them alongside members of the local and global hierarchy. There is undoubtedly an operant theology at play in all situations which may, or may not, coincide with accepted theological norms or official Church teaching. Multiple factors influence the day-to-day decisions of those in the public sphere, these may be private or public in nature, principled or pragmatic. Similarly, those involved in theological reflection and magisterial teaching also find themselves immersed in a world of often competing interests. For example, to what extent is the very attempt to frame theological judgments on all these questions conditioned first by the local culture of common or Roman law, specific regional experiences of Chinese, European or North American capitalism, or sympathies of personality to name but four? Ironically the very act of raising such problems is considered problematic—even contentious—in some Catholic quarters whether they be from the supposed 'left' or the supposed 'right'. Yet, it is perhaps only in acknowledging and, indeed, embracing the ambiguities of the reality in which social thought and action is developed and ultimately implemented that Catholic social thought can make the move from social 'thought' to the promotion and defence of a social 'conscience' with a demonstrable social impact.[13]

Indeed, in assessing that transition from 'ideas' to 'action', the move from a desire to be virtuous to the development of habits of virtue, it may again be to wider experience to which we might usefully turn.

For example, whether one agrees with their principles or not it is not an overstatement to suggest that the think tanks of the neo-liberal and neo-conservative political Right have, in proportion to their resources, achieved more cultural traction, elite buy-in and institutional impact than almost all of the local Churches in the nation's towards which their 'project' has been strategically focused. Along with ideological zeal their proponents have brought a deep and wide reading of state, market and civic institutions and a particular attention to the role of budget holders at every level. Meanwhile, the subsequent emergence of 'behavioural science' and 'behavioural economics' has begun to suggest a human instinct to develop social norms in markets even as some theologians advance (or rail against) that very neo-liberalism.[14] This attention to institutional variety and detail has been significantly underdeveloped in formal and informal Catholic approaches and, conceivably, leaves Catholic institutions and charities without an integrated approach to build business plans which do virtue, will have legs as opposed to words in the wind.

The notion of a social conscience is, of course, not only difficult to elucidate simply but also one that can be worrying to those seeking control or even simplicity. However, a 'conscience' is adaptable and responsive and may be better placed to meet challenges which arise from social sciences, natural sciences, political developments and even the impatient demands of the media seeking responses on a timescale often measured in minutes rather than the months and years taken for considerations in the past. This is not to say that these factors are total drivers of thought but that to ignore them risks placing Church teaching back to the nineteenth Century where Leo XIII found himself having to proclaim or risk being left behind completely by other religious traditions, and increasingly self-confident secular thinkers and movements whose combination of ideas-institutions and action was more able to nudge human behaviour and habits.

On a more positive level it also provides a very real engagement with the Vatican II teaching on conscience as set out in *Gaudium et spes:*

> His conscience is man's [*sic*] most secret core, and his sanctuary. There he is alone with God whose voice echoes in his depths. By conscience, in a wonderful way, that law is made known which is fulfilled in the love of God and neighbour. Through loyalty to conscience Christians are joined to other men in the search for truth and for the right solution to many moral problems which arise both in the life of individuals and from social relationships.[15]

A social conscience, renewed and invigorated opens the way for engagement with key moral issues and also for dialogue with those of other backgrounds. But it also leaves us with at least three concrete struggles for the future to which we now turn.

First, 'consciences' do not take shape very often in a 'society' in general. Concrete institutions can have a seminal effect. We are aware that some reading these words will observe that we are simply advocating here an admission of 'context' into theological thinking, and a recognition of some less than sacred sciences to reflection in saying this. But that is to miss the point. For example, upon his enthronement the new Archbishop of Cardiff, George Stack, called for the Church to address the 'structures of injustice' much as local branches of Labour parties may pass resolutions condemning 'unbridled capitalism'. Meanwhile, pro-family Catholic bodies lament the rise of social liberalism and the 'fragmentation of society'. To what extent, however, is the (relatively small) Archdiocese of Cardiff in a position to resist economic and cultural forces that are global in dimension? Or a pro-life group with even a thousand members organisationally fit to oppose those with whom it likewise disagrees? There can be nothing quite so frustrating (or disempowering), for the three to five members involved, as when a parish justice and peace group suggests it will soon be at the vanguard of some major social movement or when the staff of a tiny Catholic Bishops' Conference Secretariat behave as though they have the skills and insights of a major civil service with, even in times of retrenchment, access to major resources.

A renewed ability to refresh the Christian civic contribution may then need an enhanced attention to the habit forming potential of social institutions throughout societies. The 'state' can vary in nature, form and habits as much as firms and families. Treating them—or the varying credibility of Catholic Bishops' conference secretariats globally— normatively can distract from such variation. Meanwhile, capturing the budgets, priorities and direction of those institutions with zealous will, capacity, potential and resources may make for a more enduring protection of 'reason' than the recycling of encyclicals. From the balance sheet and profit and loss statement of a Diocese, Order, Catholic or other institution a literate reading, aware of the contingent nature of accounting norms, can determine ethics, priorities, likely success factors, potential and direction more quickly—and often more acutely—than any public utterance or exhortation by the same body.

But such a re-focusing on institutions also begs a need for a theory or theology of 'innovation' and an idea of 'success'. Not long ago an eminent Professor of Leadership asked a gathering of senior clergy what the purpose of their organisation was and how they judged if they had done

well. Their response was that they 'did not do measure-
ment' because they were supporters of 'kingdom values'.
So the eminent Professor asked them how they would
explain to a new curate how he should actually spend his
time and the parish's money when, on day one, he asked
what 'kingdom values' meant for the parish. Their answer
mirrored the answer recorded by almost every such work-
shop that the Professor had run namely 'the youth', 'the
divorced', and 'the lapsed'. When the Professor pointed out
that in the geographical area for which the clergy were
responsible the number of young people had collapsed
because of economic change, while the number of older
people struggling had leapt exponentially, the group said
' oh yes, them as well'.

If we are to strengthen the Catholic social conscience,
simply reaching for old shibboleths and institutional
approaches that protect inertia will not do. And templating
what mission, social action, and need is by burying them
into a 'programme' may not help either. And so how might
we set out what we wish to do and then be able to celebrate
when we have done it? And as forms of charity, schooling,
the state and social action which were designed for the
nineteenth Century and the immediate post-war period
begin to tire how might we unlock the new zeal of those
that would once have been Friars but will now likely be
younger or older people longing for a mission shaped life
or retirement? And will there be a budget to cloak them or
will sophisticated new fundraising techniques only go to
prop up increasingly less sophisticated and no longer
innovative responses to social and pastoral need?

Thirdly and finally, we turn to the question of ecumen-
ism. The Anglican spiritual writer and social innovator, Rev
Kenneth Leech, has often argued that the coming divide
will not be between denominations but those within the
denominations, across seemingly 'set' theological boundaries, who feel compelled and confident to reach out for
social change, and those who find such an imperative

disturbing or a distraction. To some ecumenical observers even the points of entry we have taken, the way we have presented debates, and the cautiousness with which we have raised questions and possibilities here will seem tame, even lacking in intellectual openness. While we would contest such a view it is an inclination that the development of a powerful social conscience and authentic action needs to guard against. For as culture, markets, and policy shifts at incredible speed the instinct to fall back merely on a view that identifies only a crisis of 'faith' or 'reason' as adequate for a wholehearted Christianity will be immense. The demise of European communism, the impact of the economic crisis, the debilitating shame of the cover up of the sex abuse crisis to name but three all have their role to play and it may be that ecumenical partners will become as much guardians of the light in the Catholic Church as we might, in genuine fraternity, be — on occasion — to theirs.

In any case, if the chapters here do not go far enough for some then perhaps subsequent reflection could usefully centre around 'strategies for change' in and from particular Churches as much as the common task of renewing the social conscience across all Christian communities. And may this small volume be at least a small contribution to the renewal of that task.

Notes

1   Leo XIII, Encyclical letter *Rerum novarum* (15 May 1891).
2   For example, US Catholic Bishops, *A Pastoral Message of the National Conference of Catholic Bishops on the Tenth Anniversary of the Economic Pastoral*, (November 1995) .
3   T. Kidder, *Mountains Beyond Mountains — The Quest of Dr Paul Farmer* (Random House: 2003).
4   J. Gartlan, *Barbara Ward — Her Life And Letters* (Continuum: 2010).
5   For example, see F. Davis, 'Religion and Faith Communities' in N. Yeates et al, *In Defence of Welfare: The impacts of the Spending Review* (UK Social Policy Association: 2011).
6   B. Hawke, *The Hawke Memoirs* (Heinemann: 2010). Tate, a former

Labour cabinet minister, is now a priest on the island of Tasmania.

7   See http://www.hks.harvard.edu/fs/mjbane/MJB%20biography.html. Accessed March 2011.

8   R. Jawad, *Religion and Social Welfare in the Middle East: A Lebanese Perspective* (The Policy Press: 2009) and F. Davis et al, *Moral, But No Compass: Church, Government And The Future of Welfare* (Matthew James: 2008).

9   Contrasting the views of Cardinal Murphy-O'Connor with the detailed research of the University of Kent's Professor Gordon Lynch confirms this tension.

10   It can be argued, for example, that much of the effort to define a 'distinctive Catholic economics' by groups focused on G. K. Chesterton, or by Christian Democrats such as Hungary's Professor Peter Rona is entirely self-referential because discounting subsequent developments in both Catholic thought, the experience of Catholics as CEO of major financial institutions and especially the experience of Christian Democrats in government themselves.

11   See T. Radcliffe in R. Gill, *Theology And Sociology: A Reader* (Geoffrey Chapman: 1996).

12   V. Randall and R. Theobald, *Political Change and Underdevelopment: A Critical Introduction to Third World Politics* (Duke: 1998) and also G. Guttierez, *Theology of Liberation* (SCM: 1974).

13   See F. Davis, 'A Political Economy of Catholicism' in N. Timms and K.Wilson (eds), *Authority and Governance in the Roman Catholic Church* (SPCK: 2001).

14   See, for example, the work of Professor David Halpern and his team at the UK Cabinet Office: http://www.cabinetoffice.gov.uk/resource-library/behavioural-insight-team-annual-update.

15   Vatican II, *Gaudium et spes*, 16.

Lightning Source UK Ltd.
Milton Keynes UK
UKOW051545141011

180325UK00002B/1/P